W9-CCN-123

VINEYARD TALES

VINEYARD TALES

REFLECTIONS ON WINE

GERALD ASHER

Wine Editor, *Gourmet* Magazine

CHRONICLE BOOKS
SAN FRANCISCO

The essays in this book have appeared in
slightly different form in *Gourmet* magazine,
except "Wine of the Gods," which appeared
under a different title and in slightly different
form in *Portland* magazine.

Library of Congress Cataloging-in-Publication Data:
Asher, Gerald.
        Vineyard tales : reflections on wine /
by Gerald Asher.
                P.   cm.
        ISBN 0-8118-1267-7
        1. Wine and wine making.   I. Title.
        TP548.A792   1996
        641.2'2—dc20   95-47429
                                             CIP

Book Design: Deborah Bowman
Cover Illustration: Fritz Dumville, Copyright © 1990.

Printed in the United States of America

Distributed in Canada by Raincoast Books
8680 Cambie Street
Vancouver, B.C. V6P 6M9

10 9 8 7 6 5 4 3 2 1

Chronicle Books
275 Fifth Street
San Francisco, CA 94103

IN MEMORY *of* ELIZABETH DAVID

CONTENTS

Introduction --- 12

Malmsey: A Revival --- 15

California's Edna Valley --- 23

Wine and Food --- 32

Missouri: The Return of the Native --------------------------------- 40

Barbaresco --- 52

Between Hard Covers: Wine Books in English ---------------- 62

A Carafe of Red --- 72

Napa Valley Cabernet Sauvignon---------------------------------- 82

Decanting: To Breathe or Not to Breathe --------------------- 93

Storm in a Champagne Flute --------------------------------------- 97

Ribera del Duero: A New Star for Old Castile --------------- 108

Letter from Burgundy --- 119

A Matter of Taste --- 132

Port: Years of Grace -- 137

Santa Cruz--- 148

Wine on Wine-- 155

Chardonnay: Twigs, Buds and Clones ----------------------- 160

Haut-Brion: A Most Particular Taste------------------------- 172

Hermitage and Crozes-Hermitage ---------------------------- 181

Washington State Reds: Merlot and Cabernet Sauvignon ----- 190

Sauternes: The Sweet Life -- 200

Zinfandel: California's Own -------------------------------------- 211

Portugal's "Green" Whites (*Vinhos Verdes*) ------------------- 221

California Sauvignon Blanc: A Cinderella Story ----------- 230

Celebrating Oregon's Pinot Noir ------------------------------- 239

Orvieto: Fair Lily of Umbria ------------------------------------ 249

A Vineyard by the Sea: The North Fork of Long Island ------- 261

Remembrance of Wines Past -------------------------------------- 271

Wine of the Gods-- 276

Index-- 285

VINEYARD TALES
by REGION

FRANCE
72 ------------A Carafe of Red
97 ------------Storm in a Champagne Flute
119 ------------Letter from Burgundy
172 ------------Haut-Brion: A Most Particular Taste
181 ------------Hermitage and Crozes-Hermitage
200 ------------Sauternes: The Sweet Life

UNITED STATES
23 ------------California's Edna Valley
40 ------------Missouri: The Return of the Native
82 ------------Napa Valley Cabernet Sauvignon
148 ------------Santa Cruz
160 ------------Chardonnay: Twigs, Buds and Clones
190 ------------Washington State Reds: Merlot and Cabernet Sauvignon
211 ------------Zinfandel: California's Own
230 ------------California Sauvignon Blanc: A Cinderella Story
239 ------------Celebrating Oregon's Pinot Noir
261 ------------A Vineyard by the Sea: The North Fork of Long Island

AROUND THE WORLD
15 ------------Malmsey: A Revival (Crete)
52 ------------Barbaresco (Italy)
108 ------------Ribera del Duero: A New Star for Old Castile (Spain)
137 ------------Port: Years of Grace (Portugal)
221 ------------Portugal's "Green" Whites (Portugal)
249 ------------Orvieto: Fair Lily of Umbria (Italy)

MATTERS OF TASTE
32 ------------Wine and Food
62 ------------Between Hard Covers: Wine Books in English
93 ------------Decanting: To Breathe or Not to Breathe
132 ------------A Matter of Taste
155 ------------Wine on Wine
271 ------------Remembrance of Wines Past
276 ------------Wine of the Gods

INTRODUCTION

It's ironic, now that computers tease the limits of imagination and cars are sold through appeals to romantic fantasies, that wine's age-old link to myth and poetry and breaking bread should have been abandoned. There isn't much room to dream when we are invited to appreciate a wine for its pH and residual sugar ("expressed as grams per liter"); or for an aroma described in terms of "asparagus, green olive and apple." Even as a prescription for a salad, that isn't an inspiring combination.

A glass of good wine does not need to be picked apart or burdened with jargon. It will find its echo among old memories (and sometimes help anchor a new one). Smell and taste, with a tug at the emotions, always pull the past into the present, the there and then into the here and now. Somewhere in that there and then are familiar faces, snatches of happiness, half-forgotten stories and glimpses of places now far away. Paul Claudel, the French diplomat and playwright (and, admittedly, something of a mystic) said that wine teaches us to pay interior attention—"it liberates the mind and lights up the intelligence." That could be; though I prefer what Fay Weldon, the novelist, said when interviewed about her taste in wine by the editor of the British publication *Decanter*. Living in Europe, she referred to Italian and French wines; but what she had to say can be applied to wine in a universal way. "My husband likes Italian wines," she said. "And while I like them, because they taste nice and jolly and rich and fertile, I prefer French. French wine has a kind of terrible gravitas—it always reminds one somehow of Cardinal Richelieu. There is a subtlety about French wine; it doesn't go for an easy flavor, it goes for an afterthought."

Most of us, at some time or another, are in the mood for a nice, jolly wine with an easy flavor, yet it's usually the wine with afterthought that we remember. But to experience the afterthought we ourselves must supply from memory and imagination those elements that illuminate if not the intelligence then at least the wine in hand. We get from a glass of wine what we ourselves put into it.

When I was still too young to have tasted wine, I met it in the pages of Chaucer and Balzac and Keats. Once I began enjoying wine itself my interest quickened and I read, more deliberately, the books of Andre Simon, H. Warner Allen, and Morton Shand. There are references to wine everywhere, however, and I picked up as much from the occasional aside in a novel as I did from the technical authors I was obliged to read once I had chosen wine as a profession. "This wine is too good for toast-drinking, my dear," a Hemingway character says of Champagne in *The Sun Also Rises*. "You don't want to mix up emotions with a wine like that. You lose the taste."

What I read was often charming nonsense, of course; but most of it gave wine the context without which it can neither be appreciated nor understood. I learned early that a wine isn't defined by pH and a taste of green olives but by people, place and time. What makes one wine nice and jolly and easy and another so deep that there seems no end to it? We look for explanations to the gravel and the chalk and the granitic sand. But could any Bordeaux wine fail to reflect that city's chaste classicism? Could any California Chardonnay be other than a metaphor for abundance? If we pay attention, we can find in Champagne the love of novelty at the court of Louis XV that brought such frivolity into existence in the first place. And we can taste, behind the beguiling sweetness of a glass of Port, the force of England's resolve to damage the economy of eighteenth-century France by creating, to the advantage of its ally, Portugal, a wine that would change the English palate.

In every glass of wine, I have found, there is such a story; and in every story worth hearing, there is wine. In these pages I will tell you some of my favorites.

MALMSEY: A REVIVAL

T HERE HAD BEEN VIOLENT STORMS ON CRETE ALL WEEK. One morning at Rethymno the shopkeepers had had to flush out a muddy stream flooding their shops, and on another the tiny harbor had been a great bobbing mass of tables and chairs blown into the water from the quayside cafes. The rain on the day we drove from Agios Nikolaos to Sitia near the eastern tip of the island had been too much for the windscreen wipers. Almost blindly we followed the water-slicked road through mountains that rose sheer from the seabed. The taped voice of Fleurie Dadonakis, one of the most gifted interpreters of Greek ballads and usually such a joy to hear, merely added to our sense of melancholy. Only those familiar with the Mediterranean in winter know how wet, how bone-chilling and how sad it can be.

We were on our way to Sitia's Union of Agricultural and Wine Producers Cooperative to taste the dry, slightly tannic Sitia wine—neither quite red, as it turned out, nor quite tawny—made from the local Liatiko grape. Sitia is one of Crete's four official wine appellations (the others are Peza, Archanes, and Dafnes, all in the mountainous center of the island), but most of the wine produced around the town is simple table wine. That is true of Crete generally. Though the island produces twenty percent of all Greek wine, the bulk of it, and especially the red, is blended from two or more of the island's long-established varieties and sold with neither appellation nor fuss. It appears under brand names—Minos Palace, Cavaliere, that sort of thing—likely to appeal to tourists who, in summer, crowd the *tavernas* of Chania and Elounda.

A different, and ancient, tradition of Cretan wine is only now fumbling its way towards a renaissance after being all but extinguished under more than two hundred years of Ottoman administration that came to a straggling close at the end of the last century. In the late Middle Ages, Sitia, like Rethymno and Heraklion, other ports on the island's north shore, had been famous for the production of Malmsey, a wine that had made Venice rich and England happy. It had probably resembled wines produced on Crete from time immemorial. I had heard of attempts to revive it and had already tasted one version produced on a limited scale at the Cooperative of Kastelli Kissamos at the opposite end of the island. It was dark amber, with the smoky *rancio* of an old, dry Oloroso sherry.

Yorgos Kounoulakis, the Sitia cooperative's enologist, confirmed that he too was experimenting with such a wine, fermenting separately any batches of grapes with particularly high sugars and then adding unfermented grape juice and brandy to sweeten and fortify the result. The first quantity that he had produced in commercial volume was aging in 120-gallon puncheons in a cellar. At Kastelli Kissamos they had placed their puncheons of aging wine in a shed, deliberately exposing them to temperatures ranging from 40°F in winter to 140°F in summer. The Sitia wine was a rosy amber, much lighter in color than the wine I had tasted at Kastelli Kissamos. It had a mild and unobtrusive sweetness and an aroma and flavor that made me think of a *confit* of grapes. The wines were quite different, one from the other, and I could not know which, if either, came even close to the taste of medieval Malmsey.

But the question intrigued me. I found it hard to accept that a tradition of winemaking, having survived thousands of years, could, in two hundred, be lost even to folk memory—no matter how repressive the Ottoman regime. Cretan wine had been distinguished for as long as we have records of its existence. Its reputation in imperial Rome was as great as it had been in classical Greece five centuries earlier. And at least a thousand years before that the Minoans had produced wine in the same central zones where the new appellations have recently been established.

Ancient myths suggest that the island had been a stepping-stone for the vine on its way from Asia to Europe. The story of Zeus carrying off to Crete the daughter of the king of Phoenicia, Europa, is usually illustrated, for example, with the god in the form of a bull and Europa, on his back, carrying a branch heavy with grapes. And then there is the legend of Dionysus, the god associated with wine, choosing as his bride Ariadne, daughter of King Minos of Crete. The huge wine crocks built into underground chambers at Knossos and Phaestos confirm the importance of wine implicit in the myths; one of the Minoan buildings excavated at Vathípetro, south of Archanes, revealed numerous wine jars and a press—clearly it had been a winery.

What had that ancient wine been like? Homer, entertainer rather than historian, painted everything larger than life. Dare we take his descriptions of wine literally when they were almost always qualified by words and phrases suggesting honeyed sweetness? Was he writing of wine in general or only of wine at its most heroic? His descriptions of wines are at least consistent with his account of grapes left in the sun to shrivel before pressing. And that seemed still to have been the practice when we again become aware of Cretan wine at the start of the thirteenth century.

It was the time when, as her share of the spoils of Byzantium, Venice had grabbed Crete along with some smaller islands and a string of ports useful as trading stations and naval bases. History, written as always by the victors, has drawn a discreet veil over the wickedness of Venice and her Crusader allies who, while gathered together ostensibly to protect Constantinople from the threatening Ottoman infidel, decided instead to plunder the city themselves and then to seize and share out a large part of her empire. (It was a betrayal so bitter that the hatred then generated between Orthodox Byzantium and the Catholic Venetian Republic, hence between Serbia and Croatia, their heirs, endures still.)

Venice exploited Crete by introducing to the island the cultivation of sugar, a new and profitable luxury for which European demand had been insatiable since the first Crusaders had brought it back from Syria, and by developing new markets for the island's wine. It was taken long distances by Venetian galleys after shipment through Monemvasia, one of the ports on the Peloponnese coast of Greece captured at the time of Byzantium's dismemberment. Monemvasia—as the wine was called—became Malvasia (Malvoisie to the French), a word soon further corrupted to Malmsey in English.

We can't be sure when the Venetians made their first shipment of the wine to England, but a cask of Malvoisie is listed among the provisions assembled for the celebration of the enthronement of Archbishop Robert of Winchelsea in 1295. By the 1330s Malmsey was arriving regularly, the merchants who delivered it taking raw wool in partial payment. Shipped to Flanders, the wool was exchanged there for finished cloth and cloaks, which were then sold all over Europe. This triangular trade became so lucrative that in 1349 the senate of the Venetian Republic decided to run it themselves as a state monopoly.

From this time there are references to the wine—sometimes as Cret, sometimes as Retimo (Rethymno) and sometimes as Candy (Candia being the Venetian name both for the island and for its chief city, Heraklion)—in various regulations as well as in records of wine sales and inventories all over England. The wine was a raging success. Demand led to profiteering, however, and worse. A 1350 ordinance of Edward III attempted to control prices, but by January 1353, the exasperated mayor and sheriffs of the City of London had decided that fraudulent blending was a greater problem, and they banned tavern keepers who sold Cretan wine from selling or keeping any other wine in the same establishment.

Meanwhile, the special duty imposed on what was called "sweet Levant wine" was double that collected on Rhine and Bordeaux wines, and half the revenue was reserved for the personal use of the monarch, who therefore had a direct interest in seeing the trade flourish. The City of London's restriction did not appeal to Edward III at all, especially as he was persuaded that merchants would not set up shop to sell Cretan wine in London while it lasted. Within weeks he had issued the first of doubtless many injunctions to provide exceptions to the mayor's restrictive policy.

But by the late fifteenth century the wine had become so much a part of the fabric of English life (Chaucer's Shipman tells a tale of a monk, with an eye for a merchant's wife, making himself a welcome guest at the couple's house by bringing a gift of "a jubbe," almost four gallons, "of Malvesye") that Venice thought it time to toughen its trading terms. First the Senate insisted on payment entirely in cash rather than wool; then, having increased the price per butt, it reduced the size of the measure. In 1489 the Venetians went too far, however, by imposing a heavy and discriminatory tax on Malmsey exported from Crete on English ships, a move to protect the profitability of their own merchant marine. Henry VII of England responded by imposing an identical tax on Malmsey brought to England in Venetian galleys. The Venetians, fearing that a fight over shipping rights could kill their lucrative trade in Malmsey, eventually backed down and abolished their tax in 1499; but by then Henry, a king with the mind of an accountant and the scruples of a loan shark (he had been personally responsible for taking the royal treasury out of the red and into the black at the expense of his noble peers), had come to like the color of the money, and he declined to reciprocate.

The matter seems to have ended there, doubtless because Venice was already distracted by more serious problems provoked by yet another Henry. Prince Henry of Portugal—Henry the Navigator to most of us—had planted sugar on the recently discovered Atlantic island of Madeira. By the time Venice was involved in its squabble with Henry VII of England over who would control the shipment of Malmsey from Crete, Madeira's cane crop had reached such proportions that the price of sugar in Europe had fallen by half. Furthermore, Prince Henry had clearly taken Crete—by then a golden milch cow for Venice—as his model in colonizing Madeira. In addition to sugar, he had established on the island the grape still known there as Malvasia Candida, an allusion to its Cretan origin, with the intention of making Malmsey to compete with that of Crete. It is possible that Malmsey wine from Madeira was reaching England as early as the 1450s, even though William Younger, in *Gods, Men and Wine,* says the first butt of "Malvoisie from the Isle of Madeira" arrived in London in 1537, the same year the Ottomans took Monemvasia from the Venetians.

Regardless of this new competition, the production of Malmsey on Crete remained strong. Andrea Bacci, an Italian physician writing on wine in 1596, reported that the island was then exporting 200,000 butts of it a year to the Venetian mainland. The wine's continued popularity in England is clear from the frequent references to it in seventeenth-century plays ("We have no Greek wine in the house," exclaims a horrified Lord Bornwell in James Shirley's 1635 comedy *The Lady of Pleasure.* "Pray send one of our footmen to the merchant"). In addition, Gervase Markham's how-to book for the English housewife, first published in 1649, advises the reader to see to it that "her Malmseys be full wines, pleasant, well hewed and fine."

But it all came to an end in 1669, when Heraklion fell to the Ottomans after a siege that had lasted twenty-two years. They had already taken Chania and were in possession of the rest of Crete within a year.

Had that really meant the end of Malmsey? Just from curiosity I asked Mr. Kounoulakis what wine the members of his cooperative drank. Did they, as do their counterparts in France and Italy, have the right to receive from the cooperative a quantity of wine for their household consumption?

"They always keep back some of their grapes. They know what they like and prefer to make their own wine for themselves," he said.

Oh? "Would it be possible," I asked, "to visit one of the cooperative's members and ask him how he makes his wine? Perhaps even taste it?"

A telephone call completed arrangements for us to stop, on the way back to Agios Nikolaos, at a village on the Argilos, a high clay plateau where the best of Sitia's grapes are said to be grown. The grower we were to meet had a small cafe-bar at the village crossroad and would be waiting for us there.

The rain was coming down in sheets, but we found the cafe easily enough. Though we were well into November, great bunches of grapes still hung from an almost leafless vine stretched on rods over the small terrace outside, and the rain, collecting on them, dripped with noisy splashes into the puddles below. Inside, it was pretty basic: three or four tables on a concrete floor, beer crates stacked against the back wall, a refrigerator to the side, and a sink in the corner by a table covered in oil cloth and an assortment of tumblers. It was clearly a place where a farmer in work clothes and muddy boots would feel at ease.

Three men sat at a plain wooden table, looking, in fact, as if they had been feeling at ease for much of the afternoon. The owner, it soon appeared, was the one with the cloth cap. The other two, extravagantly moustached and wild-haired, had been keeping him company while he waited for us. Each held a glass of *raki* and picked from time to time at a dish of small olives and a bowl of salted chickpeas. One of them had sliced a raw quince, which he offered to me as soon as we sat down.

They smiled a lot and spoke little until we began asking them what they did with the grapes they kept back from the cooperative for their own wine. Then they all spoke at once, very loudly, and with gesticulations that involved their entire bodies. As far as I could make out they kept back their best bunches and spread them on nets in the sun for three or four days. The concentrated juice, once pressed, would ferment until it stopped naturally, leaving a residue of unfermented sugar in the wine. When the concentration of sugar in the juice was not as high as they liked, they said, they added a little brandy to arrest the fermentation and allow a touch of natural sweetness to remain.

The bar owner's "cellar" was a small space behind the beer crates, and there he had two or three butts of wine surrounded by a litter of buckets, sacks of potatoes, baskets of walnuts and a heap of pomegranates. The sample he drew was golden brown, and drier than I had expected. It was quite nutty, almost like a sherry. He drank it as an aperitif, he told me, and with his food.

I was glad we had stopped there, even though I felt none the wiser. We agreed to give the more exuberant of the two moustached men—he really could have been playing a rustic in one of Aristophanes' comedies—a ride to the other side of the village. As we pulled up to let him out, just near a roadside shrine, he asked if we would like to taste his wine, too. Why not? We slithered two or three hundred feet down a steep and very muddy hillside into the heart of an olive grove where a tethered donkey began braying, loudly and nervously, until the man calmed it. Below us was a stone hut built half into the slope, and he explained that he spread his grapes to dry on its flat rooftop, just as the ancients had spread theirs on their threshing floors.

We stumbled farther down and round to the front of the hut, where I was surprised to find his wife and a brother-in-law sitting under a wide projecting eave snugly toasting themselves at a roaring fire set into the hut's façade. They were eating warm potatoes roasted in the embers and regaling themselves with tiny black olives piled on an enameled dish.

We sat on the bench with them to dry ourselves a little, and they explained that the fire was heating an old alembic still, unobtrusively boiling away inside the hut to convert a bad batch of the brother-in-law's wine into good brandy. From time to time they roused themselves to feed the fire from a stack of old olive wood. Regardless of the rain, they were having a little fete together, protected from unexpected intruders by their watch-donkey.

We tasted the raw distillate—it was very rough—and then my new friend produced a glass of his fragrant five-year-old for me. A busybody rooster came to see what was up and had to be chased off a bright green patch of lettuce seedlings just starting to sprout under one of the olive trees. We were beginning to feel quite cozy when I remembered that I was supposed to be tasting his wine, not his *raki*. So we went to the far side of the hut where he kept his wine, squeezing first through a cramped anteroom full of more sacks of potatoes, baskets of quince, and boxes of apples.

There were no casks in his cellar; instead, there were three big terracotta jars, just like the Minoan ones at Vathípetro, each holding, I would guess, about fifty gallons. He lifted a cardboard lid, dipped a small pitcher into the wine, and poured me a tumblerful. It was a rosy, golden brown, slightly sweet, with a mavelous flavor that just kept expanding in my mouth. Oxidation had obviously been part of the aging process, but it was not oxidized in the sense in which we use the term. This wine, he told me, had been made from grapes so rich in sugar that he had had no need to fortify it. He had pressed them; fermented the juice slowly, as usual, in the jar; and, as he needed wine, dipped into it. It was as simple as that, and the wine was delicious.

"It's my 1988," he said.

Give or take a few thousand years, he may have been right.

CALIFORNIA'S EDNA VALLEY

THE WINTER RAIN OF 1992 ENDED SIX YEARS OF DROUGHT AND LEFT CALIFORNIA LOOKING LIKE A CHILD'S PICTURE-BOOK IMAGE OF SPRING. Between vines, under fruit trees, and across hillsides that had been barren only weeks before, California poppies, flowering mustard and lupine splashed orange, yellow and blue on the bright green of new grass. At the end of a drive south from San Francisco to San Luis Obispo—about 230 miles, much of it along the Salinas Valley where crews were already bringing in the first spring crops—I was so entranced by the transformation that I overshot my freeway exit and was almost at the ocean before I realized my mistake.

Granted, San Luis Obispo, hidden from the highway that serves it, doesn't announce itself with the visual equivalent of a trumpet blast. But inattention had brought home to me how close to the Pacific the town is—as automobiles run let alone as crows fly. The fishing boats of Morro Bay and the surfing of Avila and Pismo beaches are in the town's backyard. In this special situation, open to the ocean yet a little protected from it, San Luis Obispo has what is probably California's most equable climate. It's also one of California's most agreeable places to live. Almost midway between San Francisco and Los Angeles, San Luis Obispo is compact, friendly, and independent of both. It has advantages unexpected for its size—galleries, bookshops, cafes, good movie theaters (the town's Fremont is an Art Deco gem), and lively, unpretentious restaurants—thanks to Cal Poly, with its busy and prestigious schools of engineering, architecture and agriculture.

The town's tie to agriculture in particular is made plain every Thursday, when four blocks of Higuera Street, not far from the sprawling eighteenth-century mission, are closed to traffic at the end of the business day and allowed to become, for a few evening hours anyway, a giant street market for local farmers. San Luis Obispo County is known for the quality of its fruits and deliciously tender vegetables. Bright days, cool nights and the humidity of sea fog even in the driest summers combine to give local strawberries their intense flavor, and Higuera Street vendors offer them by the crate, along with bell peppers, basil, and coriander. In season, there are artichokes and snow peas, onions and zucchini, a multitude of lettuces, bok choy and apples, broccoli and avocados, cucumbers, sweet anis, oranges and walnuts. Beef ribs and local sausages are available from huge barbecue pits set up on the sidewalks; flowers massed on all sides sell for a couple of dollars a bunch; and, at every corner, there is a musician, a juggler, or some other street performer trying, usually in vain, to divert attention from fat tomatoes and garden-grown corn sweet enough to eat straight off the cob. In fact, Thursday evenings in San Luis Obispo are as much celebration as commercial endeavor, and except when it rains, the whole town turns out for this weekly *paseo*.

Jack and Catherine Niven, whose family once shared ownership of California's Purity food chain (service- and quality-driven, it didn't survive the great wave of supermarket expansion in the fifties and sixties), already knew of San Luis Obispo's reputation for fruits and vegetables when they were looking, in the early seventies, for land suitable for vines. They were not surprised to learn that Edna Valley, abutting southeastern San Luis Obispo, had been recommended for potentially high quality wine production in the Winkler-Amerine study of California's wine regions, completed back in the 1930s. Jack Foote, San Luis Obispo County Farm Advisor (now retired), had planted an experimental plot of vines in 1968, in fact, and by 1972, when the Department of Viticulture and Enology at the University of California, Davis, made some wine from those grapes, there was general agreement that viticulture in the area was worth pursuing.

For those who cared to look for it, other evidence pointed in the same direction. The Franciscans who had accompanied Junipero Serra in his trek up the coast of California to establish the early missions had planted vines to meet their domestic and religious needs wherever they set up a community. The wine produced at San Luis Obispo was so good, however, that, as word got out, production was stepped up to a commercial scale. The mission's vineyard was extended, and by the first decades of the nineteenth century, according to Dan Krieger, history professor at Cal Poly, Father Antonio Martinez of the San Luis Obispo Mission was making over a hundred barrels of wine a year and trading it with whalers and other missions at a good price. Records show that the San Luis Obispo Mission had the highest revenues of any in California.

That vineyard at San Luis Obispo was temporarily abandoned when Mexico secularized all mission property in declaring herself independent of Spain; but then, some twenty years later, in the 1860s, it was acquired and reconstituted by Pierre Hippolyte Dallidet, a French immigrant. His son, also Pierre Hippolyte, predicted in a local board of trade pamphlet of 1887 that San Luis Obispo's vines would eventually bring great wealth to the county. By then, says Krieger, local farmers—the McCoppins and the Hays, the Andrews and the Taylors, the Atwoods and the Hasbroucks—were already shipping grapes, raisins, and wine to San Francisco from a new wharf at what is now Port San Luis, railhead of the narrow-gauge Pacific Coast Railroad built to connect both wharf and port with the town itself in 1881.

Despite skirmishes with phylloxera and the economic depression of the late 1880s, vineyards continued to flourish in Edna Valley until they disappeared completely with Prohibition. It took the Nivens and Norman and Carolyn Goss to get them started again. The Gosses (Norman was a Los Angeles restaurateur aware of the quality of San Luis Obispo produce) came to the valley independently of the Nivens but at about the same time; both families bought land in 1972 and planted vineyards the following year. In 1975 Andy and Liz McGregor planted sixty-three acres of vines; and then in 1990 and 1991 several hundred more acres of vines were planted as yet more growers moved in to join those by then already well established.

It was never the Nivens' intention to make wine. But in order to grow grapes successfully for others, they had to think of themselves as winemakers. Their Paragon Vineyard Company had had little but theory and the narrowly focused experiments of Jack Foote to guide it in planting five red varieties and three whites in different sites to see how each would react to the range of soils, altitudes, and exposures to sun and wind. As Jack Niven tells the story, it was soon evident that the valley was too cool for Cabernet Sauvignon and Zinfandel, and Merlot just wouldn't set fruit. Equally as clear was proof that any Edna Valley Chardonnay could be successful. But, as no one alive could remember having tasted wine made from Edna Valley grapes, the Nivens' attempts to sell their fruit were at first disappointing.

Their chance to show how good Edna Valley Chardonnay could be came quite fortuitously. Chalone, a winery on a limestone bench two thousand feet up in the Gavilan mountains and about a hundred miles north of Edna Valley, had a reputation for Burgundy-style Chardonnay and Pinot Noir unequalled at the time. The limited supply tended to be kept under wine merchants' counters for a favored few, and the long drive from San Francisco deterred all but the most ardent from attempting to buy directly at the winery. The last part of the three-hour drive leads up a twisting road through miles of parched mountain landscape resembling nothing so much as a Dutch primitive's idea of St. John the Baptist's habitat. In the early seventies, what's more, the winery itself, eerily remote and virtually without either water or electricity, did indeed have an almost religious austerity about it; its domestic-type well and small generator didn't come close to suppling its needs. Since then, the company that owns Chalone has brought in a power line, and that in turn has allowed the winery to install pumps to bring water up seven miles of pipeline from a well in the valley floor. Chalone extended its vineyard in 1977 and also built a new winery large enough to receive the increased crops.

From the beginning, Richard Graff, Chalone's president and its original winemaker, had a policy of using only grapes grown in Chalone's own vineyard for wines sold under the Chalone label. But he hoped to find a use for the winery's spare capacity until the new vines were bearing. At about that time, in the late seventies, John Walker, an eminent wineshop in San Francisco's Financial District, wanted Chardonnay to sell under its own label and knew that Le Central, a nearby bistro popular with Montgomery Street bankers and stockbrokers, was looking for something similar. Their need, Chalone's space, and the Nivens' grapes consequently came together in a private-label program. Begun in 1977 as an arrangement of convenience for all concerned, the program became an enormous success, launching the Edna Valley appellation among a knowledgeable and well-heeled clientele.

By 1979, when Chalone was compelled to take fewer of the Nivens' grapes in order to make room for its own, Richard Graff fully recognized Edna Valley's potential and was loath to cut himself off from it. As a result he and Jack Niven developed the idea of a joint venture between Chalone and the Nivens' Paragon Vineyard Company to make and sell Edna Valley wines. The Nivens had a winery built on their land to Graff's specifications, and this they leased to the new enterprise, Edna Valley Vineyard, in addition to supplying the grapes. Graff's Chalone undertook the responsibility of making the wine and marketing it, and the entire operation was up and ready for the 1980 crush.

If the arrangement with Richard Graff grew out of happenstance, so did Paragon's relationship with Charles Ortman. By the late seventies, Ortman was Napa Valley's Mr. Chardonnay: He had advised, consulted, or actually made Chardonnay for an impressive number of important wineries there, including St. Clement, Spring Mountain, Far Niente, Fisher, and Shafer. Whether inevitably or by chance, Ortman's involvement with Edna Valley, like Graff's, gave the region a great boost in acceptability.

Ortman remembers first working with Edna Valley grapes in 1979. "The Nivens offered me some that had lost their home," he told me recently, reminiscing, and alluding perhaps to the changed situation at Chalone. "So you could say I got the grapes by default. The wine I made from them was bottled under my own label. I was impressed by the fruit and bought again in 1980 and in 1981."

"I didn't have another opportunity to work with Edna Valley grapes until 1987. The wine I made then had still not been released when in 1988 I concluded an agreement with Beringer Vineyards, which bought my brand name, Meridian, and applied it to its new winery near Paso Robles. Beringer's management shared my enthusiasm for Edna Valley, and, as we already had that stock of the Meridian Edna Valley 1987 Chardonnay, the appellation was integrated into the new Meridian program from the start. We've continued to take grapes from Paragon every year, but we have also bought land there and have now planted a hundred acres of Chardonnay of our own."

A number of other wineries also began buying Edna Valley fruit after the 1979 vintage. Because the grapes could be relied on for flavor and texture, the grapes sometimes disappeared into a Central Coast or other blend. Over the years several wineries have earned their Chardonnay laurels thanks to a judicious proportion of Edna Valley grapes. Very few wineries have been able to offer a Chardonnay produced from Edna Valley grapes alone, however, because the quantities available have been so limited. The first vineyards planted, in 1973 and 1975, included fewer than 450 acres of Chardonnay—enough to produce a grand total of about 100,000 cases of wine when the vines could be persuaded to produce at the rate of four tons to the acre, which was seldom. A further 300-plus acres of Chardonnay have recently come into bearing. But there are still fewer than 800 acres of Edna Valley Chardonnay compared with nearly 57,000 acres of Chardonnay in the state of California as a whole.

I had driven down to San Luis Obispo to take a look at Edna Valley, to try to understand what made its Chardonnay unique. For in any Edna Valley Chardonnay certain characteristics stand out regardless of the style of the person who made the wine. The Edna Valley Chardonnay by Charles Ortman at Meridian, though not to be confused with other Edna Valley Chardonnays—whether by Steve Dooley at Edna Valley Vineyards, Brooks Painter at Leeward, Michael Martella at the Thomas Fogarty winery, Gary Mosby at Chimère, Clay Thompson at the Gosses' Chamisal or at his own Claibourne and Churchill winery in San Luis Obispo—is closer to all of them than it is to the Santa Maria Valley Chardonnay also made at Meridian by Ortman.

The phenomenon intrigues me not just because I like Edna Valley Chardonnays but also because Edna Valley, declared an approved American Viticultural Area in 1982, is one of the very few to meet what should be consumers' expectations of all such geographically defined wine regions. An Edna Valley Chardonnay is distinctive, it's recognizable, and it's consistent. And, because Edna Valley vineyards are overwhelmingly Chardonnay (more than three-quarters of the acreage planted in the valley is devoted to this one variety; the rest is divided among many), to ask for a bottle of Edna Valley wine is almost like asking for a bottle of Meursault: within reasonable limits, the buyer knows exactly what to expect.

Though I hadn't known it at the time, I'd begun to unravel Edna Valley's mystery when I'd overshot San Luis Obispo's freeway exits and found myself on the beach. The maritime influence is pervasive in the valley—to a far greater extent than in any other wine region along the Pacific coast. The very soil in which the vines grow is made up largely of marine sediment deposited 25 million years ago, when sea levels rose at the end of the Ice Age. The marine sediment is rich, of course, in the tiny shell fossils that give Champagne and Chablis in France their chalky soils. But it is supplemented here by degraded granite and tufa from a chain of fourteen ancient, greatly eroded volcanos that stretch in a line parallel with the valley from southeast of San Luis Obispo to the ocean. This spectacular formation, some of the peaks worn down to stumps while others loom to a thousand feet or more, seems to end at El Morro, at the entrance to Morro Bay, but actually continues offshore to finish under 3,600 feet of ocean with Davidson Seamount. If soil composition affects the taste of grapes, as is commonly supposed—soil stores the water and nutrients needed for growth while its form and texture control rooting patterns—then it must inevitably affect the taste of any wine. Given the unique soil of Edna Valley, this relationship is particularly relevant.

Many people would say, however, that Edna Valley's grapes and wine are affected to an even greater extent by the valley's unusual climate. California wine regions have been neatly categorized into something called heat-summation zones ever since the time of the Winkler-Amerine study. Albert Winkler and Maynard Amerine, professors at the University of California, Davis, calculated the number of degrees over 50°F—below which almost no growth in a vine is possible—in the mean temperature of each of the growing months (April to October) for a particular region. If the mean temperature for June were 70°F, say, then the excess to be counted would be 20. This they would multiply by 30, the number of days in the month, giving a result of 600. They repeated the calculation for each of the six remaining months of growth and graded California's wine regions into five categories, from cool (2,500 or fewer degree-days) to hot (degree-days in excess of 4,000). These categories have come to be viewed as indicators of which grape varieties are best suited to each region. Simple though it is, the system has been helpful to California winegrowers. But it can be misleading because it cannot distinguish between one region with fairly constant temperatures throughout the growing season and another with extremes—a freeze in April and then a heat wave in August—that balance each other out.

According to the Winkler-Amerine system, Edna Valley is a low Region II (2501 to 3000 degree-days), which ranks it with Santa Rosa in Sonoma County or Asti in Italy's Piedmont. But the actual weather and temperature patterns in Edna Valley are not at all like either Santa Rosa or Asti. In Edna Valley, spring temperatures are much warmer and summer temperatures much cooler than is usually the case in a Region II zone. Vines begin to sprout leaves in Edna Valley up to two weeks earlier than in Napa Valley (parts of which are classified, according to the Winkler-Amerine tables, as a warmer Region III). Edna Valley vines also flower earlier, and their fruit sets sooner. But the lower summer temperatures in Edna Valley allow the fruit to ripen more slowly, so grapes there are normally harvested two weeks or more after those of Napa Valley. Spending up to one month longer on the vine gives Edna Valley grapes a greater concentration of flavor, and, because temperatures have been no more than moderate throughout the summer, the grapes' fruit-sugar is offset by a ripe acidity.

This unusual balance is enhanced by the moisture of morning fogs, which become more frequent and persistent as the grapes linger on the vine into the early days of fall. Similar morning fogs drifting over the vineyards of Sauternes, near Bordeaux, provoke *Botrytis cinerea*, or noble rot, which causes a shrivelling of the grapes. That is what happens in Edna Valley, too. But whereas the growers of Sauternes encourage the botrytis, picking over their vineyards repeatedly to seek out only those grapes fully affected by it, the growers in Edna Valley, not intending their grapes for dessert wine, pick as soon as the botrytis appears.

Rarely is more than 2 or 3 percent of an Edna Valley crop touched by botrytis. But those grapes that are bring a barely perceptible but deliciously honeyed strain to the bouquet of any Edna Valley Chardonnay. More important, botryticin, a natural antibiotic produced by botrytis, moderates the pace of fermentation by impeding the yeast's growth, allowing deeper flavors to develop in the wine and more glycerol to be formed. As a result, Edna Valley Chardonnays, though fermented to be dry, are rounder, fatter and more viscous than others, and have a longer finish. These qualities are accentuated when the wine is fermented in barrel, as most of them are.

The forward, rich style of Edna Valley Chardonnays is specially good with deeply flavored or "meaty" fish, such as salmon or tuna, particularly if the fish is grilled. It's good, too, when fish is served with a cream sauce, which can make a white wine taste thin. But its compatibility is wider than the usual tag of "white wine with fish" might suggest. I've enjoyed Edna Valley Chardonnays with roast chicken; batter-dipped fried eggplant; grilled veal chops; and veal scallops in a sauce made by deglazing the pan with a glass of dry white vermouth and then adding a few sliced mushrooms, seasoning and cream. It's a mouth-filling wine that is not easily defeated.

Before I left San Luis Obispo, I stopped for lunch at a cafe by the creek that runs through the center of town. I took a table on its long narrow deck, cantilevered over the water at the side of the building. In no time at all I had in front of me fresh bread and some perfectly, delicately grilled halibut. It came with nothing but melted butter and a dressed green salad. And a glass of Edna Valley Chardonnay, of course. At that moment, anyway, there seemed to be nothing lacking in life.

31

WINE AND FOOD

Do WE FUSS TOO MUCH OVER PAIRING WINE WITH FOOD? Raymond Oliver, distinguished chef and proprietor of Le Grand Véfour in Paris, once wrote "Apart from the occasional rare and obvious mistake, there are few wines and dishes which really do not marry." Most would agree. For my own part, I have endured my share of awful food and miserable wines, but I have yet to be confronted with truly well prepared food and delicious wine in a combination so bizarre that either or both were actually ruined. Wine and food can be mutually enhancing, but they have a natural affinity in any case and are tolerant of each other to a broad degree. On occasions when I have had cause to reflect on a particularly fine wine failing to show at its best, the food has less often been the obstacle than lack of judgement in serving it on the wrong occasion or in selecting an inappropriate wine (or none at all) to precede it.

Yet seeking a perfect fit of wine and food risks becoming one more complication thrown in the path of those who simply want to enjoy a bottle of wine. The few traditions we lean on, though reassuring, are of dubious value. It is a subject that none of the gastronomic writers of the past, from third-century Athenaeus to nineteenth-century Brillat-Savarin, have even cared to discuss. There were those who cautioned us to drink Muscadet with oysters and a glass of dry Madeira after the soup, as if failure to do either would bring the social opprobrium normally reserved for those who omit to turn down the appropriate corner when leaving cards. But there neither are, nor ever were, rational rules to guide or restrain us in matching wine and food.

Formal meals were once differently composed, of course. Instead of today's well-defined progression of courses that allows all guests to be eating the same thing at the same time, for centuries grand occasions attracted a multitude of dishes to the table, in a series of arrangements that lack cohesion and meaning when seen in the structured context of the way we eat now. Each time the table was reset with a stylized pattern of new dishes, those present might choose to taste all, a few, or none. The dining table itself was a visible menu, starting with half a dozen soups or a dozen unrelated appetizer dishes from which guests helped themselves and each other. With their removal, eight or ten varied entrée dishes would arrive, followed by an assorted selection of roasts, another of vegetables and side dishes, and so on. Fish and meat, sweet and savory, could arrive on the table together, just as today they might be alternative selections on a printed restaurant menu, and, if one guest chose to eat prawns from among the first group of dishes while another helped himself to a sauté of kidneys, how could a host have hoped to plan a series of wines that would progress logically and match the food?

The answer is that he didn't, and nobody seemed much to care. Paintings of such banquets confirm that neither glasses nor wine—whether in bottle or decanter—shared the table with such elaborate food until the late 18th century. Wine bottles usually stood in coolers on the floor or were kept with glasses on a sideboard. When a guest asked for wine, he or she was brought red or white with a glass to drink from. Water was usually mixed with the wine according to preference. The glass, always emptied at one draught (no swirling, sniffing and sipping), was then either handed back to the server or placed upside down in a rinser.

After the French Revolution, Grimod de la Reynière, a former aristocrat who lived well to compensate himself for a physical deformity, instructed the new masters of Paris in the art of living by writing extensively on eating and drinking. His work, which inspired the far less useful but more widely known *Physiologie du Goût* of Brillat-Savarin, his contemporary, provides details of a way of life de la Reynière's prerevolutionary peers had taken for granted and never, therefore, would have recorded for themselves. Drawing on his privileged experience under the *ancien régime*, he explained everything from the way a menu for sixty should be planned to the manner of carving or dividing each kind of bird, fish or joint of meat. He instructed those eager to know how to eat boiled eggs in polite society always to crush the empty shells, inspired in his readers a passion to eat purée of woodcock ("the greatest ecstasy—having tasted it one might as well die," he said,

33

GERALD ASHER

innocently bequeathing a phrase still haunting us in Valley talk), and told them, doubtless with no greater success than our parents, to keep their elbows off the table. He gave excellent directions (would that they were compulsory reading today) on how to accept or decline invitations with prompt courtesy and counseled his readers not only on what could safely be discussed at dinner in the presence of strangers, but why they should avoid houses where they risked paying at cards four times the value of the meal they had eaten.

Of particular interest are his comments on wine. He explained that the beverage wines served during a meal—a Chablis for the white, perhaps, and a Mâcon Rouge for red—should be drunk undiluted only if there were to be no lingering over fine wines later. By the time he published his *Manuel des Amphitryons* (*Hosts' Manual*) in 1808, the beverage wine, water, and glasses had moved from sideboard to table, where guests, free to serve themselves, could follow their own tastes rather than that of a lackey who often premixed the wine and water in proportions to suit his own whim or in accordance with the tip he had in view.

With or without water, however, Grimod de la Reynière expected guests to drink copiously. At a lunch for twenty-five, for example, he recommended providing a dozen bottles each of an ordinary red and an ordinary white wine, to be supplemented at the final service of sweet and savory entremets and dessert with four bottles of fine red Bordeaux, four of Beaune, four of Clos Vougeot, four of white Saint-Peray, two each of the sweet wines of Cyprus and Malaga, and, for good measure, a bottle each of Rivesaltes and Lunel, golden dessert wines from the south of France, all of which would have been drunk without the addition of water, of course. Essentially, de la Reynière shows us that in his day, in the society familiar to him, wine, or wine and water, was quaffed without much thought during the progress of a meal. But at its close, there followed, at leisure, what we might consider a tasting of a few select fine wines with appropriate delicacies.

In eighteenth-century England, a diet mainly of bread and red meat was washed down with copious draughts of Port, still a coarse wine and hardly the classic it has since become. Lady Mary Wortley Montagu, wife of the British ambassador to the Turkish Sultan in Constantinople, found, on the other hand, that in Vienna in 1716 a prepared list of the wines to be offered with dinner—"often as many as eighteen"—was laid with the napkin on each guest's plate. She doesn't tell us, however, whether each wine was served successively on such occasions, whether the list was intended to provide guests with the means to select the appropriate match for any one of the variety of dishes tasted at each course, or whether guests were advised precisely of the extensive choice available merely to ensure that each would find within it a wine to meet his or her particular preference.

But regardless of the ceremony of Paris, the monotony of London, and the ambiguity of Vienna, it has been suggested that the rich bourgeoisie of Hamburg were already fumbling towards matching wines and specific dishes as early as the 1770s, even though published references to their efforts are less than reassuring. They include Malaga partnering fresh herring, Burgundy with peas, and Port with salt fish. I imagine there has been compounded confusion either in the retelling or in the translation.

The possibility of serving wines in sequence, each linked to a specific dish, came only as formal dinners changed in the course of the nineteenth century from a series of gastronomically incongruous set pieces to what was referred to as service à la russe, whereby servants carried the dishes round one at a time, offering them to guests who helped themselves.

Surviving diaries and menus show, however, that little thought was given to wine and food compatibility despite what had become feasible. At a dinner in England in 1847, provision of wines for seventeen consisted of ten bottles of Sherry, two bottles of Port, and one bottle of red Bordeaux, a selection that speaks for itself regardless of what was to be eaten. Mrs. Beeton, in her *Complete Etiquette for Gentlemen* of 1876, makes no bones about recommending Sherry as the appropriate wine for dinner, and even the venerable Professor Saintsbury, whose *Notes on a Cellar Book* is holy writ to most modern wine drinkers, says brightly that "Manzanilla [Sherry] will carry you nearly through dinner, and others of the lighter class will go all through..."

Saintsbury does not discuss wine in the context of food (except to make a passing reference to sparkling Moselle with sardine sandwiches, taken as an undergraduate at Oxford), but the menus with which he closes his book show that, though he preferred always to start with Sherry followed perhaps by a glass of white wine, on special occasions he served his guests Champagne until red Bordeaux, Port, or both appeared to bring the meal to a close. In 1899, Colonel Newnham-Davis, gastronomic correspondent of the *Pall Mall Gazette*, complained that, "In Paris no man dreams of drinking Champagne, and nothing but Champagne, for dinner; but in London . . . ninety-nine out of a hudred Englishmen . . . turn instinctively to the Champagne page of the wine-card." Anthony Trollope, the novelist, writing as a traveler in the United States in 1862, said that Americans in hotels drank mostly at the bar before they ate, but they, too, drank Champagne with dinner on the rare occasions when they did not drink water.

So much for inspiration from our gastronomic past.

Though good wines and food do have a natural affinity and a broader mutual tolerance than we usually admit (except to ourselves, when we dine alone and reach for the bottle we most want to drink without jumping through gastronomic hoops), it is also true that there is special satisfaction in achieving a compatibility so harmonious that it seems unthinkable to have paired either wine or dish in any other way.

The mistake most commonly made is to look for such congeniality by the matching of flavors difficult, if not impossible, to define. Talk of Gewürztraminer wines, for example, accompanying spicy dishes to advantage, is based mostly on the rationalization that *gewürz* means spice. The delicate aroma of a Gewürztraminer—more like the smell of damask roses than any spice I can think of—would be overwhelmed by the pungency of Madras cooking and becomes an irrelevant, even irritating, flourish when imposed on the carefully self-contained balance of most Chinese dishes.

Essentially, the response between wine and food depends on texture, intensity and scale. The texture of a dish is more often established by a sauce or the method of cooking than it is by the density of the basic ingredient. A light, white wine that happily accompanies a plain grilled sole, for example, might taste thin and pointless if served with the same sole under a creamy Mornay sauce. Charts that recommend specific categories of wine with fish, chicken, or veal rarely allow for applied variations in texture, which can make one and the same wine appear to be unexpectedly full or disappointingly light.

A California Johannisberg Riesling, often thought difficult to match to food because of its forward fruitiness and slight sweetness, presents few problems if the modest residual sugar is recognized as part of its textural balance. This natural sugar fills the wine out and makes it a match for dishes in which a ripe texture and a hint of sweetness will find an echo—a grilled veal chop garnished with slightly caramelized *confit* of onions or a *blanquette* of veal or young lamb.

Intensity and persistence of flavor in food and wine must be symmetrical or one will make the other seem fleeting and inconsequential. Veal in a cream and mushroom sauce, for example, presents a rich texture but mild flavor. It calls for the combination of full body and restrained flavor peculiar to barrel-fermented, lees-aged Chardonnay. On the other hand, a dish like chicken with garlic and fennel (from Richard Olney's *Simple French Food*), though without the texture to support a heavy wine, needs one with sustained, exuberant flavor: new Beaujolais, young Chianti, Mendocino Zinfandel. It matters less that the flavor of wine and food should echo each other (how could they?) than that they balance each other. Fish is particularly tricky because we think of it always as light and delicate, but when steamed over ginger, poached with garlic and saffron, or grilled with herbs, the flavor expands and can accept a more assertive wine.

Scale, a combination of texture and flavor intensity, is more than a sum of its parts and harder to define than either. A wine with scale is imposing: one can either match it or play it up. A sumptuous 1978 Châteauneuf-du-Pape, for example, can be matched by a truffled pheasant ("stuff it with 3 oz. of pork fat pounded with a few truffles," recommends Auguste Escoffier in *Ma Cuisine*), or be supported by a simple but succulent filet of beef. In matching an imposing wine, one must be careful not to overreach; and in playing it up, the dish must be bold even if simple. Something or other luxuriantly *financière* would upstage even the most imposing of wines, whereas two lamb chops and a mess of zucchini would be too weak and niggardly.

When serving particularly fine, old red wines it is best to err toward food with lightness of texture (this allows the wine to seem contrastingly full) and to aim for moderation of scale so that the wine's delicacy of flavor is not over-whelmed. Food lacking texture, flavor, and scale altogether would be inappropri-

GERALD   ASHER

ately insipid to accompany a special bottle, however, so careful judgement is needed.

White wines rarely age to the same advantage as red. Those that do will lose their youthful aroma but acquire a deeper flavor—what one might call a grain—allowing them to partner dishes of greater scale. An old-fashioned, mature Italian white wine, even when it's slightly oxidized, can be a revelation with pasta in the kind of creamy gorgonzola sauce that would make nonsense of a fresh, young Orvieto.

Because food affects the appreciation of a wine far more than a wine can possibly influence the taste of food, time given to assessing how the texture, intensity and scale of a finished dish, as opposed to its principal component, will modify a wine, is better used, surely, than searching through a thousand tasting notes to find a wine with an herbal aroma or an alleged hint of clove in its bouquet to support an ingredient or garnish. One man's herb is another man's green leaf, this one's hint of clove is another's geranium finish. Looking for specific and identical matching flavors in wine and food is the way to madness and perdition.

Once the principles of texture, intensity, and scale are understood, mentally checking the probable harmony between wine and food becomes automatic and uncertainties are easily resolved. In any case, there is never only one correct choice. There are usually several choices that will work very well, and an almost infinite number that will work tolerably well.

A wine and a dish might work well together and still be an inappropriate combination for the occasion, however. If, for instance, a few friends are invited to a dinner of plain, broiled steaks, the vigorous and unpretentious Gigondas recently discovered will work as well as the last, treasured bottle of Mouton-Rothschild '53 left in the cellar. In one case, however, the evening becomes an informal, relaxed get-together. In the other, the steak plays up to the Mouton-Rothschild, which therefore looms in importance and cannot be ignored. Its presence therefore could introduce an unintended focus at the table, and possibly an unwelcome formality. The choice of wine, always assuming it to be compatible, dresses both the dish and the occasion up or down.

There are times when the wine adds its own sheen to an occasion. Raymond Oliver, in *The French at Table*, wrote:

I like a wine to be presented in a given context: the vintage of a friend's year of birth, a shared memory, an anniversary or some such reason. Then the wine becomes a symbol whose value lies outside the accepted canon.

Any exaggerated or even obvious effort to coordinate such a wine diminishes rather than enhances its special role. As in so many situations, success is assured by knowing what *not* to do. If it is an imposing bottle, never match it, always play up to it. If the wine is comparatively simple except for the memories it is intended to shake loose, don't compensate by elaborating the food unnecessarily. Let the food be simple, too, but think of subtle ways in which it can be made to reinforce the wine's message.

A special wine, no matter how defined, will be appreciated all the more if a preceding bottle establishes criteria for it. Often an occasion to drink one remarkable wine is expanded into an occasion to drink two, or even more; unfortunately, rarely is one of them adequate preparation for the others. Use the first wine as a curtain raiser, to set the mood and establish a standard that will then be gloriously excelled by the special wine of the evening. A simple, light red wine, preferably one that has lost or is losing its youthful fruitiness, will show off an older red wine of great delicacy far better than an initial white wine can. On the other hand, a massive wine with subtleties that could be missed in reaction to its scale, should be preceded by a robust but straightforward wine that will make scale itself less remarkable.

Unfortunately, this preparatory sequence does not work well among white wines. In fact, I would serve one white wine with another only if there was a particular reason to do so. When young, white wines rely more than red on varietal aroma for their distinction, and, though the contrast of one young varietal against another might be interesting at the tasting bench, it is meaningless at the table. An older white wine, on the other hand, no matter how magnificent, is reduced to being merely an older white wine when seen against a younger one.

More important than remembering all these principles and examples, however, is to bear in mind that wine and food, in any combination, taste better with amiable companions. Start there, I find, and everything falls into place.

MISSOURI: THE RETURN OF THE NATIVE

I'D ARRIVED IN HERMANN, MISSOURI, TWO DAYS TOO LATE FOR THE ANNUAL GREAT STONE HILL BEAST FEAST, SO I'D MISSED THE POSSUM TERIYAKI, THE RACCOON PIE AND THE BEAVER JAMBALAYA. Every year local hunters provide for a charity benefit a selection of fauna worthy of Daniel Boone. Along with possum, raccoon, and beaver, Gary Buckler, proprietor of Hermann's Vintage 1847 restaurant, had been able to prepare other old-time frontier favorites like bobcat *bourguignonne*, marinated Montana mule deer rounds, coyote and fox salami, and stuffed water buffalo Florentine.

The wines, donated by Stone Hill Winery, were all Missouri-grown—the best of them a red made from Norton, an indigenous American grape that might yet do for Missouri what Cabernet Sauvignon has done for California. Norton is unusual, a native wine grape with no hint of the grape-jelly aroma and flavor we associate with Concord and other labrusca hybrids. But then Norton is not labrusca; it's a "summer grape," known to botanists as *Vitis aestivalis*.

More than a century ago, Missouri Norton was described as one of America's finest red wines—"full-bodied, deep-coloured, aromatic, and somewhat astringent . . . only needing *finesse* to equal a first-rate Burgundy"—by no less a wine judge than Henry Vizetelly, one of the great names of nineteenth-century wine commentary. Vizetelly, an Englishman, had tasted a Missouri Norton from Hermann at the 1873 Vienna World Exhibition, where it had taken a gold medal. In a report to the British government Vizetelly described the town of Hermann as the hub of Missouri's vineyards, "which promise to become," he wrote, "not merely the most prolific vineyards of the [United] States, but also those yielding the best wines."

That promise, alas, has yet to be fulfilled. A combination of problems had already begun to undermine Missouri's viticulture even as Vizetelly wrote of the state's imminent triumph, and Prohibition delivered the *coup de grâce*. From then on, the changed use of grapes from wine to juice and jelly meant that almost all the Norton vines of the Missouri River valley, and with them the expectations they had raised, were ripped out. Acres of Concord were planted instead on the Ozark highlands farther southwest, a site more convenient for the Welch's Grape Juice plant in Arkansas.

It was probably just as well that the dinner I shared at Vintage 1847 with Gary Buckler, Jon Held, and Patricia Held-Uthlaut (the latter two are the son and daughter of Stone Hill's owners) was less eclectic than the Great Beast Feast. I was raised on *The Wind in the Willows* rather than *Huckleberry Finn*, and I'm not sure how sharp my appetite would have been for badger pâté. But we did have venison steaks with an appropriate—considering the company—Norton red wine sauce. (In fact, the sauce was doubly appropriate: the deer had been shot by Gary Buckler, from his kitchen door, as it was munching its way through some choice Norton grapes on a row of vines planted in 1868, part of the sole quarter-acre of Missouri's Norton to have survived Prohibition.) The Helds had placed on the table four vintages of Stone Hill Norton—1989, 1988, 1985, and 1984—so that I'd have an idea of how Norton tasted both young and with a little age.

Even after reading Vizetelly, and others, I was astonished to find the wines so remarkably good. They were more meaty than fruity, with something of the Rhône about them. The 1985, in particular, rounded out by its time in wood and fully developed by several years in bottle, was quite delicious. I finally understood, as I never really had before, why Vizetelly had been so confident of Missouri's wine future.

We have lost the habit of seeing Missouri as a wine state, but in Vizetelly's day few Americans could have been surprised at Norton's success at the Vienna exhibition. Missouri's vineyards were important and the state's wines enjoyed high regard. According to United States census figures from 1869, Missouri contributed 42 percent of the total United States wine production, compared with California's 27 percent and New York's 13 percent.

In that third quarter of the nineteenth century, almost all who led in viticultural innovation and research in the United States were in, of, or associated with Missouri. They included Frederick Muench of Augusta, Missouri, whose book, *School for American Grape Culture*, is as clear a guide to grape growing as anyone might want even today; George Husmann, of Hermann, whose *American Grape Growing and Wine Making* remained the standard viticultural textbook for American growers until well into this century; and Isidor Bush, a Missouri nurseryman whose catalogue gave such detailed information on laying out and maintaining a vineyard and on the advantages, disadvantages, and correct cultivation of each grape variety named that it was translated and published internationally for use as a growers' manual. A Swiss-trained Missouri viticulturalist named Hermann Jaeger was responsible, with Husmann, Bush and Thomas Volney Munson of Denison, Texas, for finding and supplying by the million the appropriate rootstocks (both resistant to phylloxera and adaptable to French growing conditions) that saved French viticulture from the root-louse inadvertently introduced into France from America in the 1860s. The idea of permanently grafting European vinifera onto resistant native American rootstocks, the method of protection still used today, had been first proposed by Missouri's state entomologist, Charles Riley, who was honored by the French government for his timely intervention. Both Jaeger and Munson were also decorated handsomely in recognition of their exertions on behalf of French winegrowers.

If Missouri's place in the history of American viticulture has been neglected, so has the role of the Midwest in general, although American winemaking can be said to have begun there. Early attempts to grow grapes for wine on the Eastern Seaboard had failed. In his *History of Wine in America,* Thomas Pinney tells us that Midwest viticulture started with a vineyard planted at the end of the eighteenth century by Francis Menissier, a Frenchman, at what is now Main and Third in Cincinnati. Menissier succeeded in an attempt to grow grapes for wine but failed in his 1806 petition to Congress for a grant of land on which to plant more vines. His achievement nevertheless impressed Nicholas Longworth, a lawyer then recently arrived in Cincinnati from New Jersey.

According to Pinney, Longworth soon made a fortune in property speculation—at one time he and John Jacob Astor were the two largest contributors of taxes to the United States Treasury—and was devoting it to his passion for horticulture. Along with helping to develop the cultivation of strawberries, he turned his attention to viticulture and began, in the 1820s, to plant Catawba on the banks of the Ohio River. His first cuttings came from John Adlum, a Washington, D.C., grower who had discovered Catawba in a garden in Clarksburg, Maryland, in 1819.

Adlum claimed that he rendered greater service to his country by this chance discovery than had he "paid off the National Debt." But there was little profit in Catawba for Longworth until the late 1840s, when he first used the Champagne method of bottle fermentation—perfected in France not long before— to produce a sparkling version of the wine. It was an immediate and enormous success. Henry Wadsworth Longfellow, perhaps under its influence, wrote the now notorious lines in which sparkling Catawba is described as "more divine, / More dulcet, delicious and dreamy" than Champagne itself. A London journalist visiting Cincinnati in the 1850s on behalf of the *Illustrated London News* praised the wine in equally mawkish verse as "The pure and the true / As radiant as sunlight / As soft as the dew." But no matter how fatuous the endorsements, demand was overwhelming, and there were soon thousands of acres of Catawba around Cincinnati.

Disaster loomed almost at once, however, as mildew and rot, conditions to which Catawba is particularly vulnerable, took hold in the vineyards, encouraged by the warm and humid summers of the Ohio River valley. "By the end of the [1850s]," Pinney says, "it was clear that the very existence of the industry was ... problematical."

While Longworth had been busy in Cincinnati, German immigrants were settling the Missouri River valley west of St. Louis. They had been drawn there by romantic descriptions of its idyllic landscape published by Gottfried Duden, a German social reformer, who had lived in and explored the valley in the 1820s. According to Peter Poletti, assistant professor in the Department of Economics and Geography at the University of Missouri, St. Louis, thousands of Germans bought copies of Duden's report of his travels in Missouri and used them as guidebooks when fleeing to America from the harsh repression that followed Europe's revolutionary disturbances of 1830. Many had been members of what we would call the intelligentsia rather than craftsmen or farmers, but they settled into the simple life of America's then frontier. Pinney tells us that earlier arrivals from Germany called the Duden-inspired immigrants *lateinische Bauern,* Latin Peasants, a snide reference to their classical learning and intellectual pursuits.

Philadelphia's German Settlement Society, founded to establish in North America a specifically German colony where the best of the Old World could be preserved in the New, was enough encouraged by Missouri's distinctly German flavor to send an emissary to that state. He bought eleven thousand acres on bluffs above the south bank of the Missouri River, about eighty miles west of St. Louis and just downstream from the confluence of the Missouri and its tributary, the Gasconade. The first settlers arrived in the winter of 1837 and, in character with their *lateinische* education, named their new home Hermann in honor of an ancient German hero revered for defeating a Roman army. The newcomers made their aspirations clear from the start by building houses of brick instead of wood. They laid them out on straight, broad streets and planted shade trees. The town's main street was wider than Market Street in Philadelphia because Hermann was to be an important city, a beacon of German thought and culture. A German language newspaper began publication almost immediately. (Most—indeed, almost all—of the houses built in Hermann in those years are now on the National Register of Historic Places.)

Wine had not been a priority in Hermann, despite the urgings of George Husmann's father, Johann, a native of Bremen. (Bremen is far from any wine-producing region but was, and is, a port much involved with the international wine trade.) Most of the other settlers were from northern Germany, too, and had brought neither the skills nor a wine culture with them. But in 1845, a good first crop of Catawba on a few vineyards "only three years old" seems to have caused considerable interest, which was intensified by the sight of newly bearing, bunch-laden Isabella vines trained over an arbor at Hermann's Main and Schiller Streets. A report in the *Hermanner Wochenblatt,* the town's newspaper, concluded that the quantity of grapes on the vines gave hope for Hermann and its region. The town's trustees, thinking Hermann's rocky bluffs could be put to good economic use only as vineyards, had already begun to offer special lots at the low price of fifty dollars each, with five years to pay and no interest asked—provided the buyers agreed to plant vines. Six hundred lots were sold. In 1847 Michael Poeschel founded the town's first winery (eventually to be known as Stone Hill), doubtless in expectation of the considerable harvests to come.

Though both varieties were brought into Hermann in 1843, Catawba was favored over Norton. Norton's red wine needs to be aged, as do most potentially great red wines, and that would have been difficult for newly established growers with meager capital and pressing cash needs. In any case, Hermann's growers were influenced by Longworth—the first Catawba vines had come from Cincinnati. By the time sizable crops were appearing in the early 1850s, demand for the variety was already running high, thanks to the success of Longworth's sparkling wine.

John Zimmermann, Nicholas Longworth's partner, wrote to the *Wochenblatt* offering Hermann's growers the price paid in Cincinnati provided they would sell juice rather than wine. ("Winemaking is different from grape growing, and the Hermann growers do not understand the work. The problem can be avoided if we are allowed to purchase the juice as soon as the grapes are pressed.") He urged Hermann growers not to plant Norton, though it was increasingly in favor, because the grape was "not suitable for mass-produced wine.... The Catawba is the best grape," he said, doubtlessly thinking of his company's needs.

The *Wochenblatt* reported a few weeks later, on October 15, 1852, that Hermann's grape crush for the year had yielded only six thousand gallons, less than half the volume of previous harvests and barely a quarter of what was to be expected from the town's maturing vineyards. The vines, mostly Catawba, had been badly affected by the maladies to which the variety is prone, and to which Norton is largely resistant.

Norton had been "discovered" in more than one place at more than one time, causing confusion later when two differently named varieties appeared to be one and the same. The accepted origin, as given in Thomas Volney Munson's book *Foundations of American Grape Culture*, is Cedar Island in Virginia's James River, where it was found growing wild in 1835. It was named for and cultivated and introduced by Dr. Daniel Norton of Richmond (though it was not he who had found it). After the disastrous harvest of 1852, Missouri's growers increasingly turned to Norton. Frederick Muench, who thought the grape a gift to the state "worth millions," wrote that it was much in demand for the excellence of its dark red wine: "When three or four years old it is hardly surpassed." But what probably appealed to Hermann's growers was the vine's resistance to summer diseases and its tolerance of winter cold.

Norton grapes ripen evenly and resist rot. ("[Their] thin, tough [skin] never cracks," Munson wrote.) It was for similar reasons and at about the same time that Cabernet Sauvignon became the preferred grape of Bordeaux's Médoc. Norton's spread in Missouri was slower than Cabernet Sauvignon's in France because Norton is not easily reproduced from cuttings. With an alternative process, layering—the technique of burying a shoot and separating it from the parent plant when it has thrown out its own roots—years can pass before there are enough vines to set even a small vineyard. Muensch hoped that Missouri's growers would persevere. "This one state," he claimed, "could [then] supply the whole Union with red wine, cheaper than any good foreign wine can now be had."

The "other" Norton, Cynthiana, is said to have been found in Arkansas. Husmann obtained samples of it from the Prince nursery in Flushing, New York, in 1858 and urged its adoption. He thought it superior to Norton and said it would produce "the best red wine we yet have, resembling but surpassing Burgundy." Isidor Bush's catalogue called Cynthiana "our BEST AND MOST VALUABLE grape for red wine."

Even though these men and others thought Cynthiana better than Norton, everyone agreed that the two varieties—both *Vitis aestivalis*—were remarkably similar. Researchers at Cornell University's Agricultural Experiment Station at Geneva, New York, have recently published their finding that Norton and Cynthiana, at least as presently grown, are indeed indistinguishable. This conclusion suggests that either the two always were one, or, if once different, then all present plantings, under whichever name—including the 1868 plot of Norton at Hermann, which provided some of the material for the research—must have been propagated from just one version of the two.

Like the growers of the Ohio River valley, Missouri growers had to contend with mildew and rot from the start. They also had to bear constantly increasing costs as wages rose in competition with the manpower demands of Missouri's new industries. For these reasons, a pound of grapes grown in Missouri in 1899 cost twice as much to produce as a pound of grapes grown in California. The result was inevitable: from having produced 42 percent of the nation's wine in 1869, Missouri contributed a bare 3 percent thirty years later.

The woes of Missouri's winegrowers were aggravated by local Prohibitionists, whose tactics had been weakening and eroding their wine market even before the Volstead Act destroyed it altogether. In today's not dissimilar climate, it is ironic, and sad, to read of George Husmann attempting to point out, in 1870, the medical benefits of drinking red wine. America waited (and wasted) 120 years to see it on *60 Minutes* before paying attention. In Missouri, Prohibitionists, no doubt believing that their end justified any means, struck the lowest blow at their vintner neighbors toward the end of World War I by appealing to nationalist sentiment of the worst kind. The Citizens' Dry Alliance, having made much of the connection between German Americans and Missouri's breweries and vineyards, fought for ratification of the amendment outlawing the sale of alcoholic beverages by advertising in Missouri newspapers that a "dry vote is a vote against the Kaiser." "This patriotic appeal," says Poletti, "was to prove decisive in the passing of the Eighteenth Amendment."

With the onset of Prohibition, the Missouri wine industry died. At Stone Hill, the second largest winery in the country at the turn of the century and possibly the third largest in the world, the huge, carved casks—known as the Twelve Apostles—were carted away and the underground cellars stacked with trays for the cultivation of mushrooms.

Perhaps it is excessive to suggest that mushrooms sprouting in the dark under a hill that had once been covered with vines are vaguely reminiscent of those Greek myths of Dionysus dying, like all the nature gods, only to be reborn. But Dionysus *was* reborn, in Hermann anyway, and in just the sort of tell-me-a-story circumstance the ancient Greeks would have loved.

In 1965 Bill Harrison, then owner of Stone Hill, invited Jim and Betty Ann Held to use a small part of his underground cellars to make some wine. The Helds had very little land, very little money, and four small children, but they were cultivating an acre or two of Catawba on their farm near Hermann and selling the grapes to a winery out of state. Jim Held, descended from a family that had arrived in Herrmann at its founding in 1837, says he tried his best to remember what he had seen his grandfather do, and did it—with whatever primitive utensils could be found in a winery that had been dormant for fifty-odd years. The family (even seven-year-old Jon helped mangle the crush) made 1,500 gallons of wine, the first commercially significant quantity of wine to be made in Hermann since Prohibition. Harrison, having allowed the Helds to see for themselves what they could do, then insisted that they buy Stone Hill and bring the winery back to life. In 1992, Stone Hill produced 136,208 gallons of wine.

There had been about sixty-five wineries, large and small, producing three million gallons of wine a year in Hermann when Prohibition closed it all down. Wine had been the town's lifeblood. Since then, Hermann had been in fast fade: Two of its three banks had been forced to close, the population had dwindled, and buildings had been abandoned. That first creaking turn of the grape crusher at Stone Hill brought back to life more than a winery. Hermann itself has flourished, thriving along with its wineries (the town now has four) and the restaurants their revival has encouraged. Small hotels and bed-and-breakfasts bring business to art galleries, antique shops and local craftspeople. And, thanks to owners and employees who need families fed, clothes cleaned, cars serviced and plumbing repaired, Hermann, a grim statistic less than thirty years ago, has a growing tax base. It's now a daily stop for Amtrak trains running between St. Louis and Kansas City. Tens of thousands of visitors come to the town every year, and, although they arrive expecting little more than a jolly picnic, a hop to a polka band, and a few bottles to take home, most leave with a greater appreciation of the state of Missouri, possibly with a broader feel for its history and, especially in the fall at the time of the grape harvest festivals, with indelible memories of the Missouri River valley's natural beauty.

Stone Hill is the largest winery in Missouri, but there are roughly thirty others that followed its lead. They range from Lucian Dressel's elegantly restored Mount Pleasant Winery at Augusta—once the property of Frederick Muench's family—and Jim and Pat Hofherr's St. James Winery (an emporium as much as a winery) on busy Route 44 to some that produce every year, in the simplest facilities, a thousand or so cases of more than creditable wine. All these vintners, whatever their size, depend on direct sales for most of their revenues. The volume of Missouri wine distributed through stores within the state is growing, but it still represents less than twenty percent of the wine produced.

So Missouri wineries, like Mahomet's mountain, must encourage potential customers to come to them, occasionally resorting to tricking out staff in lederhosen and dirndls as attractions that would have horrified the original *lateinische Bauern*. Their tasting rooms and shaded decks, however, are not unlike nineteenth-century *guingettes*, those simple garden taverns by the Seine preserved for us forever on the Impressionists' canvases. They offer a relaxed and convivial atmosphere, with tours of the winery for those who want them. Most provide at the least a selection of sausages, cheeses, and bread, and a few are even more ambitious, offering full meals or lodging. If some—such as Montelle, on Osage Ridge near Augusta—have magnificent views of the Missouri River valley that draw crowds of tourists, others—such as Heinrichshaus or Adam Puchta, both hidden away on back roads—are destinations known only to the initiated. Every winery has its own personality.

Much of what the Missouri wineries sell, it must be said, is still slightly sweet, slightly pink, and slightly fizzy, because that's a wine formula that has never been known to fail. The state's viticultural renaissance began with Catawba, after all, because Catawba was already planted, as in the Helds' vineyard. (Advances in methods of protecting Catawba vines from mildew and rot give more consistent crops than was possible a hundred years ago.) Using what was available in the state also meant accepting Concord occasionally. And some wineries still blend fruit juices with their wine—producing a local version of the "cooler"—to create a broader appeal. Some of these practices might raise eyebrows, but if the vintners depend on those who come to the winery for their sales, then they have to be sure that those who do come will find something they like, whatever their taste.

At the same time, the winemakers understand that if there is to be more than just folklore in their future they have to produce wines with more than popular appeal. They have to restore if not the glory then at least the former good standing of Missouri's viticulture. A concerted effort was made by the state's Wine and Grape Advisory Board, by the state Department of Agriculture and by Southwest Missouri State University to fund research at the State Fruit Experiment Station into the varieties best adapted to Missouri's climate and growing conditions. The station also provides hands-on, practical counseling for the state's growers and winemakers.

The results are already impressive. French hybrids (crossings of French and American varieties tolerant of Missouri's winters and largely resistant to the region's vine maladies) rather than Catawba and Concord now predominate in Missouri vineyards. Winemaking techniques have been adapted to suit them. Seyval, for example, gives an excellent wine when barrel-fermented, as happens at Stone Hill and Heinrichshaus among others. Vidal makes a delicious Champagne-method sparkling wine, as anyone can judge at Stone Hill or at Hermannhof, where it is winemaker Al Marks's specialty. Vignoles, an unusual white hybrid genetically based in part on Pinot Noir, gives wines the rich texture and fragrance of Pinot Gris. Some producers—in particular Blumenhof, Hermannhof, Heinrichshaus and Stone Hill—make this wine in a mellow, slightly sweet style, but it is stunningly good when dry. A mellow 1991 Vignoles from Hermannhof was declared Best White Wine of the New World at the International New World Wine Competition in California last year; it was given stiff competition from a dry 1991 Vignoles, an exceptional wine from Montelle, which took a gold medal. I understand that even the judges were surprised when their blind choice was revealed to them.

When I was in Missouri two or three years ago I tasted some good wines from red hybrids, too—most notably a 1992 Chambourcin made by Blumenhof in nouveau style and a sprightly 1991 Chambourcin at Heinrichshaus. To extend the choice of black grapes available to Missouri growers, Bob Goodman, a plant pathologist and professor emeritus at the University of Missouri working as an adjunct at the State Fruit Experiment Station, has been combing the vineyards of Eastern Europe (especially those in Hungary and Moravia) for cuttings of varieties tolerant of severely cold winters. "Our summer diseases we can hope to deal with," he told me. "But no one can change this state's weather." In Missouri, evidently, even Dionysus has to wear earflaps.

Norton (or Cynthiana—some growers insist on using the other name and even insist that the two are different) already offers everything Missouri needs, of course, and has a history of success in the state. It has the obvious commercial disadvantage of needing to be aged, and its complicated acidity can set traps for winemakers. (I can't explain that without going into pH, something I vowed long ago never to do.) But it is well adapted to Missouri's climate and maladies and gives superb wine if handled right. That much is clear not only from the wines I tasted at Stone Hill, but from others produced by Hermannhof, Adam Puchta, Blumenhof, Heinrichshaus, and the Augusta Winery. The acreage of Norton has been increased discreetly in the last year or so, showing that Missouri wineries believe in this grape. (They all seem to sell out of one Norton vintage before the next is ready for release.) We should cheer them on. It could be that Henry Vizetelly is to be vindicated at last.

BARBARESCO

'VE NEVER BEEN MUCH INTERESTED IN THE LATEST FOOD FAD. Nouvelle, Cajun, South-western, Thai, high this and low that have all swept past me. I prefer familiar dishes; they talk to me. I'm happiest with lentil soup, good risotto, a roast bird, lamb cooked almost any way, beans, grilled peppers, a wild mushroom sauté and *stracotto*—that slowly cooked Italian stew that gives a glimpse of paradise. And though I enjoy wine of all kinds (How could I not?), when I eat one of those comfortable, comforting old favorites, the wine I most enjoy is a Barbaresco, preferably one with a little bottle age and an aroma that reminds me of dried apricots, damp earth and old leather.

Barbaresco, like Barolo, is made from Nebbiolo grapes grown in the Langhe hills near Alba, southeast of Turin in Piedmont. Alba is the chief market for the surrounding white-truffle country as well as a center of red wine production, a dual role that places it at the hub of a regional cooking so delicious and so bountiful that only Gargantua could really do justice to it. Mind you, in November, at the peak of the truffle season, hungry Swiss and Germans swarm through the Alpine passes and do their best. For a month they fill every hotel, inn, and restaurant within fifty miles of Alba. And there they feast. And feast.

In most other regions of the world the four or five *antipasti* served without ceremony at such Albese restaurants as La Contea di Neive, Belvedere, La Fioraia, Guido, or the new San Marco in Canelli would alone constitute a banquet of major proportions. There might be veal *carpaccio* with slivers of truffle; some rabbit liver pâté, perhaps; then, just a small filet of sea trout; a tiny soufflé aromatic with herbs; some tender cardoon in a cheese *fonduta*.... And surely one can't refuse to taste a slice of homemade sausage on creamy puréed potatoes? The tempting little dishes, so simple, so chaste, follow each other in seemingly never-ending succession from the kitchen. But then how can one manage the *risotto al Barolo* or the *agnollotti* in a meat gravy, the braised shoulder of lamb, and all the rest of the real business of dinner? Somehow, one can and one does.

Both Barbaresco and Barolo rank among the greatest of Italy's classic red wines. We are inclined to believe that anything "classic" must have been around forever, but neither of these two even existed—at least, not as we know them today—until the middle of the last century, a mere snap of the fingers against the four thousand years that vines have been cultivated on the Italian peninsula. When Thomas Jefferson visited Piedmont in 1787—a journey during which he noted down everything he saw that might be of use to the newly independent United States, from how to prepare *mascarpone* to the best way of constructing a pontoon bridge across a swiftly flowing river—he wrote that he found the Nebbiolo wine to be "about as sweet as the silky Madeira, as astringent on the palate as Bordeaux, and as brisk as Champagne."

Paris wine merchant André Jullien's 1816 book, *Topographie de Tous les Vignobles Connus*, an account of all the world's vineyards as they existed in his day, was the primary source for almost all other books on wine written in the nineteenth century. In it he described Piedmont's Nebbiolo wine in terms similar to Jefferson's, referring to its "sweet taste . . . accompanied by an agreeable sharpness." At that time Nebbiolo wines tasted sweet and sharp simultaneously because the grapes were partly dried on mats or racks to concentrate both their sugar and acid. Hence the astringency both Jefferson and Jullien noted, which was due to the resultant greater proportion of skins to juice. Much the same happens now in Valpolicella in the making of *recioto*. The "briskness" that Jefferson charitably compared with Champagne's sparkle was probably the result of poorly managed fermentation. Jullien, either less tactful or less kindly than Jefferson, simply castigates the wine as defective. Contemporary opinions of Piedmont winemaking were nowhere very high. My 1810 edition of the *Encyclopaedia Britannica* describes Piedmont wines as *brusco*—a word Italians usually reserve for bad weather and disagreeable manners—and dismisses them, without further explanation, as "very wholesome for fat people."

Matters changed in the 1840s, when Victorine Colbert, the French wife of a nobleman in Barolo, hired a compatriot, Louis Oudart, to take charge of wine-making on her husband's estate. Burton Anderson, in his *Wine Atlas of Italy,* says that Oudart's "conversion of previously sweet Nebbiolo into a dry wine aged in barrels was such a revelation that Piedmont's Prime Minister Cavour hired him to do the same" at his property nearby. Oudart's work for Cavour (later the architect of Italy's unification) was followed by a spell at the Castello di Neive, near Barbaresco, where the lever-screw presses Oudart used for the then owner, Conte Castelborgo, still stand in a corner of the castle's cellar.

Oudart's ideas were more quickly adopted in Barolo than in Barbaresco, some twenty miles distant, giving Barolo a lead in the market that developed for this new style of Nebbiolo wine. Barolo's place on the best tables was assured, in any case, once Victor Emmanuel II installed his special friend, a Barolo girl known to all as La Bella Rosín, in a royal hunting lodge nearby. There was more than a little nudge, nudge, wink, wink behind the promotion of Barolo as the "wine of kings," but then the court was still a novelty in late-nineteenth-century Italy even if mistresses weren't, so the association—of the king with Barolo, that is—was too great an asset to be wasted.

The winemaking changes Oudart initiated were consolidated in the 1880s by Domizio Cavazza, founder of both Alba's wine school (still one of Italy's best) and, in 1894, of a wine cooperative in Barbaresco that helped complete the transformation there. Barbaresco remained for some time, nevertheless, a sort of junior partner to Barolo. Not only had it entered the market later but it also had only half the acreage of vines.

Cavazza's cooperative was forced to disband during Italy's fascist era, but its revival was instigated in 1958 by parish priest Don Fiorino to encourage young men, drifting away to the booming Fiat factory in Turin, to stay at home. The cooperative's new building, erected in 1961, takes up one side of the tiny piazza by the church at the top of Barbaresco's only street. With fifty-seven members, the association of Produttori del Barbaresco now incorporates half the growers and half the vineyards of the village (but not of the Barbaresco appellation, which includes the neighboring communities of Treiso and Neive). Its members contribute grapes grown on some of Barbaresco's most favored sites, but the quality of even the finest grapes would be squandered without the strict control imposed by the cooperative's president, Celestino Vacca. Members are required, for example, to bring their grapes to the winery in small baskets rather than by the truckload so that an appropriate selection, almost to the bunch, can be made before any fruit passes to the crusher.

It is standard practice for cooperatives to insist that every member deliver his entire crop of grapes to the winery. A cooperative doesn't want to be just a useful dump for imperfect grapes growers prefer not to keep for themselves. The Barbaresco cooperative goes further. It requires its members to deliver their best grapes but reserves the right to refuse any of them it considers substandard. Members are encouraged by a system that rewards specially fine lots. As a result, the cooperative's wines, impeccably made and appealingly plump, have a ripe, concentrated style. Were André Jullien to return to Piedmont now and taste them, he would have to drink his words.

The cooperative's wines also point up the differences among Barbaresco's discrete vineyard sites because it receives grapes from just about every one of them and processes each batch separately. In good years it bottles them separately too, labeling each wine with the name of the vineyard location—the "cru," as they say, using a French word for which there is as yet no official Italian equivalent—where it was grown. (Dialect words like *sorì*, for "sunny place," and *bricco*, meaning "hilltop," are now commonly used in Piedmont to designate a site with a distinguishing microclimate.)

Cavazza had drawn up a map of Barbaresco's vineyards a hundred years ago, basing it on exposures and microclimates. Aldo Vacca, Celestino's son and the cooperative's vineyard advisor, talked to me about the differences among the sites and slopes when I visited Barbaresco not too long ago. "Alba's wine producers and bottlers have always taken such distinctions into account when buying grapes here," he said. "They buy grapes from one section for body, look somewhere else for structure. They get aroma from here, strength from there."

In the 1960s Prunotto and Vietti, two particularly respected regional producers who have long-standing relationships with Barbaresco growers, started to give their wines "cru" designations. Allowing the consumer to become familiar with the vineyard names stimulated interest and demand. The producers didn't seem to mind that it gave more power and control to the growers. The greater prestige and added value of the wines were what counted most.

By and large, Barbaresco wines are assumed to be softer than Barolo, more fragrant and more delicately finished. But the choices we now have among "cru" wines allow us to see that Barbaresco varies from one vineyard to another almost as much as Barolo does. Nebbiolo ripens late, when autumn days are already shortening and mist drifts through the valleys, so the more southerly a vineyard's exposure the better the fruit will be. That's why it has always been the rule in Piedmont to plant prime vines where winter snow melts first. But because even south-facing slopes have shoulders exposed to the east or southeast, west or southwest, variations of style are inevitable.

A wine from a grower with vines on Barbaresco's Montestefano, for instance, is indistinguishable from the firmest Barolo; it is closed, even austere, when young and a serious mouthful only when mature. "But there are many contrasts," Aldo Vacca told me. "Though Montestefano wines are difficult at first, Pora wines, which age just as well, are forward and easier to enjoy from the beginning. Those from Ovello are much the same. Wines from Moccagatto, which faces southeast, have less power but are more flowery; they have finesse rather than body.

"The best, and best known, of the sites here in Barbaresco, however, are probably Rabajà and Asili. They are really two halves of a single slope, with Martinenga, owned entirely by the Marchesi di Gresy, nestled between and below them. Rabajà wines can be as aromatic and as graceful as those of Moccagatto but with more substance. Asili wines have the best of everything: austerely tannic when young, just as Montestefano wines are, they soften with time and develop a wonderfully intense perfume. Montefico and Rio Sordo have the same exposure as Montestefano, and they too need age before they mellow. But, unlike Montestefano, they never lose a certain rustic quality."

The wines of Barbaresco's Pajè (sometimes listed as Pagliere) can be rustic, too, even angular. But thanks to good acidity they remain fresh over the years even as they develop the typical Barbaresco aroma of the forest, of mushrooms and game. Among those growers with vines on the Pajè slope, the best is Alfredo

Roagna. Roagna's wines have a hand-hewn quality typical of Pajè; but the one he bottles as Crichët (a dialect word) rather than Barbaresco, aged entirely in new French oak barrels, is so rich and unctuous, so atypical of a Barbaresco Pajè, that the official tasting commission won't allow Roagna to sell it with the Barbaresco appellation on the label. Not that he minds. "My customers are willing to pay more for Crichët than they pay for my Barbaresco," he told me.

Barbaresco wines produced on the hills of Treiso and Neive have characteristics of their own. Treiso's vineyards are higher than those of Barbaresco (1,400 feet as opposed to 800), with cooler temperatures and thinner soil. But what a Treiso-grown Barbaresco might lack in body it makes up for in aroma. Neive wines, on the other hand, are particularly muscular, even to the point of seeming clumsy if the fruit isn't handled well.

Through their good example, the Produttori del Barbaresco have helped raise the standard of all wines in Barbaresco. But it is Angelo Gaja, a grower with skill, enthusiasm, boundless energy, and a flair for promotion, who has pulled Barbaresco into the international limelight. If, as many think, Barbaresco has now taken the starring role from Barolo, it can only have been thanks to him. His superbly crafted wines reflect an intense, lively and focused personality as much as they do a contemporary style of winemaking—a style that owes much to Gaja himself and to the ideas he has brought back from extensive study in France and California.

Some time ago, when I spent a day with Gaja discussing his aims, he told me that he began developing his philosophy in the early seventies. Gaja speaks rapidly, passionately, and without pause, switching from Italian to French to English without seeming to notice. "The quality of any wine comes from the vineyard, obviously," he said. "Making sure the quality is in the fruit in the first place is exhausting work. We can't control the weather, so we must constantly adapt to it.

"The key problem, however, is to transfer that quality from the grapes to the wine. To make that happen, yet leave behind any hard, green tannins, is easier to talk about than to do. For a start, the winery must be suitably equipped. We decided to do away with wood and concrete fermenting tanks and replace them with stainless steel. Stainless steel tanks with water-cooled jackets allow control of the temperature at which our wines ferment. That means we can monitor the speed of fermentation and therefore the time the juice spends on the grape skins. Because grape skins are the most important source of tannins, this was a first step toward their better management.

"Still, even though we switched to fermenting in stainless steel, we continue to age our wines in wood. Wood aging helps stabilize the color of a red wine, for one thing, and, curious though it seems, the tannin in wood helps soften the wine's own tannins once they combine. We give a new wine six months in small barrels made of French oak and then transfer it to larger, wooden casks for another year or two before bottling. The size of the container—a sixty-gallon barrel against a sixteen-hundred-gallon cask—makes a difference because in the barrel the ratio of wood to wine is higher."

Eager to experiment, to test his latest idea, to meet the newest challenge, Gaja has sought constantly to align his wines with the best the world offers. In his search for perfection no detail escapes him. When I visited him in Barbaresco a few months ago, for example, I saw stacked in the open behind his winery thousands of barrel staves waiting to be assembled in his own cooperage. Buying staves from France, holding them in Barbaresco, and then making the barrels himself was the only way that Gaja could be sure the wood would be adequately air-dried.

As the demand for barrels has forced up the price of oak, along with the cost of holding inventories of drying staves, coopers in France have found themselves under pressure to move their stocks a little faster. But the benefits of long air-drying are real—two or three years is considered the minimum for rain, sunlight and bacterial action to leach out bitter components—and it's just the kind of thing Gaja would not leave to chance. His wines reflect his obsession with detail, with polish, with technical control. Their flavors are pure, their structure is elegantly logical, and their refinement is absolute.

Bruno Giacosa, a Neive producer whom some think of as tradition personified, does not use barrels for his Barbaresco. I visited him, too, when I was last in Piedmont. "We tried putting our Barbera in barrels a few years ago and we weren't satisfied," he told me, with a certain calm finality.

Gaja and Giacosa are a study in contrast. Where Gaja—an affable man usually dressed in a chic Missoni sweater—receives his visitors in a sophisticated, artfully lit, high-tech setting, Giacosa's office, with bare white walls and a barred window, opens off a bottle-packing floor in a drab concrete blockhouse on a busy main road. He is retiring in manner, and in appearance is indistinguishable from any of the other middle-aged, plainly dressed men—brokers, merchants, growers—who discuss prices and make deals over lunch at Neive's busy Trattoria Ferroveria on the Piazza Garibaldi. Where Gaja is voluble, Giacosa is laconic. Where Gaja is highly visible on the fashionable wine ciruit, Giacosa is almost reclusive, sending his daughter Bruna in his place to visit distributors around the world. And where Gaja is ready to discuss the whys and wherefores of his numerous winemaking theories, Giacosa shrinks from being too precise about anything. "Winemaking involves a great many small decisions," he says, "each affecting the next. One can only hope to get them all right, to capture what was there in the grapes to begin with."

Giacosa, who buys all his grapes from growers with whom he has long-standing relations, ferments his wine, as does Gaja, in stainless steel tanks. But then he transfers it directly into huge wooden casks—no barrels—to be aged for three or four years. The wines for which he is best known, Gallina and Santo Stefano, are made from grapes grown in namesake vineyards on the extensive domain of Castello di Neive. In good years Giacosa's Gallina is as violet-scented as textbooks say a good Barbaresco should be. And year after year his Santo Stefano is a wine against which all other Barbarescos can be judged.

Both Gallina and Santo Stefano have the structure and the elegance of the best of Gaja's wines, and the robust fleshiness of the best of the cooperative's. And like every wine Giacosa produces—even his Dolcetto and Barbera—they have a rich harmony of aroma and flavor that is his alone. Castello di Neive makes a Santo Stefano of its own with the same grapes, and remarkably good it is, too. But it doesn't have the resonance of Giacosa's wine. I would compare Giacosa's Santo Stefano with a Beethoven symphony if I thought I could get away with it.

The wines from Marchesi di Gresy's estate are different again. Alberto di Gresy's grandfather bought the present family property essentially as a hunting retreat, leaving the cultivation of the vineyards to his tenant farmers. When Alberto assumed management of the part of the estate he and his siblings had inherited through their father, he soon concluded that merely selling grapes meant he would always be growing a crop for a buyers' market. "It would have been difficult to keep the place going for the family on the income," he told me. "There's a payroll to meet, social-security payments, taxes. I had to increase the value of what we produced. Do you know that by transforming my crop from grapes to wine my revenues increased as much as tenfold? Even allowing for all the necessary additional investment and the cost of labor, bottles, corks, and so on, the change from selling grapes to making wine made it possible for the family to keep the property." Di Gresy, need I add, trained as an economist.

"But I wanted to make wine anyway," he went on. "I had spent all my summers here as a boy, close to the farmers, and I knew how good our Martinenga grapes were. It upset me to sell them to producers who just mixed them in with others. We started to make wine ourselves in 1973. I had no preconceived ideas except that wine, first and foremost, is a pleasure. It exists to be enjoyed. I wanted each of our wines to be agreeable, elegant, harmonious. But—pride of ownership, I suppose—I also wanted each wine to reflect the personality of the vineyard. So, although our chief concern is to produce wines that make people happy, we never force their styles in ways that would divorce them from the vineyards themselves."

Di Gresy succeeds in imbuing his wines with his own engaging charm while preserving the distinctive, spicy personality of the Martinenga vineyard. His wines' grace and discretion, furthermore, mask a structure every bit as firm as Gaja's.

The Produttori del Barbaresco, Gaja, Giacosa and Di Gresy are the Big Four of Barbaresco. But there are forty or fifty other producers. Some, like Alfredo Roagna, are small growers in Barbaresco, each with a few acres of vines. Three of the best have vineyards adjacent to each other on Rabajà, just above Di Gresy's Martinenga: Romano Marengo; Giuseppe Cortese, an inveterate winner of gold medals; and Bruno Rocca, who, with his wife and mother, goes through his vines three or more times for each harvest so that every bunch is picked when it is perfect. ("I don't do it to impress people," he says, "I just want my wine to give joy.") Some, like Castello di Neive, are large growers but small producers, preferring to sell outright a large part, if not most, of their grapes. And others are producers elsewhere, particularly in Alba and in the Barolo area, who either buy Barbaresco grapes or who own vineyards there. Among them, the finest Barbarescos are produced by Prunotto, Pio Cesare, Vietti and Fontanafredda.

I had gone to Barbaresco to compare the 1988, 1989 and 1990 vintages and found myself liking all three. Each year was better than the one before. As in Bordeaux, the 1988 wines were classically elegant, the 1989s more exuberant, and the 1990s were the biggest, richest and fleshiest of them all. Among the several dozen wines I tasted, there were few I wouldn't be happy to drink, in the fullness of time of course, with a garlic- and rosemary-scented loin of lamb or a pheasant braised with cabbage. Or perhaps a *stracotto*. With a wine like one of these, that would be as good as glimpsing paradise twice over.

61

BETWEEN HARD COVERS:
WINE BOOKS IN ENGLISH

Books for those who buy rather than make wine tend to be compendiums of maps and facts: they define appellations, list growers, measure vineyards, and quantify wine production. Lively, readable commentary, experiences of wine or just personal reflections on wine in general, is much rarer, even—perhaps I should say especially—in France. Pierre-Marie Doutrelant's *Les bons vins... et les autres* (Good Wines... and the Rest), published in Paris in 1976, was a sparkling exception.

Perhaps it is because the English didn't produce wine until quite recently, and so were never able to take it for granted, that they have been more willing than others to share their experiences and opinions of it between hard covers. Needless to say, their stance has always been essentially consumerist. Neither Andrew Boorde (*The Breviarie of Health*, 1547) nor William Turner (*A Book of Wines*, 1568), physician-authors of the first texts on wine in English, had much to say on the water-holding properties of soils or on the advantages of alternative pruning methods. Both approached the subject in terms of wine's contribution to good health—nourishing the brain and scouring the liver, that sort of thing—finding their justifications in the ancient wisdom of Galen, Aristotle, and Pliny.

Firsthand accounts of wine regions and winemaking, of differences of taste and style, and of the fluctuations of quality and price from one vintage to another began to appear in English toward the close of the eighteenth century. The letters and travel diaries of Thomas Jefferson, one of wine's earliest and most acute English-speaking observers, are richer sources of information about late-eighteenth-century Bordeaux, for example, than the journals and ledgers written by local vintners themselves. They took their craft and business for granted and saw no reason to describe, let alone record, much about them.

By the nineteenth century, however, such reports had blossomed into wine travelogues and consumer guides. Physician Alexander Henderson's *History of Ancient and Modern Wines*, published in London in 1824, was obviously inspired more by Jullien's tersely instructive *Topographie de Tous les Vignobles Connus* (from which Henderson borrows freely), first published in Paris in 1816, than by the obscure accounts of intestinal hygiene presented by Boorde and Turner. Henderson had first intended to revise and reissue the *Observations* of his fellow physician Sir Edward Barry, published some fifty years before. But fortunately for us he abandoned that plan in favor of researching a book of his own, the earliest in English to use assumptions we share in discussing wines still familiar to us.

Henderson, a joy to read and a model for writers on any subject, provides insight as relevant today as it was a hundred and fifty years ago. His book is distinguished specially for its accurate reporting and intelligent discussion. Among the many minor benefits, Henderson helps shed light on why published tasting notes are so boringly repetitive. "The English language," he says, "is particularly limited in this department; and when we have gone through about half a dozen phrases, we find that our stock is exhausted." His thesis that tastes and smells reside not in objects themselves but in the unreliably fluctuating senses by which they are perceived should be taken to heart by those inclined to accept the numerical rating of wines by critics as something other than fallibly human.

Henderson makes no mention of American wine. But then in 1824 there was hardly any to be found, even though John Adlum's book, *A Memoir on the Cultivation of the Vine in America, and the Best Mode of Making Wine*, had been published in Washington the year before. Apart from its importance in the history of wine on this continent, Adlum's book has significance, too, as the first book written in English to instruct farmers in vineyard practices and in the art of winemaking. His approach to the subject was as unassuming as it was practical:

> I would advise every person having a farm or garden, to plant some Vines, of the best he can procure in his own vicinity, and others, where hardy kinds might may be had. A garden may produce enough for the table and some to make Wine. There ought to be one Vine planted for every pannel of fence he has round his garden.

As Americans took Adlum's advice, vineyards spread west to Missouri and north to New York's Finger Lakes, thereby encouraging a succession of books on growing grapes for wine. John Dufour's *American Vine-dresser's Guide* appeared in Cincinnati in 1826; Alphonse Loubat's, similarly titled, in New York in 1827; and Alden Spooner's story of success with native American vines after repeated failure with European varieties was published in Brooklyn in 1846. More followed, the most important of which were Frederick Muench's *School for American Grape Culture* (St. Louis, 1865), George Husmann's *American Grape Growing and Wine Making* (New York, 1880), and Thomas Munson's *Foundations of American Grape Culture* (New York, 1909).

Munson, whose experimental vineyard of hybrids was near Austin, Texas, made a valuable contribution to salvaging the vineyards of France from phylloxera through the grafting of European vinifera varieties onto the rootstocks of native American vines. It is today the standard protection from phylloxera all over the world. In recognition of his work he was decorated with the *Mérite Agricole* by the French government.

Perhaps the best known of all nineteenth-century American wine books—and, despite its forbidding title, the one with most appeal for the layman—was Agoston Haraszthy's *Grape Culture, Wines, and Wine Making with Notes upon Agriculture and Horticulture*. Haraszthy's book, published in 1862 as a report to the Senate and Assembly of California on the state of viticulture in Europe, together with an account of current practice in California, contains vivid descriptions of all Haraszthy saw and experienced in 1861 during a European tour of investigation, on which he was accompanied by his son Arpad. Along with detailed information on vineyards and cellars, almond orchards, silk making, the drying of figs and prunes, and the production of sugar beets and other crops that he felt could be profitable in California, Haraszthy gives insight into subjects as diverse as the social conventions of matchmaking in a German spa and the most comfortable seats to procure when travelling in a Spanish public conveyance.

Haraszthy's flamboyant reporting was exceptional, however, among nineteenth-century American wine books. Most were severely technical, written to provide novice vintners with practical instruction. Little was published in the

United States specifically to inform, let alone beguile, the consumer. That is largely because the interest in wine in the expanded English-speaking world had shifted to production.

But even in England, the perception and use of wine had changed in the centuries between Boorde and Henderson. Though still recommended for its nutritional value, wine in England was unabashedly accepted by an enriched gentry as one of life's pleasures: its geography, its history, even its chemistry were subjects for agreeable intellectual curiosity. Henderson's book had been followed, in 1833, by the first edition of British journalist Cyrus Redding's *History and Description of Modern Wines*, the most detailed world viticultural tour that had until then been published. From France and Spain, Redding's account led eventually to Greece, Persia and India, where he found Australian wines "made so successfully as to sell in the market at Calcutta for thirty-two shillings per dozen." Though with no opportunity to have tasted them, Redding mentions favorably wines produced in Ohio and Indiana, where "the crop in 1811," he says approvingly, "was as much as twenty-seven hundred gallons."

Of a piece with the prevailing interest in antiquity, eighteenth-century and early-nineteenth-century authors in England, like Barry, Henderson and Redding, drew on the works of Columella, Hippocrates, and Athenaeus to discuss wine. They assumed in their readers a more than passing acquaintance with the classical world (Henderson's text is strewn with footnotes in Latin and Greek), which implied a fairly restricted market for wine books—and for wine.

That was indeed the case. Almost two centuries of using wine duties as a means of waging economic warfare with the French had made a luxury of table wine in England, leaving those of modest means to wallow on gin lane. But in the early 1860s, Gladstone made sharp, successive cuts in wine duties while extending wine licenses to village grocery stores. Gladstone, moved to help change social behavior by easing wine onto the family dinner table at the expense of spirits taken in the freer atmosphere of the tavern, helped create a vast new market for wine among those who would not have known Athenaeus from Charley's Aunt. Imports of French wine into England more than tripled between 1859 and 1862.

In this booming but inexperienced new market there was both a need and an opportunity for books on wine. Charles Tovey, with his *Wine and Wine Countries: A Record and Manual for Wine Merchants and Wine Consumers*, published in 1862, sought to use his own experience as a wine merchant to educate both the new consumer and the untutored grocer who served him. To set the High Victorian tone of admonition then conventionally used for instruction, Tovey, in the preface to his book, quotes a member of the Board of Trade who spoke before a select committee hearing of the House of Commons in 1852: "The wine trade itself is much altered from the respectable character it used to bear; persons of inferior moral temperament have entered into it, and tricks are played, which in former times would not have been countenanced." (Tovey conveniently ignored contradictory court records that showed the wine trade to have had its share of "persons of inferior moral temperament" at least as far back as the thirteenth century.)

A reader looked in vain to *Wine and Wine Countries* for elegant phrasing and classical references. He found instead the excessive drinking of the doubtless jolly but uncouth Saxons pointedly compared with the more moderate and refined habits of their Norman conquerors—seen by the English upper classes as their own forbears. Where Henderson was careful and showed respect for his reader ("The description of the mode of conducting the fermentation of the grapes in Burgundy is partly copied from notes made on the spot, in the autumn of 1822: but as I unfortunately did not arrive there in time to witness the vintage, my information is less satisfactory than I could wish, and possibly, in some respects, erroneous"), Tovey is authoritarian and patronizing ("As it is next to impossible for a stranger to judge with precision and accuracy of the promising qualities of Bordeaux Wine in wood, or even in bottle, when young . . . and as deception is always easily practised, we should advise the trade to apply only and exclusively to firms known in this country as being of *high respectability.* . . .")

He puts in a depressing plug for Champagne ("We know of remarkable instances of persons who having been prostrated by illness to almost the last extremity, were resuscitated by taking Champagne"), repeats with relish every tale ever circulated to the detriment of Port, and despatches American wine with brief ambiguity:

Before proceeding to notice the wines of our own colonies, we will just mention that North America is cultivating the vine to a considerable extent; and that, in the United States, the native wines, especially the sparkling kinds, are fast supplanting the foreign . . . they are even said to exceed in purity and delicacy any other known wine, whilst it is their peculiar property that no spurious compound can be made to resemble them.

It is a relief to turn to Robert Druitt, in his time a well-known London physician, whose *Report on Cheap Wines . . . Their Use in Diet and Medicine*, first published in book form in 1865, is both encouraging and entertaining. It was based on articles Druitt had been prompted to write for the *Medical Times and Gazette* in 1863 and 1864, because, as he says in his introduction to a later edition, "rivers of strange wines were coming in from all parts of the world [thanks to Gladstone's reduction of wine duty], and both the medical profession and the public wanted to know what they were good for."

Druitt's tone is cheerfully good-natured even when he exhorts his fellow physicians to prescribe wine as a tonic for their patients instead of the "filthy mixtures" prepared in hospital dispensaries. "We must take people as we find them," he says, reasonably enough. "Man, as a social animal, requires something which he can sip as he sits and talks, and which pleases his palate whilst it gives some aliment to the stomach, and stimulates the flow of genial thoughts in the brain."

Elsewhere, in a passage that should be printed as a government warning on every page of every edition of every newsletter that picks wines apart, he says "Wine should have an absolute *unity*, it should taste as one whole." It is only in bad wine, he goes on, that "here a something sweet meets one part of our gustatory organs, there something sour, there something fruity, or bitter, or hot, or harsh, just as if half-a-dozen ill-blended liquids came out of one bottle, with perhaps a perfume atop. . . ."

His asides are as delightful as they are pungent. For instance, in describing the effect on wine of even a trace of some substances, he pointed out how small a quantity of garlic will give "a rich, full, savory fragrance to a leg of mutton," and then adds gratuitously: "The same in excess would be pronounced detestable by any one who had not got over his Anglican prejudices."

And, though fervent in the cause of table wine, he was ready to throw in all but the kitchen sink to condemn Port, then probably the most popular fortified wine in England: "The reign of Port coincides with the growth of the national debt, the isolation of the English from continental society, the decay of architecture...."

For Druitt, though with more humor than Tovey, could hector his readers when necessary. Apart from castigating them for drinking Port, he complained rather sternly that they were apt to keep their Burgundies and red Bordeaux beyond the time when they had arrived at their prime. He therefore recommended a cellar weeding from time to time and suggested that the surplus bottles be sent to "widows of limited income, girls at cheap boarding-schools...." He pressed his fellow physicians to encourage their patients to drink red Bordeaux. "You will add ten years to your patient's life and to your own fees."

Just as Gladstone's tinkering with duties and licensing had expanded the market for table wine (and for wine primers), so pressure from London importers on their suppliers in France to ship dry rather than sweet *cuvées* doubled the annual shipments of Champagne between 1860 and 1865. Champagne had been a sweet, sparkling dessert wine, therefore competing, in England, with Port and sweet Sherry. Several houses, including Veuve Clicquot, had shipped dry versions of the 1857 vintage in 1860. By the late 1870s almost all the producers were shipping dry *cuvées* to London, and the heyday of Champagne had begun.

Henry Vizetelly, engraver, writer and publisher (he was sued for obscenity for publishing translations of Émile Zola's work in London), launched his *Wines of the World* in 1875, and followed it with the first specialized consumer book on wine: *Facts about Sherry*. The success of the Sherry book must have helped him see the potential for just such another specialized book, one more extravagantly produced, dedicated to the prestige of Champagne. He first published the abundantly engraved *Facts about Champagne and other Sparkling Wines* in 1879, but by 1882 he had revised and expanded it into his *History of Champagne*, still one of the most remarkable, most beautifully produced, and most sought-after wine books in English.

Inevitably, after such bravura, other new wine books seemed anticlimactic for a while. But at the same time that a stream of technical books in English was being published for the growing number of wineries in Australia and South Africa, let alone the United States, Silas Mitchell, a Philadelphia physician (it is to be noted how many lay writers on wine have been medical men), produced his classic *Madeira Party* in 1895. The book is a fictional re-creation of the conversation of a group of men at a Madeira-tasting party, supposedly taking place in Philadelphia in the earlier part of the century. Of social historical value, apart from its interest to those researching the use of Madeira wine in the early 1800s, the book's rather self-conscious and high-minded exchanges (somewhere in it one of the group observes: "I have noticed that the acquisition of a taste for Madeira in middle life is quite fatal to common people") nevertheless suggest that wine pretentiousness has never been an exclusively English vice.

In the first years of the new century, before World War I, the then very young André Simon, later to found the International Wine and Food Society, produced both his *History of the Champagne Trade in England* and his *History of the Wine Trade in England*, thereby beginning a flow of books on wine (and on food) that continued until his death in 1970 at the age of ninety-three.

Simon's published work ranges from reprints of his straightforward lectures to students of the London Wine Trade Club (which he also helped found) to learned papers as diverse as his descriptions of dinners of the powerful sixteenth-century Star Chamber, and an analysis of the private cellar book of J. Pierpont Morgan. Simon's personal charm comes through in all his books, but in none more than in the brief comments he attaches to each of the menus and wines served at lunches and dinners with friends, compiled and published in 1933 as *Tables of Content*.

One of the most successful of Simon's works, in terms of the number of repeat editions, has been *Vintagewise*, a book first published in 1945 as an informative postscript to George Saintsbury's *Notes on a Cellar Book*.

It is ironic that Saintsbury's entire, voluminous and distinguished body of work, published both before and during his tenure as Professor of Rhetoric and English Literature at the University of Edinburgh (it included important histories of French and English literature as well as innumerable articles for the

Encyclopaedia Britannica), is overshadowed by one small anecdotal volume written in his retirement. Though no more than a collection of thoughts provoked by a review of the cellar book he had kept for most of his life, *Notes on a Cellar Book* is nevertheless the work for which he is remembered, and is probably the book in which he most stands revealed. In table talk of the greatest urbanity, it fuses Saintsbury's twin loves of wine and literature.

Perhaps, in those frenzied years of the twenties, nostalgia for the prewar pace and the amenities Saintsbury had taken for granted gave the book added attraction. In any case, it was an enormous success, ran to three editions within a year, and has been repeatedly reprinted in new editions ever since.

Along with André Simon's books, *Notes on a Cellar Book* set a high standard. Whether by way of inspiration or challenge, both men have encouraged more than one following generation of writers on wine. Outstanding among them are Morton Shand, dazzlingly well informed and entertainingly opinionated; Cyril Ray, who, apart from the books he himself wrote, was responsible for compiling the twelve annually issued volumes of *The Compleat Imbiber*, each an enticing anthology of stories, essays and poems on wine (and sometimes food) now hard to find and dear to collectors everywhere; Edmund Penning-Rowsell, whose regular revisions of his *Wines of Bordeaux* are accepted as the first and last word on the subject; William Younger, whose extraordinary review of wine history in *Gods, Men and Wine,* has been, until now, an unequalled accomplishment; Hugh Johnson, André Simon's successor as editor of the *Wine and Food Society Journal*, whose work has changed the way we think about wine books, let alone wine, and whose *Vintage: The Story of Wine* makes him a fit contender for Younger's crown; and Jancis Robinson, whose *Vines, Grapes and Wines*, one of the best and most original wine books of the last decade, has appealed alike to professional and amateur, grower and consumer, because of its seductive combination of unobtrusive scholarship and literary grace.

Happily, on this side of the Atlantic, too, the useful thicket of technical books and encyclopedias for which we have long provided fertile ground is now blossoming with reflective commentary, the sharing of experience and opinion, and the kind of anecdotal ornament that both enhances and is enhanced by the pleasures of a glass of wine.

A few that spring to mind include *Notes on a California Cellar Book: Reflections on Memorable Wines*, by Bob Thompson, a worthy borrower of Saintsbury's plumage; *Thinking About Wine*, by Elin McCoy and John Frederick Walker, a wide-ranging collection of essays and stories; and *Making Sense of Wine*, a book in which Oregonian Matt Kramer, musing under chapter headings taken from Bossuet and T. E. Lawrence, at first suggests expectations of his readers as daunting as Alexander Henderson's quotations from Martial and scattered allusions to Timarchides of Rhodes and Philoxenus of Cythera. But deploying with skill analogies as diverse as musicology and prizefighting, Kramer grips his readers' attention as he illuminates some of the more abstruse aspects of wine. Occasionally the eyes do glaze over—he goes on at great length about the perils of shipping wine in uninsulated containers, for example. Then suddenly, apropos of the drinking of great Sauternes and Beerenauslese Rhine wines, Kramer makes the brilliant play of offering a recipe for bread pudding. The reader, from them on, is eating out of his hand.

71

A CARAFE OF RED

WE HAD STOPPED FOR A QUICK LUNCH AT A PASTRY SHOP NEAR THE PLACE DE LA MADELEINE. My friend sniffed approvingly at her glass of red wine. "This is good," she said. "What is it?"

It was a Corbières, a wine from a block of wind-riven mountains between Carcassonne, Narbonne and Perpignan on the French Mediterranean coast. She was right: it *was* good.

And what did she think of the Bonington watercolors we'd seen that morning at the Petit Palais? She knows far more about pictures than I do, but she brushed Bonington aside. "Is that all you're going to tell me?" she asked.

How much did she want to know? The Corbières is the oldest wine region of France. Its story is virtually the story of French wine.

"Why don't you start at the beginning," she suggested. So I did.

The Romans planted their first vineyards in the Corbières soon after they built a harbor at Narbonne. In passing a decree establishing the colony in 118 B.C., the Roman senate intended to secure for Rome the passage from the Mediterranean to the Atlantic by way of the Aude and Garonne River valleys. It was the route by which wine, much prized by the Celts, was bartered for Cornish tin. Rome, ever belligerent, needed tin to produce bronze for weapons and preferred to see her enemies (and victims) deprived of it.

The Seventh Legion was sent to protect the traffic (hence the region's ancient name of Septimania), and veteran soldiers, usually married to Celtic women, were encouraged to settle there when they retired from active service. It was probably veterans who planted those first vineyards. But they chose to trade their wine not to Cornwall but back to Italy in exchange for the small luxuries only Rome could provide. There, their wine was so highly prized that Rome's speculators rushed to extend the vineyards. Wine from Septimania was soon competing successfully with that grown on the Italian estates of Rome's most powerful families. Cicero left for us a record of the furious debates in which senators demanded that the vineyards and olive groves of Gaul not be allowed to render their own valueless. The emperor Domitian was prevailed upon in A.D. 92 to order half of them ripped out.

"Why had the wine been so good?" my friend wanted to know. All the usual reasons, I assured her: soil, climate, the care taken by men whose survival—let alone their prosperity—depended on what they could produce from a patch of vines. Then as now, the Corbières farmer had little choice beyond vines, sheep and goats.

Most of all, though, it was and is a unique combination of Mediterranean and Atlantic influences. Like the northern Rhône valley, the other wine region that flourished in the first century of Roman Gaul, the Corbières sit at a climatic crossroads. The mistral, the fierce wind that blows down the Rhône valley, has its equivalent in the *cers*, a powerful wind that blows through the Carcassonne gap from the Atlantic to the Mediterranean. Atlantic weather patterns reach far into the Corbières, and the climate, less predictable than that of Italy, can run to extremes. The Romans were surprised that vines and olive trees native to Italy would grow there at all. Saserna, the leading agronomist of the time, saw it as proof that the world was getting warmer.

"Global warming in the first century?" my friend murmured as she refilled her glass. "Is nothing new?"

Bordeaux, at the other end of the Aude-Garonne connection, had to wait another century or two until the Romans stumbled onto grape varieties able to resist the spring frosts and summer rains of its unabated Atlantic climate. But no matter how strange it might have seemed to Saserna, vines that did well elsewhere in the Mediterranean did well in the Corbières too. Growers had to choose among varieties available, of course. Some that were successful on the maritime plain could not be relied on to ripen their fruit at higher altitudes exposed to the *cers*.

The rugby-playing, garlic-fancying winegrowers who now live in the high valleys of the Corbières are descended from those Gallo-Roman farmers, many of whom had taken refuge there at some time during the Languedoc's turbulent past. The region's great sweep of mountains, gorges, and maritime plain fell prey to Visigoths, Arabs (who seized it after their conquest of Spain), and Franks under Charles Martel. In the early fifth century the Visigoths, fresh from sacking Rome, just walked into Narbonne. The inhabitants, perhaps under some illusion of the permanence of Pax Romana, had left the city gates open and the walls unguarded while they went to the vineyards to pick their grapes. An ancient illuminated manuscript recording the event, displayed in a Narbonne museum, expresses tersely the economic importance of wine to the region. "War can wait," it reads. "The vintage cannot."

But neither vineyards nor trade prospered in the uncertainties of the dark age that followed. This troubled time ended for the Corbières in 800 when Charlemagne, Charles Martel's grandson, approved the foundation there of Lagrasse Abbey. Among the objectives listed on the document of grant was the planting of a vineyard. Over the next two centuries fifty such abbeys were established in the area, and every one of them had extensive vineyards. They became, for hundreds of years, the sole repositories of viticultural knowledge and wine-making skills in the region.

It is usual to say that an abbey's vines provided wine for celebrating mass. But more than that, they were a principal source of wealth. As the abbeys' vineyards were extended into formerly uncultivated woodland, the descendants of Rome's veterans were tied by contracts that obliged them and their children to work land they would never own. The arrangement brought order but provoked a resentment that still colors the fiery politics of the region. My friend would not have needed me to remind her of the great cruelty in the Corbières and in neighboring parts of the Languedoc in the thirteenth century. The Inquisition was born right there and was used, in the name of religious orthodoxy, to help consolidate the power of the Roman Catholic church and of the French crown. The *vignerons* of the Languedoc have been chopping trees, blocking roads and raising hell for a long time since then.

The horrors can blind us, however, to two events during those centuries that had enormous impact on the region's wines. The first was the introduction of distilling. In the late 13th century, Arnau de Villanova, a Montpellier physician, was the first in Europe to produce alcohol from wine heated in an alembic. Distilling had been known to the Arabs since the tenth century—both *alcohol* and *alembic* are Arabic words—and it is thought that De Villanova had learned the process from his friend Raymon Llull, a scholar of Arabic sciences at the University of Montpellier.

The second was the completion, in 1680, of a canal linking the Mediterranean and the Atlantic. Jean-Baptiste Colbert, Louis XIV's finance minister, improved on what the Romans had started by using the Aude-Garonne passage to cut what is now known as the Canal du Midi. He hoped it would give the manufacturers and farmers of southern France easier access to the markets of northern Europe. An extension of the canal continued to the Rhône. Sète, the town founded by Colbert as the canal's Mediterranean port, became a center of the international wine trade.

Just as Colbert had intended, the canal gave impetus to other economic activity, including distilling. The Dutch, in particular, bought huge quantities of Languedoc spirits. To keep the stills going, vineyards were soon spreading from the hills onto the plain, where Aramon and other common, high-yielding varieties (later to be the undoing of the Languedoc) were first introduced.

It needed only one hard winter to divert these thin, coarse wines from the distilleries to the blending vats. From October 1708 until February 1709, temperatures in much of Europe rarely rose above freezing. To relieve the shortage of wine in Paris caused by the widespread destruction of vineyards normally supplying the capital, a royal decree of 1710 suppressed taxes on Languedoc wines shipped there. Languedoc vineyards had been barely affected by the winter's severity.

But once those cheap wines started flowing into the blending vats, it became difficult to keep them out. Bordeaux's landowners were far from pleased and used every legislative trick to block the annual arrival and sale of Languedoc wines until their own crop had been sold. Disputes over shipment of Languedoc wines through the Canal du Midi continued until 1776 when Anne-Robert-Jacques Turgot, briefly Louis XVI's comptroller general of finance, abolished Bordeaux's privileges along with the special export taxes and myriad petty regulations imposed by the city to obstruct the free movement of Languedoc wines through its port. Turgot, some of whose ideas anticipated those of Adam Smith, was a similar curiosity: a modern economist at large in the eighteenth century. Had vested interests not succeeded in forcing him from office after only twenty months, it's possible—even likely—there would have been no French Revolution. One of his urgent projects had been an attempt to abolish the taxes that inhibited free trade of grain among the provinces—the principal cause of frequent, sometimes severe, local famines and therefore a major factor in the 1789 riots.

"Aren't we wandering from the point?" my friend said.

Wine is a subject that leads everywhere, but it clearly wasn't the time to say so. Instead I explained how the effect of the Canal du Midi was as nothing once the railways arrived in the 1850s. Spawned by the industrial revolution—the first tracks in France were laid to move coal and ore, not people—the railways then fed it, literally, with calories garnered from Languedoc vineyards. French industrial workers of the nineteenth century, and for much of the twentieth for that matter, relied on wine for the high-calorie diet their physical exertions demanded. Every liter provided seven or eight hundred additional bulk-free calories, and the cheapest of the wines arrived in the northern industrial cities by rail from the south. From the late 1850s until the mid-1870s, money poured into the Languedoc as fast as wine gushed out. It was said at the time that a man could pay off the price of vineyard land there with the profits from his first two crops.

At the height of local euphoria, in 1867, a Languedoc grower reported to a meeting of the Central Agricultural Society in Paris a mysterious sickness affecting his vines. The problem was identified by the University of Montpellier as the insect *Phylloxera vastatrix*—the devastator—and the appropriateness of the name was soon made evident. In 1875 the wine harvest in France was larger than it had ever been or was ever to be again. One year later, in 1876, standing vines in the Languedoc's Gard *département* alone were reduced by more than 100,000 acres to less than half of what had been thriving there before. Within thirty years, phylloxera had destroyed almost every vineyard in France.

The University of Montpellier was in favor of using resistant American rootstocks quite early in the course of the epidemic. Unfortunately, the American rootstocks available at that time could not tolerate the high chalk content of the best vineyards in the Languedoc hills; and on the plain (where the mass of cheap wine was grown) flooding the vineyards seemed to work just as well, cost a lot less, and was quicker. But flooding was the same thing as heavy irrigation. Yields rose fantastically and quality fell in just proportion. But no one cared: As the infested vineyards of other regions disappeared, demand for these wines of the Languedoc plain—whatever their quality—continued to grow. The wine sold in 1875 for sixteen francs a hectoliter had been of better quality than that sold for forty francs in 1880; but bouquet and finesse had become irrelevant. The industrial working masses simply needed the calories.

Once it became possible for the Corbières growers to replant, they found themselves unable to compete with the wines of the plain. There could be no question of flooding hillside vineyards, yet the merchants of Narbonne, Sète, and Béziers (now blending and shipping on a huge scale) refused to distinguish between the small production of quality wine of the Corbières and wine of the over-irrigated, high-yielding vines elsewhere.

In 1907 the Languedoc's uncontrolled production, aggravated by fraud, caused the French market in cheap bulk wines to collapse. Government troops fired on growers rioting in the streets of Narbonne, but in Béziers an artillery regiment mutinied rather than obey orders to do the same. The Corbières growers realized they had to protect their common interest by distinguishing their wines from those of the plain. It took them until 1923 to win a judicial decree by which they were defined as a region separate from the rest of the Languedoc. But even so, their wine was not officially recognized, even as a *Vin Delimite de Qualite Superieure* (a very junior version of a controlled appellation), until 1951; and the Corbières was not raised to the distinct status of a full controlled appellation until 1985.

Until the 1960s Corbières wines sold at prices hardly different from those paid for the grossest of *gros rouge* of the Languedoc. To live, many growers found themselves obliged to adopt the high-yielding varieties of the plain—especially Carignan. Though never as productive in the hills, these varieties drew the growers into the same vicious circle of lowered quality and falling revenues from which the growers of the plain had been unable to extricate themselves.

"But if this wine is anything to go by," my friend said, helping herself to the last of the carafe, "it looks as if they have somehow been able to do just that."

They had indeed. A turnabout began in 1967 when a small group of growers in the Val d'Orbieu between Narbonne and Lézignan came together and planned a coherent strategy to pull themselves up by their own vine-shoots. With seemingly quixotic pretension (at the time Corbières had no reputation at all, and nothing seemed likely to change that), they defined what a Corbières wine should be, agreed on mutually binding standards of quality control, and invested together in equipment that each on his own might not have been able to afford.

As this growers' association grew, so it took shape. The original group drew into it some of the region's wine cooperatives, along with the best of the independent growers. They kept standards high and objectives clear by admitting new members only after careful evaluation of vineyard, cellar, wine quality and personal drive. A crucial step was to bring into the association a viticultural and enological research laboratory in Narbonne to which all members might turn for assistance at all stages of planting, caring for their vines, and winemaking.

With the support of the regional chamber of commerce, the association established an experimental vineyard domain where they researched which varieties formerly planted in the Corbières should be brought back, which clones should be used, how vines should be trained, and how pruning should be done.

Aramon and a host of hybrid varieties have virtually disappeared from the Corbières. Those Carignan vines that remain are old: the variety offers worthwhile fruit only when the vines are over thirty, and the yields are meager. New plantings are discouraged, and the regulations are regularly revised to reduce the permitted proportion of Carignan as old vines become uneconomic and must be replaced.

Increasingly the growers depend on Grenache, Syrah, Mourvèdre, and a little Cinsault—the grape varieties of Châteauneuf-du-Pape. Syrah and Mourvèdre, in particular, are referred to as "aromatic varieties" because of the flavor and character they bring to Grenache or Carignan. Growers in the mild maritime zone of the Corbières closest to the Mediterranean use Mourvèdre rather than Syrah; it gives depth of color and backbone. But farther inland, moving west towards the Atlantic (the coast of Mediterranean France runs north-south at this point as it drops down towards Barcelona), growers use Syrah for the same reason that their colleagues in the northern Rhône do. It resists wind, and, even in mountainous conditions at the limit of its tolerance—perhaps I should say *especially* in mountainous conditions at the limit of its tolerance—it gives grapes of particularly fine flavor where Mourvèdre would hardly ripen. Some growers have planted Merlot and Cabernet Sauvignon as a shortcut to market acceptance, but sentiment in the Corbières is generally in favor of restoring a Mediterranean tradition and not borrowing from elsewhere.

Though Marsanne and Roussanne, known for the role they play in producing white wines in the northern Rhône valley, have also been reintroduced to the Corbières, most Corbières wine remains red, richly colored and sumptuous. But then the Languedoc is, after all, *daube* country, the region honored for that slowly braised beef dish of which Robert Courtine says in his *Hundred Glories of French Cooking*, "one finds oneself talking in terms of music, of poetry."

"That was a *tarte provençale* we were eating," my friend reminded me, just as I was ready to quote from the scene of Proust's *Remembrance of Things Past* in which Monsieur de Norpois becomes ecstatic over a cold *daube* "spiced with carrots...couched...upon enormous crystals of jelly."

"Wouldn't it be more helpful to tell me if I shall be able to find any of this wine when I get back home?" she asked. Not only could I assure her that she would, but I could give her the good news that most of it sells on the sunny side of $10 a bottle. Distribution of individual Corbières estate wines will always be patchy. Most of them are small, with limited production. But on a slightly larger scale, the cooperative cellar of Les Vigerons d'Octaviana are shipping three or four wines to several markets in the United States under the brand name Guy Chevalier. The Guy Chevalier Syrah, the most admired of them, comes from a vineyard with the curious name of Le Texas. Because the Corbières appellation does not provide for a one-hundred-percent Syrah wine, it must be labelled Vin de Pays de l'Aude.

The group that started it all back in 1967 has recently set up a sales office for Val d'Orbieu Wines in Dallas to oversee the national distribution of its Réserve

Saint Martin and Resplandy brands. For the present, to conform to what they judge to be American expectations, they are concentrating their efforts on wines prepared from single varieties so that they can be labelled Syrah, Grenache, Marsanne and so on. In this country we have been conditioned to pay more attention to a wine with a varietal identity and to place a higher value on it. Val d'Orbieu's Syrah is one of their finest wines—though less fleshy than the Syrah of Guy Chevalier, it is more intensely flavored. These Mediterranean varieties are usually at their best, however, when used to complement each other, as they do in most of the individual estate wines. Val d'Orbieu's Cuvée Mythique (a blend of Syrah, Mourvèdre, Grenache, Cabernet Sauvignon, and old Carignan) is based on this principle. The first vintage, 1990, was launched successfully in 1992.

If, in the Corbières, one can talk of an equivalent to Napa Valley's Rutherford or of the Médoc's *route des grands crus*, it would be a long, narrow, gravelly slope with an area of perhaps eight hundred acres near the villages of Boutenac and Gasparets. Exposed to the southwest and protected from the *cers* by a thick grove of pines at its back, it was the site of the first Roman commercial farm in Gaul. No one in Corbières would dispute that wines made from grapes grown there are always among the best and usually are the best of the Languedoc in any given vintage. The slope is divided among five estates which, not surprisingly, led the Corbières' revival in the 1970s: Villemajou, Les Palais, Château La Voulte Gasparets, Fontsainte and Les Olliex. All are producing excellent wines. Other Corbières estates to watch for include the Domaine Serres-Mazard, Château Saint-Auriol, Domaine du Trillol and Château Beauregard.

Where Corbières growers have led, others have followed. Scattered all over—in the Minervois, in the hills north of Pézenas, and in secluded bays and valleys near Perpignan in Roussillon—there are other growers who have made tremendous efforts in recent years. Many of their wines, too, are available—spottily—in the United States. I am thinking of wines like the red Collioure of the Clos du Moulin and the Clos des Paulilles; the red (and white) Côtes de Roussillon from the Château de Jau; and the outstanding Saint-Chinian of Château Coujan and of the small cooperative at Berlou (their brand name is Berloup), the last and highest village in the Minervois where the vine will grow. The most impressive of them all, though, are the red Coteaux du Languedoc wines made by Olivier Jullien at his Mas Jullien. His small production is much in demand in Montpellier; in the United States his wine is available, as far as I know, only in New York City.

"Aren't there also Muscats and dessert wines produced in the Languedoc?" my friend wanted to know. "I am sure I read somewhere that a proprietor of Château Yquem in the eighteenth century went to the Languedoc to discover the secret of making sweet wines."

"Now, come on," I said. "It's past two o'clock and we were supposed to be out of here at half past one. When am I going to hear about Bonington?"

"How much do you want to hear?" she asked.

"Why don't you just start at the beginning," I suggested, and waved to a passing waiter to bring another carafe of Corbières.

81

NAPA VALLEY CABERNET SAUVIGNON

I CAN'T NOW REMEMBER THE FIRST BORDEAUX WINE I EVER TASTED. It's sure to have been something quite modest. Neither can I remember my first glass of Burgundy, my first Chianti nor my first Champagne. But, perhaps because I started at the top, I remember very well my first Napa Valley Cabernet Sauvignon: It was the Georges de Latour Private Reserve 1954 of Beaulieu Vineyard and it was poured for me at a dinner on my first visit to San Francisco in 1967. I could hardly have had a finer welcome to the city.

Since then, thanks to friends who had the foresight to buy wines largely under-esteemed when released, I've had other opportunities to taste Napa Valley Cabernet Sauvignons of the fifties, and of the forties, too.

The most memorable occasion was a dinner in San Francisco in 1979, at which we drank the 1951s of both Louis M. Martini and Beaulieu Vineyard's Georges de Latour, the 1956 of Charles Krug and the 1941 of Inglenook. The color of the Charles Krug and the flavor of the Louis M. Martini belied their age. The Georges de Latour, like every Georges de Latour I had had before and have had since, was impressively concentrated, a sign of the maturity of Beaulieu Vineyard's vines even then. The Inglenook, more dense, and dark almost to the point of blackness, was unexpectedly elegant. All four of the wines were striking for their depth, their balance and their harmony. Each finished as it began, without the least discord.

The wineries that had produced them were among a mere handful functioning in Napa Valley long after Prohibition had been repealed. The Depression and World War II had done little to improve the status of California wine; most Americans preferred to reacquaint themselves with the European wines of which they had been deprived. The situation seemed hardly to have changed in the sixties, although, with the opening of Heitz cellars in 1961 and with the first vintage of Cabernet Sauvignon of Mayacamas Vineyards on Mount Veeder in 1962, there were already signs of renewed interest. The extent of that renewal became clear only when Robert Mondavi, having quarreled with his family at Charles Krug, founded in 1966 the Oakville winery that bears his name. The clean lines of its now familiar arch and tower, visible up and down Route 29, still define that moment. They have become as much a symbol of a change of era in Napa Valley as they are of the winery itself.

By the early seventies several newly established producers were already releasing admirable wines, often from young vines, which are notorious for their failure to provide depth and concentration, let alone stamina. And yet, though hardly equal to those intense examples from the forties and fifties, they had a classic refinement and, perhaps surprisingly, they, too, have held up well.

For many years Robert Mondavi's 1974 Napa Valley Cabernet Sauvignon Reserve served as a benchmark for other valley wineries; eighteen months ago I brought conversation at a London dinner table to a halt with a bottle of Caymus's 1976 Napa Valley Cabernet Sauvignon; and last February, also in London, a fragrant Joseph Phelps's 1975 Cabernet Sauvignon I had carried from San Francisco lost nothing to the magnum of Château Cheval Blanc 1978 that preceded it.

No one who had been paying attention was all that surprised as another moment was defined for Napa Valley at the blind tasting of French and California wines organized in Paris in 1976 to mark the bicentennial of the Declaration of Independence. Napa Valley Cabernet Sauvignons from wineries that had not existed fifteen years earlier were accorded top honors when tasted alongside *crus classés* of Bordeaux by a jury of distinguished and well-qualified French tasters. Because their judgement was held in such respect, there were enormous repercussions when it was revealed that the jurors had preferred a Stag's Leap Wine Cellars 1973 Napa Valley Cabernet Sauvignon to Baron Philippe de Rothschild's Château Mouton-Rothschild 1970. Sophisticated arguments were put forward to explain away their choice, but allowing for every extenuating circumstance, it was clear that Napa Valley Cabernet Sauvignon had arrived. Everyone who could jumped in, including Baron Philippe himself.

"You should buy land in Napa Valley," one of his banker cousins said to me, generously, over dinner at about that time. "It's cheap." He was right, of course. But, living in California, I was too close to what was going on, and land prices in Napa seemed already inflated to me. I did nothing, but scores of others agreed with him. Earlier this year, when I asked the Napa Valley Vintners' Association for help in putting together a representative tasting of 1990 and 1991 Napa Valley Cabernet Sauvignons, the Association's director, the late Elaine Mackie, was able to assemble on short notice samples of both vintages from each of more than fifty wineries. And even that considerable number represents barely a third of those whose wines could have been considered. Instead of the four hundred acres of Cabernet Sauvignon bearing fruit in the Valley thirty years ago, there are now more than nine thousand. No other wine region has grown so rapidly while simultaneously taking its place with such assurance in the front rank of the world's wines.

Success brought its problems. If the initial revival was auspicious, its consolidation was erratic. Some wineries found themselves immediately and their success has endured. Others were first praised excessively (and sometimes with dubious cause), then condemned as they lurched from tough, oversized Cabernet Sauvignons to vapid, empty ones in a vain attempt to hold onto the good opinion of those hardly entitled to one. Wineries with difficulties were often victims of the years of Prohibition, in which grape growing had been divorced from wine making. A grape grower, whose revenues, after all, were based at the time on tonnage and sugar concentration, was concerned only with producing a healthy, abundant crop that would bring him the maximum sugar bonus. His involvement ended once the crop was delivered to the buyer and he gave little thought to its ultimate purpose. As a result, even Napa Valley grapes often lacked both balance and character.

The valley's rapid expansion, with its unprecedented demand for qualified winemakers, meant that the young man or woman taking possession of those grapes rarely had the experience to judge the fruit beyond its healthy appearance and the results of a simple analysis for acid and sugar. Recently trained, and more often than not in his first full-charge position, the new winemaker saw the fruit delivered by giant truck rather as a potter might see a fresh load of clay dropped off in his yard: It was up to him to make something of it.

The wines he made would become his résumé. Taught not to take risks, he went by the numbers and followed the rules, leaving nothing to chance. He pushed the grapes to a desired end rather than bend the desired end to take advantage of whatever potential the grapes might have had. Available technology included presses and filters, the latest centrifuge, high-velocity pumps, and tanks that cooled and stirred and aerated themselves. Most Napa Valley wineries established in the seventies described themselves in their press releases as "state of the art." What that usually meant was a miniature version of a Central Valley grape processing plant—but in gleaming stainless steel. The equipment was designed for efficiency, and, unless the winemaker stood ready to temper its effect, the grapes, having first been smashed and chewed up, were beaten, pumped, and spun from the moment they arrived.

The worst of it was that inexperienced winemakers, and even some who should have known better, would often burden wines already bereft of character (let alone delicacy) with unnecessarily brutal tannins. They learned quickly that such wines, though completely unbalanced, would be praised for their potential longevity by critics who probably knew less than they themselves. Such wines earned stars and medals and high ratings. And they sold. With more experience the winemakers would have known that neither bulk nor excessive tannin but balance alone ensures the reasonable aging of a bottle of wine; and even time couldn't conjure up quality if it was lacking to begin with. Meanwhile, consumers soon grew bored with wines that gave no pleasure. Many now wonder what's to be done with closets full of bemedalled wines unlikely to be drinkable in this or any other lifetime.

Those producers who got it right, however, shared an important attribute. From the start they understood that making wine was the last stage of growing it, one in which every effort had to be made, every care had to be taken, not to undo in a day what nature had achieved in a season. Wasn't that how the first Europeans to plant vines in Napa Valley had seen the situation? In French and German, as in Italian and Spanish, there is no word for winemaker, only for winegrower. Bernard Portet at Clos du Val and Walter Schug at Joseph Phelps were Europeans and already understood that the growing of grapes and the making

85

of wine are but a single process. But they were hardly alone. Many valley pro-ducers—Charles and Chuck Wagner at Caymus, Joe Heitz, Warren Winiarski at Stag's Leap, the Trefethens, and Robert Mondavi himself, to name only a few—were growers. They, too, understood the making of wine as neither more nor less than realizing, in the fermenting vat, the full potential of their fruit.

Eventually the point was understood by just about everyone, although, ironically for a valley of which Cabernet Sauvignon is the greatest glory, the lesson was learned by winemakers having to come to terms with Sauvignon Blanc and Pinot Noir. Both varieties, less tough than Cabernet Sauvignon, are unforgiv-ing of mistakes in the vineyard and rough treatment in the winery.

The persistent taste of green stems in Sauvignon Blanc ("grassy" was the marketing term for it) made winemakers realize that they ignored the vineyard at their own peril. In the winery nothing could be done to change or eradicate what was a direct result of the way in which Sauvignon Blanc grapes were being grown. Uncomfortably aware that Sauvignon Blanc was, in fact, "made" on the vine, they became fully cognizant at last of the vineyard.

To preserve their reputations, winemakers were obliged to contribute to cultivation decisions, and the gap between growing and winemaking began to close. The lesson learned from Pinot Noir was, in some ways, even more radical and touched winemakers even more directly. Years of effort to make good Pinot Noir had brought few worthwhile results, less because of the often repeated claim that the wrong clones were planted in the wrong places than because winemakers had attempted to make Pinot Noir as if it were Cabernet Sauvignon of a different flavor. The rigorous procedures used to produce clumsy Cabernet Sauvignon were disastrous when applied to Pinot Noir. It was not easy for winemakers to under-stand that releasing the weaker concentrations of color, flavor, and tannin of Pinot Noir needed less force, not more.

In due course, though, winemakers discovered what could be achieved simply by handling this fragile variety gently and by refraining from overwhelming its delicacy with tannin—usually coarse tannin, derived from the stalks rather than the fruit—that served no purpose. Thrilled with their discovery, they soon questioned why it had taken so long to realize the futility of being so harsh. It was only a matter of time before they would ask whether it was necessary, let alone beneficial, to be as harsh with Cabernet Sauvignon.

It was a question I'd often posed to myself. Twenty years ago, when I first came to work in the California wine industry, I was confronted daily with ideas about growing grapes and making wine opposed almost 180 degrees to all I had been taught and had observed in Europe. In California, any suggestion that soil composition could affect a wine's style and quality was dismissed as unproven. Single vines were expected to produce three times as many grapes as in Europe, while maintaining the same intensity of flavor. And basically nature was held at bay in the winery—no indigenous yeast, no barrel fermentation, no malolactic (the bacterial action that softens a wine and draws its divergent flavors together), and as little contact as possible between a wine and its lees. In California wineries the words "clean it up" were a universal mantra that had little to do with cellar hygiene.

Actually, now that I think of it, there was never any claim about intensity of flavor. What I was told was that a vine in California could bear and ripen three times the grapes generally acceptable in Europe with no loss of quality. The University of California's experiments proved that the levels of acid and sugar— and therefore of alcohol—were the same in California wines whether the yield was heavy or light. "European vines are less vigorous, less productive," I was told, "because the soil there is exhausted. Besides, we have more sun in California, so a single vine here easily ripens more fruit."

I saw no reason to argue. Why shouldn't things be different in the New World? I was impressed by the confidence with which everything was scientifically justified and didn't have the wits to ask myself, let alone anyone else, why there is an obvious difference between Bordeaux Rouge and Château Margaux, even when the acidity and alcohol are identical. I didn't see immediately that in California, balance, always an ingredient of quality, was being confused with quality itself. But then I wouldn't have known, in any case, how to define the "obvious difference" between Bordeaux Rouge and Château Margaux in terms acceptable to those who believed only in numbers. No matter what I might have said, it would have sounded like an alchemist mumbling about the effect of the moon on his potions. Indeed, when I mentioned once that growers in Europe preferred to bottle their wines when the full moon began to wane, I was made to feel that I had just proclaimed the earth to be flat.

There have been great changes since my early days in California. Vineyards are now being replanted more densely and with less vigorous rootstocks; an increasing number of wineries, including some of the most distinguished, are again allowing natural, indigenous yeast (as opposed to laboratory yeast selected to work within predictable parameters) to play its role in fermentation, restoring depth and subtlety to the wines; and there is a freer attitude about lees, with more emphasis on their protective and enhancing roles. Tony Soter, proprietor of Etude and consultant at Spottswoode and a number of other wineries specializing in making Cabernet Sauvignon, says of his generation "We have learned a lot, and we have unlearned a lot, too."

There is now, too, a greater willingness to take risks for the sake of quality. I was hardly surprised to learn that many wineries have installed gentler presses, traded in their violent-action pumps, retired the centrifuge, and changed their methods and frequency of "pumping over." (It's necessary, as red wines ferment, to keep the liquid and the floating mass of grape skins in appropriate contact to extract color, flavor, and tannins. There is more than one way to do it, but a gentle-handed discretion is always essential.)

What would the two most recent vintages reveal of these changes? Both 1990 and 1991 had been affected, of course, by the ongoing drought in California, though stress on the vines had been less than might have been the case because of other vagaries of weather. In 1990 heavy rain over the Memorial Day weekend had saturated the soil, at least temporarily, giving the vines relief for most of that growing season. It had brought problems, on the other hand, by encouraging vigorous shoots and leaves that then had to be repeatedly restrained or removed. Also, by arriving when the Cabernet Sauvignon (and the Sauvignon Blanc) were in flower, it caused much of the blossom to fall instead of setting to fruit, leading to a considerable loss of potential crop.

When a warm July followed a warm June, growers expected an early harvest. But August started off cool and became even cooler. Picking, repeatedly delayed, began sporadically only at the end of the month. The lower temperatures and the longer time on the vine as the fruit came to maturity intensified its flavor, however, and gave better balance.

California's summer of 1991 was described as temperate, but that was surely a euphemism. Fog-bound San Franciscans, used though they are to what Mark Twain called their winter-in-August, were ready to leave en masse for Hawaii. In Napa Valley, not affected to quite the same extent, the fruit nevertheless hung long, changing color and accumulating sugar very slowly. Many growers had already thinned their crop—something the rain had achieved for them in 1990— to give the remaining bunches the best chance of ripening when September brought warm and even hot weather that persisted until well into October. The grapes were splendid, and after tasting the wines, I must say that the high hopes expressed for both vintages appear to have been amply fulfilled. Just about all the wines are very good, and some are superb. Though a few wineries produced their better wine in 1990, to my taste the majority did marginally better in 1991. That long, cool summer seems to have given wines of greater vivacity and longer, more concentrated flavor.

But the bigger question is: Did I find the wines, overall, fundamentally different from those made under the old régime, so to speak, five and more years ago? I did, undoubtedly, and in ways more far-reaching than can be attributed to the circumstances of vintage alone. I must generalize, of course: after all, there are Napa Valley wineries that never suffered an "old régime," and there are others that will evidently need yet more time to adjust to change. But the 1990 and 1991 Napa Valley Cabernet Sauvignons are striking, first for their accessibility, and then for their depth. They have better structure—*real* structure as opposed to tannin corsets—yet they are more supple. Furthermore, though true to their vintages and to their Napa Valley origin, the wines show more diverse personalities than I remember when tasting any similarly extensive range of wines from earlier vintages. And there were remarkably few I would have rejected out of hand.

I hadn't the chance to taste everything, so not much should be read into my mentioning some wines and not others. I am not giving out awards, after all, and even less am I deliberately passing over someone's mistake in tactful silence. I can't comment on wines I haven't tasted. It's as simple as that. Among those I have tasted are some I like very much. They include, in no special order, Shafer's Hillside wines (I prefer the 1991 of the two current vintages, but I also like very much the 1988 still current in most parts of the country); Beringer's Chabot Vineyard (I prefer this wine, once called Lemmon-Chabot, even to Beringer's Private Reserve); and the new Cabernet Sauvignon now being produced by S. Anderson—a winery better known for its white and sparkling wines—from grapes grown on the Richard Chambers Vineyard in Stags Leap District. The 1990 makes a brilliant red wine debut for both the vineyard and the winery. The 1991 is every bit as good.

Both Randle Johnson of Hess Collection and Craig Williams of Joseph Phelps are of the minimal intervention school of winemaking and it shows in the seamless quality of their wines. Williams told me he has never worked so hard trying to do so little. Bernard Portet works equally hard at Clos du Val where his wines, it seems to me, have become somewhat more Californian as others have become more French. "At this winery," Portet told me, "there is a constant battle between the principles of French winemaking and the California climate." Personally I see no battle at all, just a remarkably successful fusion of the two—as anyone can see from the winery's 1990 and the 1991 Cabernet Sauvignons.

Other wines that caught my attention were Johnson Turnbull 1991, a Cabernet Sauvignon with something of the intense eucalyptus aroma we associate with Heitz's Martha's Vineyard; the graceful SLV 1990 of Stag's Leap Wine Cellars; the Silverado 1990 and 1991; Duckhorn 1990; Far Niente 1990; both the 1990 and the 1991 of Diamond Creek's Volcanic Hill (where presses turned only by levers and human muscle have been used from the beginning), Spottswoode 1990 and 1991; Truchard 1990; and Etude of just about all available vintages. Three 1987s tasted recently on separate occasions deserve mention: Heitz's Martha's Vineyard, Cafaro, and Caymus Special Selection. And I must give special credit to the 1989 Corison. Cathy Corison's production is small, but her 1989 is surely the single most beautiful expression yet of Napa Valley Cabernet Sauvignon. It is a study in what is possible with the right approach, even in a vintage not considered one of California's most generally successful.

At a winemakers' meeting on natural fermentation last summer, I heard John Williams of Frog's Leap say, "I found most of our red tanks had started fermenting anyway by the time we were ready to inoculate with a selected yeast, so I just stopped inoculating—with great results." It is this growing reliance on natural yeast, whole or in part, that is giving greater depth of flavor and texture. Frog's Leap 1990 is as good an illustration as any, and so are Newton Vineyard's 1990 and (especially) its 1991. The 1990—finely nuanced, fruity and tender—is the first Newton vintage for which natural fermentation was used. The winery's earlier Cabernets, good though they are, do not compare with it. The 1991 is even more concentrated, more elegant, and more distinguished.

Bill Dyer of Sterling Vineyards is the latest to be converted to natural fermentation, starting with his 1992 Cabernet Sauvignon. It will have a richer style than Sterling Cabernet Sauvignons have had in the past. Dyer's wines have always been precise, and, more often than not, tightly austere when young even though maturing with a meticulous elegance. I think that is what we can expect of his Sterling Diamond Mountain 1990 and of the Sterling Reserve 1991.

Von Strasser, also on Diamond Mountain, is making its debut with its 1990 Cabernet Sauvignon and will follow with a 1991 that will be no less captivating. The mature vineyard, established on steep terraces more than ten years ago, looks across at those of Diamond Creek. Von Strasser Cabernet Sauvignons have intense fruit and great finesse and are certain to cause considerable excitement.

Two wines from Robert Mondavi, his 1990 and 1991 Reserve Cabernet Sauvignons, stood head and shoulders over most others at the tasting. "The character of the reserve is basically unchanging," Charles Thomas, then Mondavi's winemaker, assured me, "because the grapes have come from the same vines on the west side of Oakville just about from the beginning. But the style does change. We pick by taste, not by numbers; we have learned to be gentler with the grapes; we pay greater attention to details, no matter how small, rather than concentrate only on the big picture.

"People don't understand, for example, that the decision whether or not to filter a wine can't be made at the time of bottling. A wine destined not to be filtered must at every stage from fruit to bottle be handled in a way that will make

91

the whole question of filtration superfluous. We have learned to be sensitive to things we once ignored. Atmospheric pressure, for instance. Do you know that we now work according to the phases of the moon? We bottle our wines, for instance, when the full moon begins to wane."

92

DECANTING:
TO BREATHE OR NOT TO BREATHE

THE MYSTIQUE ATTACHED TO DECANTING—VISIONS OF A HAWK-EYED BUTLER WATCHING THE BOTTLE AGAINST A CANDLE FLAME AS THE DEPOSIT SLIPS FORWARD TO ITS NECK; ONE MISTAKE AND THE VALUABLE WINE IS RUINED—CAN BE SO INTIMIDATING THAT WHAT IS ACTUALLY A SIMPLE OPERATION IS THOUGHT TO BE COMPLICATED AND DIFFICULT, NOT TO MENTION AFFECTED. But anyone who can pour wine into a glass can decant a bottle of wine.

When I was young I was skeptical of the need to decant wine, any wine, and though I wasn't sure what the "risks" of decanting were, I thought they outweighed any possible advantage. I was converted by everyday experience: any remnant of red wine left over from dinner always seemed to taste better with lunch next day. That's how I came to accept the basic logic of decanting—that red wine needs to be aerated to be enjoyed at its best.

The popular notion that a wine can be aerated merely by drawing the cork a few minutes before serving ("to let the wine breathe" is the way waiters usually put it) is an example of useless wine lore. The University of Bordeaux established years ago that the limited surface of wine exposed to air in the neck of a full but open bottle allows the absorption of almost no oxygen at all, even after twenty-four hours. In a restaurant, or anywhere that decanting is not a convenient option, the wine will begin to aerate—"to breathe"—only when poured into the glasses. When a good waiter pours the wine before the food arrives at the table, it's not because he wants to encourage you to drink up and order a second bottle. (Well, there could be a little of that, too.) It's to prepare the wine for drinking. He would be an even better waiter, however, if he poured the wine into a carafe and let it breathe there until needed. Recently I was impressed by a waitress in a popular New York City bistro on a busy Saturday night because she decanted the bottle of wine I'd ordered without being asked to do so—perfectly and without fuss.

Anyone who tastes a red wine poured straight from the bottle will be surprised to find how different—how much better—that same wine is when poured into a jug and allowed to stand, if only for just twenty minutes. As a young red wine is poured from the bottle, its aroma expands; in older wine the bouquet is released. Furthermore, the change affects the tannin, making the young wine, particularly, seem both softer and broader. An older wine seems also to fill out, its angles disappear and it darkens slightly in color. Then, too, decanting an older wine helps keep it clear of any sediment. That's one reason (there are others) why, when decanting, we handle an older wine slightly differently from a young one.

It's never a good idea to treat wine roughly, but a young red can be poured without ceremony into a decanter, a carafe, a jug, or even another— clean—bottle. Those who have a sure hand can just pour, and those who prefer to make the job easier for themselves can use a small kitchen funnel. In either case the stream of wine will fall directly into the middle of the decanter where it will certainly make a splash. For a young wine that can do no harm and, in fact, probably does some good.

A mature wine, on the other hand, needs gentle handling, even when the sediment is minimal. California Cabernet Sauvignon wines and wines like those of Bordeaux, to which Cabernet Sauvignon or similarly tough-skinned grapes have made important contributions, will always throw a limited sediment while they age over several years. (To some extent that can be true of any red wine, but most are not really made for aging.)

The sediment in a Cabernet Sauvignon or a Bordeaux is usually loose and will settle at the bottom if the bottle is allowed to stand upright for few hours. In vintage Port—and in some Rhône wines, too—the sediment attaches itself to the lower side of the bottle as it lies on its side aging. It's easier to handle if left undisturbed by keeping the bottle horizontal from cellar (or closet) to table in a decanting basket. I'm not referring to one of those silver-plate, latticed bottle-holders so often the pride and joy of expensive gift shops and silversmiths. I mean the simple wicker version that most wine stores have for sale. A decanting basket also helps keep the bottle steady while the cork is drawn and the contents poured.

A red wine's sediment is a mixture of tartrates, heavy tannins, and coloring matter—organic compounds that in falling free leave the wine softer, silkier, and more elegant. Wines in which sediment is expected to form—Bordeaux and Port especially—are traditionally sold in bottles with a well-defined shoulder, as opposed to the slope-shouldered bottles in which we expected to find Pinot Noir, Beaujolais, and other wines that we neither age to the same extent nor expect to throw a heavy sediment. The shoulder in a Bordeaux bottle is there by design as well as tradition: it helps retain sediment as the wine in the bottle is poured.

The actual decanting is simplicity itself. Light a short candle placed in a holder on a table or a counter low enough to allow the flame to be seen from above through the shoulder of the bottle being decanted. Take the decanter in the left hand at an angle about midway between vertical and horizontal and grip the bottle with the right hand. Hold it in the middle to leave a clear view of its neck and shoulder as the wine flows into the decanter. The wine should be encouraged to run down the side of the decanter so that it splashes as little as possible—the angle at which the decanter is held will help.

The operation is even easier, of course, if a decanting funnel is available. The decanter can then stand on the table because the tip of the decanting funnel is curved and directs the flow of wine to the side of the decanter's neck.

I usually find it difficult at first to see the flame clearly through the wine and the dark green glass, but as the wine flows from the bottle its level becomes more shallow. It's then easier to see the surge of dark sediment as it moves towards the shoulder. Once having started to pour, one must continue to do so steadily, so it's best to take it slowly from the beginning. Hesitating or stopping the flow by tilting the bottle back will stir the deposit into the wine, something best avoided.

Stop pouring when the sediment arrives in the shoulder and just before it starts to flow into the neck itself. A tablespoonful of wine will stay with the sediment, of course, but that would be lost in the heel of the bottle anyway—we would never pour the last of the wine, complete with sediment, into someone's glass. Occasionally, of course, even the most experienced hand will inadvertently let a little of the sediment through into the decanter. It will sink to the bottom, however, and be no more than a slight nuisance when the wine is poured into the glasses. The wine is not "ruined."

Though there are exceptions (I wouldn't decant a young Beaujolais, for example—its lively fruit aroma usually needs to be restrained by cooling rather than expanded by decanting), I now decant red wines as a matter of course. My rule of thumb is to decant older wines just before we sit down to eat and younger wines an hour or so earlier.

Not too long ago I served a Beringer Napa Valley Private Reserve Cabernet Sauvignon '86 at a dinner party. The wine was tough and decidedly tannic when I first drew the cork, but two hours in a decanter tamed the tannin and brought out a rich aroma and flavor we might not otherwise have enjoyed. The wine was gorgeous when it could have been what is politely called a challenge.

A couple of nights earlier I had tasted at a special dinner a series of Château Latour vintages ranging from the 1949 to the 1961. They were poured for us to taste as soon as they had been decanted. At first I thought there was something wrong: the wines were tough and blunt. But within minutes the decanting had the desired effect and we were captivated by the bouquet, the elegance, and the charm of those wines.

Captivated, that is, by all except the 1952, one of my least favorite Bordeaux vintages. There are limits to what even decanting can achieve. But that's another story.

STORM IN A CHAMPAGNE FLUTE

A FRIEND OF A FRIEND HAD TAKEN A LONG LEASE ON A HOUSE IN WEST LONDON IN ONE OF THE FEW JOHN NASH TERRACES—FOR ALL I KNOW, THE ONLY JOHN NASH TERRACE—OUTSIDE REGENT'S PARK. In Nash's hands, elegance had been more than an abstraction, and the house, built in the early years of the nineteenth century, had been carefully restored and handsomely decorated. Carpets had been laid and curtains hung. On the morning when a few of us were shown around the house, it stood empty but ready.

On the spur of the moment my friend's friend decided to throw a party. A black-tie party. The next night. Ten o'clock. We were all invited. And so, we later discovered, were at least a hundred others.

An exuberance of jazz musicians—I could hear them playing long before I reached the front door—had been hired. Someone had distributed folding chairs about the rooms. The catering was superbly confident and magnificently simple. On every floor, from basement to attic, were open crates of perfectly ripe, perfectly aromatic peaches brought straight from Covent Garden. The whole house smelled of peaches. And next to the crates of peaches were ice tubs filled with bottles of Lanson Champagne. I was twenty-two and life was in Technicolor. We talked, we danced, we ate peaches; we listened to the music, admired each other, and drank Champagne.

What is it about Champagne? Clearly not just the physical effect of the alcohol lurking behind the bubbles. In most circumstances even the sound of a cork popping lightens the mood and provokes an immediate sense of expectation. With a flute of Champagne in hand, the young feel wisely witty and the old feel young; everyone is better looking. Robert Smith Surtees's character Jorrocks observed that Champagne "gives one werry gentlemanly ideas," which may or may not be so. I can only say that one glass of Champagne will raise the morale and two will fuse the most ill-assorted group into a dinner party.

Champagne began as a still, light red wine in the valley of the Marne, east of Paris. In the sixteenth century, thanks to a powerful sponsor, it captured the loyalty of the court of Henri IV. The king's own chancellor, Nicolas Brûlart, owned immense vineyards at Sillery-en-Champagne, north of the Marne, on what is now known as the Montagne de Reims. Brûlart knew the tastes of the court and taught his growers how to meet them. He commended them to pay special attention to delicacy, urging that the grapes be picked no later than ten o'clock in the morning to ensure their fresh and cool arrival at the press. The clear juice was separated from the black grape skins quickly to keep the wine as light as possible. Though it was elegance that interested Brûlart, not lightness of color for its own sake, Champagne destined for the court soon ceased to be red; by the late seventeenth century, it was no more than the palest bronze-pink, and was known as *vin gris*.

Shipped in barrel with traces of unfermented sugar remaining in the wine—at the time, both knowledge and equipment were spare—the wine inevitably resumed a slow fermentation as soon as spring temperatures set the yeast in motion. But by then the wine had been transferred into bottles and closed, the better to preserve its fresh qualities. Most wine in bottle in those days was protected by a film of olive oil or a loose cloth to allow the gas of any continuing fermentation to escape. But in the tightly bunged bottles of Champagne, carbon dioxide generated by the renewal of fermentation was trapped in solution. As the wine was poured, it sparkled, captivating a court addicted to novelty and artifice. Just as Champagne's pale color had acquired importance without having been Brûlart's main objective, so its accidental sparkle became a mark of high fashion.

But the quality of the sparkle in a Champagne bottled at destination remained unpredictable. In 1724 the growers of Champagne appealed to the government for the right to ship their *vin gris* in bottles rather than barrels, the better to ensure and control the *mousse*, or foam. With permission given in 1728 and the development of the Saint-Gobain glassworks to provide the vast number of bottles that would be required, real sparkling champagne, though still not quite as we know it, made its debut.

By the early nineteenth century, experience had taught Champagne producers to calculate the pressure of gas that would be generated by a given presence of sugar. They were then able to blend their wines and provoke a second fermentation by adding sugar and yeast before bottling instead of just hoping that the first fermentation would continue. Further improvements in the manufacture of glass bottles allowed, with greater safety, an increased pressure of gas, and Champagne came closer to the wine we drink today.

The last step before its full commercial success was a process introduced by Madame Barbe Nicole Ponsardin Clicquot (the *veuve* of the eponymous Champagne), which removed the inconvenient debris of bottle fermentation without losing the wine's effervescence. She had the idea of inverting the bottles into holes in a steeply sloping tabletop. Repeatedly shaken and gradually turned during several weeks, the bottles were gradually brought from an oblique to an upright position as the debris in each was coaxed into a compact mass settled on the cork itself. Once the retaining wire was removed, the cork, with the debris adhering to it, flew from the bottle, propelled by the pressure of gas within before the operator's thumb stopped the flow. The slight loss of wine was made good and a new cork secured so swiftly that the sparkle was barely diminished.

French law recognizes the importance of the changes that occur during the time a bottle of Champagne is allowed to retain the yeasty lees of its second fermentation. That is why it imposes minimum aging for Champagnes with bottle lees intact. A vintage Champagne (one proclaiming the year in which the grapes were grown) must age with its lees for at least three years before being disgorged. Nonvintage Champagnes must spend a year, a minimum that might soon be raised and that, in any case, is already usually exceeded by quality-conscious producers.

Once disgorged, Champagne begins to lose freshness. Producers usually recommend that nonvintage blends, rarely assembled with the idea of long-term development, be consumed once released for sale. Vintage Champagnes continue to evolve in ways that depend on the style of the year. Some people do and some don't like their Champagne with this additional aging. The English were always notorious for liking theirs "old landed"—aged, that is to say, in English cellars for several years after being disgorged. For most tastes, however, a vintage Champagne

99

aged for three or four years with its lees and a further three or four without is amply ready to be consumed, even though there are exceptional wines that age superbly for fifty years or more. The best of them, especially if allowed to age on their lees for a late disgorging, acquire a bouquet of freshly baked biscuits or of toasted almonds.

Credit for "inventing" champagne is often given to Dom Pérignon, the cellar master of the abbey at Hautvilliers in the Marne Valley from 1668 to 1715. (His name is now used for a prestige *cuvée* produced by Moët & Chandon.) In fact, the evolution of Champagne as a sparkling wine had started long before his time and was to continue long after. Dom Pérignon is properly credited, however, with identifying the dominant characteristics of the wines from the various sites in the valley and on the hills north and south of it. He started the practice of blending grapes of disparate origin within the Champagne region to arrive at a balance of qualities superior to any that could be found naturally in one place. According to his contemporaries, he was so sensitive to the possibilities of each of the abbey's vineyards that he could say, from tasting a single grape, where the basket had come from and decide, on the spot, to which vat it should be consigned.

Because the second fermentation, in Dom Pérignon's day, had really been no more than a resumption of the first, he had had to balance his blend from the start. Today's master blenders, thanks to their ability to control, stop, and provoke fermentation at will, can spend days tasting the year's new wines, the *vins clairs* as they are called, and can test-blend them before committing themselves. If wine of a particular vintage is deficient in some way, the blenders can restore the weak or missing quality with earlier vintages stored as still wines in tank, in cask, or in magnums. (Each firm has its preference.) A *cuvée* today, therefore, starts with hours of tasting and discussion. Dom Pérignon, poor fellow, had only a few seconds with a grape crushed against his tongue to make his decision.

Dom Pérignon probably worked with black grapes only, though his would have been a wider range of varieties than the Pinot Noir and its more rustic cousin, Pinot Meunier, used today exclusively. White grapes had earlier disappeared from Champagne, but in the eighteenth century Chardonnay began to

100

appear among the Pinot Noir and Pinot Meunier vines in the Marne valley. Chardonnay contributed to the delicacy of the wines, as one might expect, and was also found to improve their sparkle. It spread north onto the Montagne de Reims, and then entire vineyards of white varieties were planted south of the Marne, earning the hillsides there, formerly known as the Montagne de Vertus, the name by which they still are known: the Côte des Blancs. These three—the Montagne de Reims, the Marne Valley, and the Côte des Blancs—supported by vineyards still farther south in the Aube *département*, are the principal divisions within the Champagne region. Pinot Noir, Pinot Meunier, and Chardonnay are the three grape varieties grown there.

The individual *crus*—the village names once used to distinguish one Champagne from another—have largely disappeared from public notice in favor of the names of the Champagne houses. Early in the nineteenth century one would have chosen between, say, a Sillery or an Avize, just as, in Burgundy, we still choose between a Beaune and a Volnay. But the art of blending contributed so much to the commercial success of Champagne that by the century's end one chose not between *crus* but between a Mumm, say, and a Pol Roger. As a result, consumers are relatively unfamiliar now with the names of the villages and the specific characteristics of their wines, even though the *crus* still play an important role.

All *crus* are graded by the Comité Interprofessionel du Vin de Champagne—the professional organization that represents both the Champagne houses and the grape growers—on a scale from 100 percent down to 80 percent. (The scale formerly went down to 50 percent.) Until 1989, when a thirty-year collective contract between the growers and the Champagne houses expired, the percent rating affected the price paid to each grower for his grapes. Here, roughly, is how it worked. If the price for the grapes of a particular year was agreed at, say, 28 francs a kilo, that is what the owner of a vineyard in a village at the top of the scale would get. The owner of a vineyard in a village rated 95 percent would get 95 percent of the agreed price per kilo, and so on down to those who received the minimum of 80 percent. The rating applied to the vineyards of a particular village as a whole, and one doesn't have to be a viticultural expert to recognize that a favored and well-cared-for vineyard in a village rated 95 percent could be

101

giving better grapes than the least-favored vineyard in a village rated 100 percent. As a result, to secure the best grapes, Champagne houses occasionally offered premiums above the percentile of the negotiated price.

Those villages rated 100 percent—there are 17 of them and they account for 4,317 hectares of the 27,500 hectares of vineyard presently planted in Champagne—are known as *grands crus*. The 45 villages rated from 90 to 99 percent—accounting for 5,249 hectares of vines—are known as *premiers crus*. Together, the *grands* and *premiers crus* of Champagne represent 32.4 percent of the total area under vines.

It is wines from these *crus* that earned for Champagne its reputation. Used in combinations of villages, of the special sites within each village, or of Champagne's three grape varieties as affected by those special sites, they make possible the subtle variations that distinguish the style of one Champagne house from another. Chardonnay lightens a wine, Pinot Noir gives it weight, and Pinot Meunier brings a fresh quality useful in heavy years. But the wine of each village also has its particular characteristics, as Dom Pérignon well knew: Bouzy and Ambonnay give a blend body, for instance, Cramant, Ay, and Le Mesnil finesse, Mailly power, Verzenay flavor, and so on.

Henri Krug emphasizes the role of the *crus*. "People are always asking about the varietal composition of this or that Champagne," he said to me recently, "But one can discuss blends only in terms of varietals from *specific villages*. For example, we use Pinot Meunier only from certain places, like Leuvrigny.

"A *cuvée* can have fifty wines in it from half a dozen vintages. We have to think ahead. We must project what it will have become after bottle fermentation and six years in bottle with its lees. By that time each wine must have made its contribution to the overall effect, and the wine should have the harmony of a symphony where nothing jars but every note has its place."

According to André Lallier, head of Champagne Deutz, the work of assembling the *cuvée* should be no more than a last fine-tuning. "The real decisions should have been made long before, when a producer chose to buy this rather than that vineyard or decided with which growers to sign long-term supply contracts."

But buying vineyards and signing grape contracts have both become extremely difficult in Champagne. A hectare (roughly 2.5 acres) of *grand cru* vine-yard sold for 10,000 francs in 1960. By 1988 its value had risen to a million francs—when the land was available. A single hectare at Ay recently sold for five million francs. At today's rate of exchange, that is $400,000 an acre for agricultural land.

Other numbers help explain this. In 1945 Champagne sales amounted to 22 million bottles. In 1990 that figure had catapulted to 230 million bottles. Though sales have increased, Champagne's geographic appellation is finite, and production is just about as large as it can be. Producers who depend on bought grapes have a difficult time, especially as the supply has been further reduced by growers who prefer to add value to their crop by turning it into Champagne them-selves (or making an arrangement with the local cooperative to do so on their behalf) and then selling it by mail order. The French market for Champagne is now dominated by just such private-producer sales.

The big Champagne producers, usually referred to as the *grandes marques*, have cannibalized each other simply to acquire vineyards. Some have established affiliated and similarly named wineries outside France to help deflect some of the worldwide demand for their brands. These sparkling wines, in California particularly, have done well and now frighten the Champenois, who are uneasy at the thought of having to compete with the very brand names that once carried the global reputation of Champagne. The situation has been brought to a head by a drop in sales coincidental with a sagging world economy, and, although Champagne has in the past always presented an elegant and unruffled façade to the world, whatever its inner turmoil, this time we are being given a glimpse of problems usually dealt with behind Champagne's firmly closed doors.

In Britain, long Champagne's largest customer outside France itself, sales began to slide in 1990 after years of steady growth. Then in 1991 shipments fell 40 percent. Sales in France were also down by 12 percent, and shipments declined to greater or lesser degrees to all other markets.

There have been similar setbacks before, most recently in the mid-1970s, but the anxiety was more widespread this time because the quality houses were affected as much as the volume producers. Firms that would normally have three or four years' inventory maturing in their cellars are presently financing five or six. The call on their resources has been further aggravated not only by the big harvests of 1990 and 1991 (contracts between the Champagne houses and their growers usually bind buyer and seller to the yield of so many acres, whatever that yield might be) but by the unprecedented prices paid for grapes when the industry-wide contract ran out.

A formula under that group contract had put limits on the quantities of grapes the larger houses could buy, a plan designed to prevent their offering premiums over the negotiated price only to draw grapes away from smaller rivals. When the contract's term ended, each house negotiated for itself; the limits were off. What the large producers wanted, in any case, was to offer prices that would encourage growers to sell their grapes rather than process them for direct-mail sales. Everything conspired to send up grape prices, which in turn put immediate pressure on current Champagne prices. The revenues to buy the grapes had to come from somewhere. As things turned out, it was an unfortunate time for prices to have been increased.

In 1992, at a sedate but unprecedented press conference, Christian Bizot, president and director general of the venerable house of Bollinger, announced that Champagne was at a crossroads. He said what everyone knew: that problems created by falling sales were compounded by high grape prices, excess inventories, and disappointment (expressed mostly in the British press) with the quality of much nonvintage brut. The region, he said, had lost its sense of direction.

Though critical of no one in particular, Bizot pointed out that a trade once dominated by family firms was now largely controlled by four groups (Louis Vuiton-Moët Hennesy; Rémy-Martin; Seagram; and Marne et Champagne, a conglomerate of cooperatives). "I'm not saying that the change is for better or worse," he said, choosing his words carefully in French and translating them himself into impeccable English, "but change it certainly is."

Bizot said he saw Champagne's role eroding along with its distinction. He accepted, he said, the challenge of a rise in the quality of sparkling wines made elsewhere in the world, but he regretted the confusion sown by Champagne houses lending their names, and, with their names, a credibility that belonged not to them but to the region of Champagne.

"California sparkling wines would not have the reputation they now have in the United States," he argued, "if French names had not been used to launch and support them.... Now more than ever," he said, "the producers of Champagne must demonstrate the distinction of their product."

Champagne Deutz's André Lallier, with whom I lunched the day after the Bizot press conference, agreed that California sparkling wines, including his own Maison Deutz in San Luis Obispo, were helped, when they started, by the credibility of the Champagne houses sponsoring them. "But the second bottle of any wine," he said, "is sold on the quality of the first. Our people in California are setting their own very high standards, and, yes, that is a challenge. But we don't think our development in California has worked against our interests in Champagne. Producing good wine in a country helps make it more accessible. That is as true for sparkling wine as it is for still wine. In France everyone has a cousin, an uncle, someone, who has a vineyard somewhere and makes wine. Champagne is a step up, but it is an easier step for people who are familiar with good sparkling wine. That must help Champagne. I would say that if there is a problem it is not in California but here in Champagne. We now have wines of a quality below the expected standard. Perhaps we need two classifications to make that clear."

"I am not anxious about our Champagne industry, however. On the contrary, I am very optimistic. I see the production of good sparkling wines around the world as a positive development that will stimulate and help Champagne."

Christian Bizot, presenting to the assembled press Bollinger's Charter—a statement of the firm's own commitment to what it considers to be the basic ethical and qualitative tenets of a *grand vin de Champagne*—seemed also to suggest that it was time to restore distinctions within Champagne, between the *grands* and *premiers crus* and other Champagnes for a start.

"The *grands crus* of Bordeaux and Burgundy give credibility to those regions as a whole," he said. "Basically, the situation is the same in Champagne, but consumers don't know this because few are familiar with the *crus*. The needs of blending, a fundamental part of Champagne, make it difficult to offer a wine that is assembled only from 100 percent *grand cru* grapes. But at Bollinger we think it is time to prepare a back label for wines blended from *grand cru* and *premier cru* wines only. Champagne must find a way to explain to the world what its distinctions are, how its quality is defined. The *grandes marques*, particularly, must define themselves and the role they play."

The difficulty is that many consumers are dazzled by well-publicized names, and others are deterred by Champagnes with real character when they have become used to rather bland wines produced on the same principles that give us flavorless food.

Antoine Gosset, head of the small, quality house of Champagne Gosset at Ay, gets quite heated on the subject. "Standardization is robbing Champagne of its character. Character costs money—money spent on quality grapes and aging. It is expensive to age a product that was expensive to produce in the first place.

"Those making fine wines find themselves at a disadvantage. This doesn't just affect wine, of course. Butter no longer tastes like butter; chicken doesn't have the true taste of chicken. Quality is lost in the name of producing these things more cheaply. But those who promote a product with the slogan 'It's cheaper' neglect to add 'and it's not as good.' Sometimes it's not even recognizable for what it is supposed to be. People are settling for shadows."

There is no need for that. Whatever the current brouhaha, there are plenty of superb Champagnes. For what it's worth in these confused times, here are those I hold in highest esteem and which give me most pleasure. The choice is subjective, of course; and is neither particularly unusual nor original.

Everyone agrees, for example, that Bollinger and Krug stand apart from all other producers; even their competitors are in agreement on this point. At both establishments, fermentation in barrel plays an important part in establishing style, though Henri Krug maintains that what counts is not just the matter of fermentation in wood but of fermentation in small volume. I enjoy all Krug *cuvées*, and usually pick a Bollinger Vintage R.D.—the R.D. for *récemment dégorgé,* or recently disgorged—for my own family celebrations.

I am never disappointed by Deutz. The Cuvée William Deutz is consistently a perfect example of all that Champagne should mean: elegance, harmony, refinement, length. I have great respect for Veuve Clicquot; the wines are always reliably delicious. Clicquot's Gold Label Brut Vintage can sometimes surpass the prestige *cuvées* of other houses. I think that was the case with the Brut 1982.

I am also devoted to Roederer Cristal (who isn't?), to Taittinger's Comtes de Champagne (a prestige *cuvée* made of white grapes only, its delicacy and freshness more than Brûlart would have dared dream of), and to Perrier-Jouet's Belle Epoque, known in the United States as Fleur de France. Fleur de France is packaged in such a charming bottle that it is easily (and often) dismissed by critics as a marketer's *cuvée*. I was all the more pleased when the French *Guide Hachette des Vins* gave the 1985 *cuvée* its prestigious *Grappe d'Or* for 1991. *Hachette's* juries taste their way through thousands of wines presented "blind" each year to find the one recipient of that annual award.

I asked earlier: "What is it about Champagne?" yet didn't and can't answer my own question. But I remember many years ago watching a play in London's West End and hearing one character say to another: "Take a glass of Champagne with you while you dress for dinner, my boy. It'll give the right fillip to your tie."

And I bet it did.

107

RIBERA DEL DUERO:
A NEW STAR FOR OLD CASTILE

O N A PITCH-BLACK NOVEMBER NIGHT AND IN THE TEETH OF A HOWLING GALE I DROVE ACROSS NORTHERN SPAIN TO PEDROSA DEL DUERO, A VILLAGE IN OLD CASTILE, TO JOIN THE PEREZ PASCUAS BROTHERS, BENJAMIN, ADOLFO AND MANOLO, FOR *CORDERO LECHAL AL HORNO*, THE LOCAL SPECIALTY OF SUCKLING LAMB BAKED IN A WOOD-FIRED OVEN. The warmth of their open hearth and the appetizing smell of the lamb would have been welcome enough—it was a relief just to be snugly inside, behind shutters and a stout door—but there was ready on the table a platter of an invitingly aromatic sliced sausage and some equally fragrant hard sheep's milk cheese.

Benjamin's son, José Manuel, poured for me a glass of the family's 1989 Ribera del Duero, a red wine that had taken honors a few weeks before in a national competition. It was fresh, enticingly fruity, and brought with it a reminder of summer that quickly dispelled all further thought of the rigor outside.

As a wine region, Ribera del Duero is both old and new. Old because vines were first planted there by the Romans, then reintroduced by Cistercian monks in the eleventh century; and new because recently (in 1982) it was formally recognized as a distinct wine region—or *denominación*, as the Spanish say. It brought together what had once been two separate but adjacent wine-growing areas on the Duero, a river possibly better known to the world as the Douro, its Portuguese name once across the border. One of those areas had been scattered around the small town of Peñafiel, huddled at the foot of its improbably white, improbably perfect, Walt Disney castle. The other surrounded Aranda del Duero, a messy but lively manufacturing town about twenty miles away. The new region, seventy miles long and twenty-five miles deep, incorporates both of them.

Did the wines' new distinction inspire a change in style and quality, or had just such a change justified the wines' new status? Either way, praise lavished on the wines of Ribera del Duero in the last decade has provoked outsiders to buy land there and encouraged growers to extend their vineyards. The region, about eighty miles north of Madrid, now has thirty thousand acres of vines—about the same as Napa Valley, California—with more than half of them concentrated in the communities of Roa de Duero, Pedrosa de Duero, La Horra and Sotillo de la Ribera. But if I mention the surrounding historic cities of Burgos, Segovia and Valladolid—probably more familiar and certainly easier to find on a map—identifying the region becomes simpler.

There had been a buzz of interest in this new *denominación* even before wines of the first "official" vintage—the 1982—were released. Though wines of the 1980 and 1981 vintages made by those planning to meet the requirements of the (then) proposed new regulations were sold as plain table wines, they were greeted with considerable curiosity because everyone knew they were essentially what Ribera del Duero would offer. Fortunately, 1980 and 1981 were good vintages; and, more fortunately, 1982—an auspicious year with which to launch a new appellation—was an overnight success. Within weeks an official of the royal household in Madrid had arrived at Pedrosa to arrange for a regular supply of the Perez Pascuas Ribera del Duero, under a private label, for the king's own table.

Nevertheless, the extent of what Ribera del Duero would offer was revealed in stages. That is because regulations defining the new appellation provide (as do those applied to most Spanish red wines) for a hierarchy ranging from *joven* (young) through *crianza* (mature) to *reserva* and *gran reserva*, distinctions related to time spent in cask and bottle before release. At one extreme, the *joven*, aged in neither wood nor bottle, is sold as soon as the producer deems it ready; at the other, a *gran reserva* must spend a minimum of two years in barrel and three years in bottle before release. In fact, the differences depend on more than time alone: both producers and their customers know very well that if a wine is to be aged for two years in wood and three in bottle before sale, it must have qualities beyond those expected in a wine to be drunk within the year.

At any rate, when those 1982 *joven* wines (already released in 1983) were followed by the 1982 *reservas* (released in 1985), earlier admiration turned to acclaim. This was specially so in the United States, where one critic compared a particular 1982 *reserva* to Château Petrus—a sure way to drive the market to frenzy.

For the growers of a region largely ignored (indeed, largely unknown) until then, this was heady stuff, to say the least; and for everyone else, the wines came as a revelation. Although Vega Sicilia, an estate at Valbuena del Duero, east of Valladolid, had been producing extraordinary wine for more than a century, its production had been so spare and so difficult to find, and the price so high when one did, that the wine had taken its place among legends like Tokay Essenzia and pre-phylloxera Bordeaux. Even those who knew of Vega Sicilia and might even have tasted the wine, perceived it as unique—unrelated to anything else in Spain, and certainly to the unlikely terrain of Old Castile.

It is in fact Old Castile itself that most of those tasting these new Ribera del Duero wines find most difficult to accept as the improbable source of such sumptuousness. Nowhere in Spain, nowhere in Europe that I can immediately think of, is quite as bleak. Wind-whipped and frozen in winter and mercilessly sunbaked in summer, it is virtually without trees, totally without charm, and austerely indifferent to any human presence. Though cities like Burgos and Valladolid have something of the grandeur appropriate to former capitals—Valladolid was the seat of government for much of the sixteenth century, Spain's golden age—the small towns and hamlets seem isolated and forlornly colorless. Forget smiling wine villages, real and imaginary; those of Old Castile appear to have been pulled together, stone by stone, as raw evidence of survival against all odds.

These villages had to survive more than a harsh climate. The drawn-out combat—could it really have lasted two hundred years?—between Christian and Moor as well as Christian and neighboring Christian, with repeated burnings of enemy crops and an incessant slaughtering of each other's livestock, had reduced Old Castile to little more than a desert. It was revived and resettled only in the late Middle Ages, when colonized by monks sent from Cluny in France. Not that there was much joy for the inhabitants even then. Castile was sucked dry for the royal treasury and remained, for centuries, a byword for misery. Even lesser noblemen, preoccupied with honor while living wretchedly in tumbledown manors, had little, save their pride, with which to nourish themselves. To this day, the classic dish of Castile is simply a bread soup flavored with garlic, sometimes simmered with a ham bone, and for festive occasions enriched with an egg dropped in each bowl and allowed to poach there. (It is beside the point, and will therefore not be allowed to brighten this diversionary wallow in historic gloom, that *sopa castellana* happens to be uncommonly delicious.)

From a decidedly narrow perspective, the years of wreck and ruin before the arrival of the Cistercians had one thin silver lining. Because vineyards originally planted by the Romans had long since been hacked and burned away, all notions of tending a vine and making wine had been forgotten. So the monks' experience and knowledge of Burgundian viticulture (brought from Cluny, along with the skills and techniques necessary to build monasteries and churches and to copy and illuminate manuscripts for their libraries) was put to use immediately, without having to supplant other practices.

Though much farther south than Burgundy, the Ribera del Duero is at an altitude of two to three thousand feet above sea level, and this presented problems similar to those already overcome in that part of France. There, too, a risky spring, an unpredictable fall, and a summer shorter than was common around the Mediterranean had obliged the monks to plant vine varieties that would bud late, minimizing the dangers of a spring frost, and ripen early. The monks in Ribera del Duero were up against a similarly difficult climate—below zero Fahrenheit in winter and over a hundred degrees in summer—and the vines they planted, severely controlled by pruning in the French manner to concentrate the flavor of the fruit, were robust enough to withstand these extremes. All this was contrary to the practice of neighbors across the border in northern Portugal, for example, where prolific vines were simply allowed to run rampant up into the trees in the ancient Roman fashion.

Following again the Burgundian example, the monks made and stored their wines in wooden containers rather than in the giant terra-cotta amphorae more customary in Spain and still, though now made of concrete, in regular use there. Whether by judgement or good luck, then, the Cistercians brought to Ribera del Duero the combination that has been crucial to the nuanced character of most French red wines through the centuries: pruning and oak barrels.

In the discussion of oak and wine, the most important point is either ignored or forgotten. Oak barrels are not used—or shouldn't be—to introduce a flavor of oak. They are used—or should be—for an effect that becomes fully apparent only when the wine has been aged for a while in bottle. Though our knowledge of precisely what happens and why is still scant, a wine, held in barrel, changes in ways that are both subtle and complex. Many explanations could be true, even when apparently in conflict. The results, at any rate, are plain enough: Wine aged in wood is less angular (it tastes "rounder"); its components are better integrated (the acidity, tannin, alcohol, and so on are bound together more harmoniously); and both aroma and flavor are richer and deeper (they seem to be released from within the wine rather than from its surface). Most important of all, however, the time a wine spends in wood before subsequent aging in bottle is a major factor in the development of those aromas and flavors we call bouquet—though the floral associations of "bouquet" are usually less appropriate than others we can best call nostalgic. Alonso de Herrera, whose treatise on agriculture, first published in 1513, remained in everyday use in Spain until the late nineteenth century, recognized the connection between the aging of wine in wood and its subsequent bouquet. "Wine from barrels," he said, "is more fragrant than wine from jars."

Bouquet, however, unlike the aromas and flavors of the grape itself and the short-lived fruity aromas induced by the modern techniques of cold fermentation with selected yeast in stainless-steel tanks, can be as difficult to describe as it is to analyze. It is composed of hundreds, possibly thousands, of barely stable compounds, and the degree of our individual sensitivity to them can vary considerably. Little wonder, then, that a wine's bouquet shakes loose a different response from each of us. Few people go so far as to attempt to define that response (except in specialized publications) or to give voice to the associations a particular wine might provoke, even when they seem to be quite specific. But then they rarely *are* specific except when we are persuaded to accept the verbalized impressions others are foisting on us. Smell bypasses the rational intellectual processes and goes straight to our core of emotion, memory and nervous reflex. That's why the pleasure we get from a mature fine wine can be quite intense yet conceptually vague at the same time. On many levels the bouquet of a mature wine (as opposed to the grapey aromas of a young one) finds in each of us—or we find in the bouquet—a uniquely personal mnemonic echo.

Always supposing, of course, that the wine was of a quality that would allow the kind of transformation aging implies, we mostly owe the pleasure of that response to the alchemy of oak before bottling. Sometimes a wine will indeed also benefit from oak flavor, but, as with garlic in the kitchen, when the oak is obvious, it's obviously excessive. No matter how palatable, a wine that smells of nothing but oak and tastes of little else, too, is the equivalent of an ordinary cotton t-shirt sporting a prominent designer's logo. They're both marketing gambits.

It's been said often enough in books and articles on Spanish wine that little changed in the way wine was made in Ribera del Duero from the time the monks came in the eleventh century until the middle of this present one. Through all that time the wine was known as *clarete* because, like the medieval wine of Bordeaux, it was light red, made from a mixture of black and white grapes. White grapes were there as part of the insurance provided by mixing many grape varieties, of both colors, in any one vineyard. Today one black variety, the Tinta del País, is the principal and sometimes the only variety used.

Clarete began to change in the 1950s. An exodus from the wine villages of young people in search of opportunity in Burgos and Madrid left no one to tread the grapes, to throw his weight on the levers of the ancient screw presses, to hoist the skin residue from sixty feet underground (there are miles of wine cellars burrowed under the towns and villages of Castile), and to rack the wines from vat to cask after heaving each barrel into place. The shortage of labor drove the growers into cooperatives, where together they could acquire equipment none could have afforded singly. They largely abandoned their underground cellars, though some are now being reclaimed, enlarged, and refitted as part of the region's rebirth.

At the cooperatives, mechanical crushers allowed the removal of the stalks before fermentation, something not possible when the grapes were crushed by treading, and this reduced the need for white grapes to attenuate the harshness of grapes fermented with their stems. Gradually, white grapes began disappearing from the vineyards. Those that remain are mixed with a small

113

proportion of black grapes—usually Grenache rather than the Tinta del País—to make a rosé wine. In turn the traditional *clarete* has become less aggressively rustic, yet of deeper color. Few of the cooperatives had barrels, and those that did lacked the resources to renew their supply. But although the subtlety of the wine disappeared, its technical quality and consistency improved, thanks to managers who were usually trained enologists.

By 1978, the year before the region's growers applied for their *denominación*, ninety-eight percent of them belonged to cooperatives. But for some reason, the cooperatives—with the sole exception of the oldest, at Peñafiel—failed to seize their opportunity to make the most of these wines and to market them in a way that could secure their members' future. Almost until yesterday, all but Peñafiel lacked even rudimentary bottling facilities. Whatever the quantity, whatever the quality, their wines were sold off in bulk anonymity. A few growers were concerned at the lack of foresight, but most of them, having surrendered their winemaking to the cooperatives, appeared to have lost interest in what happened to the fruit of their labors once they had dumped it at the reception docks. Throughout the fifties, sixties, and seventies, most Ribera del Duero wine simply disappeared into the great national blending vats of Spain.

The Perez Pascuas brothers had been among the founding members of their village cooperative, but, as they explained to me that night over our succulent quarters of lamb, they pulled out in 1980 because they had been unable to convince their fellow members that red wine sold as a raw commodity was a losing proposition.

"We went back to making and bottling our own wine," Benjamin Perez Pascuas told me. "That first year we sold it to anyone who would buy from us. Now we sell exclusively through regional distributors, each of whom approached us as the wine became better known. Even our overseas importers, somehow, found us before we either needed or had time to look for them."

My visit to Pedrosa had been to take a look at the newly completed Perez Pascuas bodega as well as to eat. The operation included both a well-equipped laboratory—the pride and joy of José Manuel, a recent enology graduate from the University of Madrid—and a magnificently vaulted hall with a thousand new

American oak barrels already in place. Manolo told me they had borrowed the money to build. "To some extent the bank lent to us against the value of our vineyards and on the strength of our reputation. The family has been in Pedrosa for a long time, after all. But its real security is the future it sees for us here."

The Perez Pascuas family, and doubtless its banker, had possibly been inspired by the example of the cooperative at Peñafiel: an enterprise, founded in the 1920s, that had put aside each year a small volume of its best wine for aging and later sale in bottle under its Protos label. But another source of inspiration was surely Vega Sicilia. A region that could produce such a wine could undoubtedly do better than sell the rest of its production in anonymous bulk.

Vega Sicilia had sprung from one of the Cistercian monasteries established at Valbuena del Duero in the twelfth century, but the history of the estate as we now know it began only in 1864, when it was acquired by Don Eloy Lecanda Chaves. It was he who brought from Bordeaux cuttings of Cabernet Sauvignon, Merlot, and Malbec to mingle with the region's indigenous Tinta del País. The estate was given the name Vega Sicilia, a corruption of the name found on old maps of the property, when the Herrero family took over in 1890. Since then the property has been through other hands, but each owner has paid such scrupulous attention to the wine that its high quality, scant production, and enviable reputation have attracted prices that were long the envy of the owners of Bordeaux's top châteaux.

The estate's Bordeaux varieties have contributed to more than the mystique of Vega Sicilia's wine, but, whatever their proportions in the vineyard, the regulations defining the *denominación* Ribera del Duero allow no more than fifteen percent of the grapes used to be other than Tinta del País. When necessary to keep the varieties in balance, the estate buys Tinta del País grapes to supplement its own. But, whatever the role of the Bordeaux varieties, most people would agree that an important, if not the critical, factor in maintaining the style of Vega Sicilia's wines has been the careful use of oak—both American and French—for its vats and barrels. The owners buy staves rather than barrels and have them air-dried on the estate under their own supervision. Vega Sicilia's barrels are then assembled in the estate's cooperage.

Vega Sicilia's winery and cellars are a curious mix of ancient and modern, a tangible statement of the owners' determination to retain what is good and add whatever is better. For example, though the stainless steel fermentation tanks gleam with a mirror finish I have seen in no other winery, the original brick-vaulted bodega, to which the wines are transferred after fermentation, is virtually unchanged (but scrupulously maintained) from the time it was built. "We've had to retile part of the floor," Felix Nieto, the manager, pointed out to me, almost apologetically, when I visited him there recently. "The original bricks were too far gone."

There are two wines made at Vega Sicilia. The best lots—usually about a third of the crop, but sometimes less and sometimes, as in 1977 and 1984, none at all—are selected for a lengthy aging, first in large and then in small barrels. They are assembled and bottled after seven years, and the wine is then allowed to mature in bottle for three more years before it goes on sale. That wine, the cream of the crop as it were, carries the Vega Sicilia name and is sometimes referred to as Vega Sicilia Unico. (In other words, for those who might have seen the two references elsewhere and wondered, Vega Sicilia and Vega Sicilia Unico are the same thing.) The estate puts aside a quantity of each vintage of this wine for release in later years. Those subsequent releases now include a small number of magnums.

The rest of the wine spends a shorter time in wood (usually in new barrels, to season them for Vega Sicilia Unico) and a shorter time in bottle before release under the estate's Valbuena label. There are years—1963 and 1971 among recent vintages—when the estate makes neither Vega Sicilia nor Valbuena; and in any year there might be lots not included in the selections for either. So Valbuena should not be thought of as the estate's catchall. An extension of the vineyards several years ago has allowed a gradual increase in production. Nevertheless, the 1982 Vega Sicilia, an opaque, deep garnet-colored wine with a marvelously dense flavor, just released in accordance with the estate's usual aging policy, will probably sell in New York for about $140 a bottle. The 1987 Valbuena sells—when it can be found—at prices up to $100 a bottle.

Although the Peñafiel cooperative and Vega Sicilia had been models for the growers of Ribera del Duero for a long time, what finally brought about change was one remarkably dynamic man: Alejandro Fernández. Largely self-educated, Fernández is a natural engineer akin to those who, out of sheer necessity, invented America's agricultural machinery in farm workshops early in the century. He invented a machine to harvest sugar beets—a government-sponsored crop introduced to the region in the 1940s when Spain was isolated—and from that and other patents Fernández made a modest fortune, which he invested in vineyards in his native Pesquera del Duero. He was convinced of the area's viticultural potential, and believed it could be achieved without the support of non-indigenous grapes like Cabernet Sauvignon.

His first wine, the 1975, was impressive; but no one knew what to make of it. Dark, strong, and tannic, it was evidently not *clarete*. The wines of the vintages that followed, all in a similar vein, were so "difficult" that the 1978 was dismissed summarily and publicly by one of Spain's leading enologists. Fernández loves to tell how she came to taste it again, ten years later, at a national wine conference, and, without even remembering having tasted it before, she analyzed and celebrated the qualities of that wine from a public platform for half an hour. (I tasted that same deliciously lively wine in the Fernández bodega in Pesquera in late 1992. It was indeed superb, but I think I would have run dry of words in less time than she.)

Luckily, Fernández's enthusiasm, energy, and uncompromising standards were infectious. It was as if other growers, equally convinced of the potential of their own vineyards and of Tinta del País, had been waiting for a signal. While Fernández's wines are improving with each passing vintage (he says his 1991, an impressive wine I first tasted from barrel, is his best yet) other growers are now also releasing excellent wines. They offer Fernández strong competition, though no one is yet producing wines in a style to match his.

Some twenty estates are now making and bottling their own wines in Ribera del Duero, and doubtless we shall see more of them. Several of the cooperatives, too, have invested in new equipment, including bottling lines and barrels for aging their *crianza* and *reserva* wines. Ironically, they include the cooperative at Pedrosa del Duero that the Perez Pascuas brothers had felt constrained to leave in 1980.

Ribera del Duero wines are, it must be said, not cheap. Nor can they be if they are to maintain their present high quality. But, however costly the wines of Vega Sicilia, or the *gran reservas* of Alejandro Fernández's Pesquera, most *crianza* wines distributed in the United States sell at more approachable prices in the $15 to $20 range, with *reservas* from $20 to $30.

Producers whose wines I specially recommend and who have some distribution here include (in addition to Vega Sicilia and Alejandro Fernández, of course) Perez Pascuas Pedrosa; the Peñafiel cooperative (for its wines under the Protos label); Balbas (the carefully made wines of Juan José Balbas have a patrician style that quite distinguishes them from other Ribera del Duero wines); and Ismael Arroyo and his sons for the elegantly seductive wines sold under their two brand names: Mesoñeros de Castilla for *jovenes* and *crianzas*, Val Sotillo for *reservas* and *gran reservas*.

Curiously, though quite a few *crianza* and *reserva* wines are being shipped to the United States, hardly any *jovenes* come here. It's a pity, not only because they are less expensive than the selected and barrel-aged *crianzas* and *reservas* but also because they burst with fruit and offer a different kind of pleasure.

Valduero, a producer in the village of Gumiel del Mercado with an able young enologist, Margarita Madrigal, in charge of winemaking, is offering splendid *reservas*—any of her recent releases offer proof enough of that—and truly delicious *jovenes* wines too. Though presently not widely available, they are worth watching for.

It was the 1991 Valduero *jovén* that had bid me welcome to Ribera del Duero last time I was there in the fall of 1992, much as had the 1989 Perez Pascuas *jovén* two years before. Tired from a long and difficult journey, I'd decided to eat in the dining room of my Burgos hotel rather than venture out into the night. It was no hardship: apart from finding the Valduero *jovén* as the house jug wine, I soon realized that the Mesón del Cid deserves the reputation that ranks its *cordero al horno* with those of the Mesón Mauro in Peñafiel and the Asador El Ciprés in Aranda del Duero, two of the best places in Castile to eat the local *lechal* lamb. But the truth is, I didn't have much choice in the matter. Outside, there was a howling gale.

LETTER FROM BURGUNDY

A GREAT BOTTLE OF BURGUNDY IS ONE OF THE STRONGEST ARGUMENTS WE HAVE IN FAVOR OF WINE. Pierre Poupon, a Burgundian merchant and writer, once said there is something in a great wine (by which, of course, he meant Burgundy) that transcends wine itself. It's the sort of observation that always sounds better in French, but even those on this side of the mystical would agree that Burgundy is one of life's finer compensations.

The problem for most of us, though, is to *find* that great bottle of Burgundy. Viticulturally, Burgundy is small: even if one adds the vineyard areas of Chablis, the Mâconnais and the Côte Chalonnaise to the 21,000 acres of vines in the Côte d'Or, the French administrative *département* that lies at its heart, there are still barely 60,000 acres of vines entitled to one or another of Burgundy's controlled appellations. The Gironde, the *département* that surrounds Bordeaux, has 260,000 acres of controlled appellation vineyards. In Bordeaux, furthermore, a château is a château. Every year it produces its principal wine in substantial quantity and its reputation, based on that one wine, is recorded in numerous books and over many years. There's a track record, in other words.

A Burgundy *domaine* is small, too; but having been stitched together by several generations of judicious marriages—each adding a few small scattered parcels of vines, a few rows here, an acre or two there—the *domaine* is likely to produce and sell, despite its size, not one wine but a collection of them.

The best of its vines will be in privileged sites known colloquially as *climats* (the meaning is obvious) and officially as *crus*. The grower usually makes and bottles separately a wine from each, though he (or she—there are increasing numbers of women in the business these days) is rarely able to produce more than four or five hundred cases of any one of them. Sometimes he might have only twenty-five or fifty cases of a wine from a highly prized strip of land he owns in a particularly prestigious *cru*.

The *climats*, or *crus*, are for the most part defined by law and carry appellations that distinguish them from one another and from wines produced under the general village appellation. A *grand cru*—Richebourg, say, or Bonnes-Mares is considered so distinct that the name of the village is not even mentioned on the label. A *premier cru*, such as Beaune Bressandes, is always identified by the names of both the village—or, in this case, town—and the *cru* (Les Bressandes vineyard lies within the boundaries of Beaune). Other *climats* are recognized in ordinary usage but not in appellation law. They are no more than localities in a village— the French use the expression *lieu-dit* to describe them—and they appear on labels, if at all, as window dressing. Strictly speaking, wines so labelled are entitled to no more than the general appellation of the village. Of the Côte d'Or's 21,000 acres of appellation vineyards, about 5,300 acres rank as *grand* or *premier cru*.

With rare exceptions, every *cru* is divided up among several, and sometimes many, growers. It is this multiplication of *crus* and growers that not only results in a fragmented production of hundreds—no, thousands—of different wines with overlapping names but also ensures the frustration inevitable when small numbers mean scanty and unpredictable distribution. At any given place at any given time there can never be more than a limited choice of Burgundy, so that even after studying form conscientiously one still has to choose from among what is available. The odds against finding a particular bottle—the specific vintage one might want of a specific *cru* from a specific grower—are so high that there is, when everything does work, a special serendipity added to the intrinsic pleasure of the wine. On the other hand, the exasperation of finding oneself once again with a dull bottle, after having tried hard to make an intelligent assessment of the *crus* and the vintages and the names of unfamiliar growers, is hardly transcendental.

The present 21,000 acres of Burgundy's classic varieties—Pinot Noir, Chardonnay and Pinot Blanc—are a substantial increase over their acreage in the Côte d'Or in the last century. In 1855, at the height of Burgundy's nineteenth-century boom, the Côte d'Or had little more than 6,000 acres of them. Of far greater consequence then were the 60,000 acres of Gamay, the prolific variety used to produce Beaujolais that was later banished from the Côte d'Or as it had been many times before. Part of the land that supported Gamay in the nineteenth century supports Pinot Noir and Chardonnay in the twentieth.

This extension of the acreage of classic varieties has helped increase the supply of wine entitled to Burgundy appellations. (Since the end of World War II, the area in the Côte d'Or under vines has been increased by 40 percent.) But it hasn't necessarily helped produce more wine of the quality on which Burgundy's reputation has always rested. In fact, Burgundy possibly has less wine now of that quality than it had fifty years ago. Well-intentioned research that has led to the use of high-yielding clones, especially of Pinot Noir, and classroom teaching that promoted the generous use of fertilizers have allowed and encouraged crop yields to increase to levels now more than double the 1855 average of eighteen hecto-liters of wine per hectare of vines. One doesn't need to know how many gallons there are in a hectoliter or how many acres in a hectare to get the point. (For those who *do* want to know, a hectoliter is 26.4 U.S. gallons; a hectare is 2.47 acres.) In Burgundy, moderate yields, concentration and quality are usually found together.

Anyone taking the trouble to check would probably find a correlation between the 6,000 acres that were all Burgundy's nineteenth-century growers thought worth planting with Pinot Noir and Chardonnay and the 5,300 acres of today's *grands* and *premiers crus*. These few thousand acres have emerged from centuries of trial and error, so it's hardly surprising that for a real experience of Burgundy one really does need a wine from one of the *grands* or *premiers crus*. I've enjoyed many bottles of Burgundy with simpler appellations, but rarely has a village wine really stood out. When it has, there has usually been a reason.

Recently, for example, when a village 1989 Aloxe-Corton from Domaine Tollot-Beaut was so good that I felt compelled to ask questions, I discovered that the family blends wine from its *premier cru* holdings in the village of Aloxe-Corton with its village wine (and is therefore obliged to sell the lot under the name of the lesser appellation). Otherwise there wouldn't be enough of either wine to make an adequate bottling.

Burgundy of any kind is expensive compared with most other wines— a matter of supply and demand—and there is no getting around the fact that a bottle of a good Burgundy *cru* from a reliable grower sold across the counter (let's not talk about restaurants) will most likely cost from forty to a hundred dollars and up. But that's no more than the price of a fillet of beef. Just as most households don't buy fillet very often, I buy a good *cru* only for the sort of occasion when skirt steak won't do. (Red Burgundy has an affinity for beef, by the way; Bordeaux is for lamb. There's no such thing as lamb *bourguignonne*.)

When the opportunity presents itself to taste side by side the wines a grower produces from his separate *crus*, it's not difficult to tell them apart. Yet I've learned to expect that any grower's wines will usually have more in common with each other, regardless of the *crus*, than any one of them will have in common with a wine produced from another grower's vines in the same *cru*. There is, in short, less consistency among the various wines produced from a particular *cru*, whatever the texts say, than there is among the wines of an individual grower. The Clos de la Roche of Jacques Seysses's Domaine Dujac is much closer in style to other Domaine Dujac wines than it is to the Clos de la Roche made by Charles Rousseau of Domaine Armand Rousseau, another proprietor of vines in that particular *grand cru*.

For that reason, when faced with a restaurant wine list or a display of Burgundy, I start by looking over the growers represented. Some restaurants fail to give growers' names, listing their Burgundy wines by village and *cru* only. Some restaurants don't mention the vintage either, or they list one and serve another. Even in a wine store, one finds the name of village and *cru* prominent on the bottle—French law sets minimum type sizes for appellations on labels— whereas the name of the grower is given in a typeface sometimes so small as to be almost illegible.

But no matter how difficult it might be to get at them, or how much list and label might conspire to give the impression that the particular *cru* is most important, the grower's name is in fact paramount. It is worth taking the trouble to remember or to write down a few that have been found to be reliable or that have been reliably recommended. It's necessary to know both first and family names: as one might expect, cousins and cousins of cousins bottle wines under similar names. Sometimes this gives rise to confusion, as with the Domaine Armand Rousseau just mentioned. Everyone talks and writes of Charles Rousseau, but it's

122

the name of his late father, Armand, that appears on the Rousseau label. One is just supposed to *know*. In a restaurant, if at all unsure, ask to see the actual bottles before making a choice.

Even when both the growers' names and the vintages of the wines are clearly shown in a wine list, it's safest to pause long enough to take a good look when the bottle is presented at the table before being opened. Restaurants have been known to list a *cru* from one grower and then substitute the same *cru* from another when supplies of the first run out. (This is one of the reasons restaurateurs may prefer to avoid giving a grower's name in the first place, even though it's the most important information they have to offer.) I prefer to take an alternative *cru* from the grower I know, unless the substitute is from a grower I can rely on equally. I might even prefer to take a village wine from a good grower rather than a *cru* from one I'm unsure of. But the vintages available will also influence my decision. I put both grower and vintage ahead of *cru*, and would rather drink a 1985 village Burgundy than a 1983 from a famous *cru*.

The significance of vintage is widely misunderstood. What sets the wines of one year apart from those of another is as much style as quality. In wine both terms are hard to define, but the distinction between them is obscured by the way in which vintage charts grade years in a simple hierarchy from "great" down to "mediocre." One needs to be particularly careful with Burgundies because those who compile such charts tend to favor years which produce "big" wines. In Burgundy those are the years that most often yield more disappointment than pleasure: it is not in the nature of Burgundy, or of Pinot Noir vines in general, to produce "big" wines. When it happens—even naturally, as a result of hot, dry conditions that stress the vines and possibly dehydrate the grapes—it is almost always a sign that the wine is out of balance. Seldom will anyone acknowledge, however, that a wine can be extraordinary without being the better for it.

Consumers in Britain and the United States in particular have been led to believe that clumsy, tannic wines offering little pleasure when young are certain to develop in time into something wonderful. The harder and more graceless the wine, the greater its promise. "Will need at least ten to twelve years to come round," critics say, as if that in itself were somehow commendable. I've been aston-

123

ished to read descriptions of such wines that include approving references to "mouth-searing" tannins. There's nothing good about "mouth-searing tannins" in *any* wine, and least of all in one made from Pinot Noir grapes. One must ask not only what it is that such tannins are supposed to be promising but what it is they are intended to mask. Usually they are there to compensate for a lack of concentration, a lack of depth, or a lack of "flesh" in the wine.

This bizarre attitude has encouraged the Burgundians themselves to put a gloss on some of their most awkward vintages, selling intractable wines at higher prices than more delectable ones. Difficult wines improve with the years about as often as difficult people do. It's a drum I bang frequently, but I must say again that only a wine balanced and agreeable when young is likely to be balanced and agreeable as it ages. Too often a red Burgundy vintage is dismissed by the charts for being too delicious too early and too easily.

It's true there is little point in aging the wines of vintages like 1987, but there was no need to. The question is, was there really any more sense in aging the much vaunted 1983s and the expensive 1988s? At least the 1987s gave their moment of pleasure to those who, ignoring the charts, bought and drank them. And those I continue to drink I still find very attractive. Yet even the Burgundians are coming to the conclusion that the 1988s, most of them now more gawky than when they first went into bottle, will never turn out as well as had been promised. The 1983s didn't turn out as had been hoped either. I have drunk and enjoyed old Burgundy often enough and find a kind of poetry in its woodsy aromas and fleeting nostalgia, but I view with caution, even suspicion, any Burgundy wine I'm told *must* be aged for this or that amount of time. I avoid such wines when they are young and have no confidence in their future.

The fancy for such wines is not new: it goes back to the early nineteenth century. For long ages before then, any dark, heavy wine would have been rejected as coarse and unacceptable. Red Burgundy had held a special place in the world of wine for its fragrance and silky texture. Though made essentially from black grapes, it was often straw-colored or that particular hue of pink known as partridge eye. None of it was more deeply colored than strawberry juice. Varying proportions of Pinot Blanc and Pinot Gris were mingled in the vineyards with

Pinot Noir to contribute to the wines' pallor and delicacy. Skins were left together with the juice only briefly once the grapes had been crushed, so that the least possible color and tannin were released into the wines, which were intended to be consumed within the year. Those wines were made from vines more densely planted and more severely pruned than is the case today, of course, and, though more delicate, they were probably more concentrated, too.

Principally to satisfy a demand from foreign markets for wines of a deeper hue, Burgundies began to change in the late eighteenth century. The British, in particular, weaned from light wines by a century of patriotic tax differentials calculated to persuade them to strengthen their ally Portugal by drinking her Port and Madeira, began to insist on similar weight and a "high color" in their Burgundy. Growers abandoned the straw-colored and partridge-eye wines. "If the buyer wants color and durability rather than finesse," wrote Pézerolle de Monjeu in his *Conseils que Donne un Vieux Vigneron aux Habitants de Pommard et de Volnay*, published in the late 1700s, "he must be given what he wants as far as the vineyard will allow." As a result of this thinking, Pinot Blanc and Pinot Gris vines were progressively eliminated from the vineyards and Burgundy's centuries-old tradition of winemaking was changed to intensify the wines' color, regardless of the effect on style.

"The taste of this century is dictating how we make our wines," wrote the Abbé Tainturier, whose book, *Culture des Vignes à Beaune et Lieux Circonvoisins*, published at about the same time, gives an even clearer indication of what was going on. "Are we not fortunate," he asks rhetorically, and perhaps with conscious irony, "to have grapes that can adapt to fashion?"

By 1825, when an official survey of Burgundy wines summed up their ideal qualities as "1, a fine color; 2, body; 3, aroma or bouquet as appropriate to our wines; 4, alcoholic strength; and, lastly, finesse," the eighteenth-century preference for delicacy, taking little account of color, had been completely reversed.

Not everyone accepted the change in the spirit of Pézerolle de Monjeu. Jean-Jacques Lausseure, a Paris wine merchant originally from Nuits-Saint Georges, gave vent to his feelings in a book, *Les Grands Vins de Table*, published in 1850, in which he placed responsibility squarely on English taste and influence.

"Burgundies have been completely deformed," he complained. "The majority of consumers has been persuaded that these wines should be strong and alcoholic; that's why, under the name of Burgundy, one can get only some dense, heavy liquid. Most of the English, without bothering to find out how any particular French wine should be, insist that it have body, lots of taste, and be thick."

Lausseure had it largely right; and what was true of the nineteenth-century English is today also true of many others. But carried away, perhaps, by an exaggerated Anglophobia, he allows himself to ignore the role that the French market itself played in deforming Burgundy. The Revolution of 1789 had brought an end to most internal tolls and duties formerly hindering the free circulation of agricultural products within France. Vineyards everywhere, including those of the Côte d'Or, expanded to supply wine to the increased populations of the major cities. Despite Philip the Bold's famous interdiction of Gamay in 1395, the Côte d'Or was again smothered with it.

A thinking man or woman might ask how the light wines certain to have been the result of planting the abundantly productive Gamay on former pasture-land could become the dense, heavy Burgundy deplored by Monsieur Lausseure. Part of the answer, of course, is that following the innocent, if regrettable, changes already reported by the Abbe Tainturier and Pezerolle de Monjeu in the eighteenth century, the nineteenth had seen the invention of the saccarometer to measure sugar content and of Jean-Antoine Chaptal's process of correcting from the sugar sack the deficiencies of over-cropped—that is, watery—grapes. (The new process of extracting sugar from beets made it cheaply available.) The mid-nineteenth century had also seen the establishment of the railways with a direct line to Beaune from the southern Rhône valley. "Burgundy"—often fraudulently blended with wines from a more southern clime—became an end appropriate to these highly profitable means, whether destined for the British market or any other. The combination of all this led to nineteenth-century "Burgundy" that was alcoholic, highly colored, and "thick."

Though reading history helps us see through the nineteenth-century murk to Burgundy's essential style—fragrant, supple and delicious even when the year allows it also to be plump and full—we probably wouldn't want to go back to those eighteenth-century wines. The industrially produced, regularly shaped bottle that permits wine to be "laid down" wasn't available then. A bottle—or rather, the time spent in it—has never been as essential to Burgundy as it is to Bordeaux and Port, but a short sojourn there, preceded by the almost imperceptible access to oxygen that a wood barrel allows, melds a young Burgundy's flavors and refines its bouquet in ways we now take for granted but which the eighteenth century could hardly have known.

There's more to be learned from the past. Philip the Bold's attack on Gamay was just as much an attempt to forbid the planting of vines in the well-watered fields at the base of the Côte d'Or's slopes—where yields were inordinately high—as it was a salvo against the grape itself. He wanted to restrict vineyards to the hillsides, where the resulting smaller crops were the surest guarantee of quality. Modest yields are still the foundation of quality in Burgundy and are most often the factor that distinguishes one grower from another. Recently, when I had congratulated a grower on a particularly fine wine he had given me to taste—it had to perfection Burgundy's unique combination of delicacy and sumptuousness—he modestly brushed my compliment aside and said: "You could have done it. Anyone can do it. To make good wine you need a good *terroir*, of course, and clean fruit. You must be careful. But the essential thing is to keep the yield below twenty-five hectoliters to the hectare. That's what it is. It's no secret. It's yield every time."

We each have our favorites, I suppose, among the Côte d'Or's most serious growers. To list all mine would take up too much room, but here are a few worth remembering.

In Côte d'Or whites I watch for Meursault from Domaine Pierre Matrot, Chassagne-Montract from Domaine Ramonet and Puligny-Montrachet from Domaine Etienne Sauzet and Domaine Leflaive. Olivier Leflaive's merchant offshoot of Domaine Leflaive—called Olivier Leflaive—also produces some attractive *cru* wines, but his village wines are too heavily oaked for my taste. Of course, some people like that.

Thierry Matrot of Domaine Pierre Matrot, a good natured, typical Burgundian *vigneron*—whose occasional adornment with a single jet ear-stud is therefore all the more disconcerting—describes Meursault as fat, supple and powerful. "A Meursault is a Rubens," he says. "A Puligny is more delicate, with floral tones—a Fragonard. Puligny is best with fish, steamed or quickly seized in butter. No unctuous sauces. Meursault, on the other hand, goes well with sweetbreads and richer foods. A really mature Meursault Charmes is so unctuous, so powerful, that you have to drink it with the kind of rich, creamy dish we eat less often these days."

I'm not sure where Matrot would place the wines of Domaine Ramonet of Chassagne-Montrachet in the roll of art history. Titian, perhaps? Noel and Jean-Claude Ramonet's wines are singularly intense and bold, and the brothers' Bâtard-Montrachet '92, tasted from barrel at six months, was one of the most splendid young white Burgundies I'd ever tasted.

In reds I watch for wines from Domaine Marquis d'Angerville and Domaine Michel Lafarge, both of Volnay; Domaine de Courcel of Pommard; Domaine Tollot-Beaut of Chorey-les-Beaune; Domaine Simon Bize & Fils and Domaine Chandon de Briailles of Savigny-lès-Beaune (Savigny wines are particular favorites of mine: they have the finesse I most appreciate in Burgundy and are better value than wines of most other appellations); Domaine Daniel Rion of Prémeaux; Domaine Méo-Camuzet and Domaine Jean Grivot of Vosne-Romanée (to some a controversial grower, but truly one of the best); Domaine Georges Roumier and Domaine Comte de Vogüe of Chambolle-Musigny (which, after some lackluster years, is producing superb wines under François Millet); Domaine Dujac of Morey-Saint Denis (I suspect that Jacques Seysses's delicately plump wines come closest to showing us what eighteenth-century Burgundy might have been); Domaine Rossignol-Trapet and Domaine Armand Rousseau of Gevrey-Chambertin; and Domaine Gelin of Fixin.

Of recent vintages, 1985 is presently my first choice for reds, but 1987 produced wines that were fragrant, balanced and attractive. Whites were better in 1986 than in 1987. I don't much care for the 1988s, but I tasted recently an elegant and attractively developed Vosne-Romanée Beaumonts '88 of the Domaine Jean Grivot that was enough to serve as a warning to those who generalize (but we must).

Most 1989 reds are now very attractive, despite a slightly dry finish. The problem with many of these wines is not excessive tannin but insufficient flesh. As I've said, that is not something that can miraculously reappear, so one must ignore those critics who refer to their tannic finish as a sign of potential. "Just taste that tannin," they will say. "There's a lot of life in that wine." They are wrong.

The summer of 1989 was hot and the grapes, ripening with difficulty, never quite attained the degree of maturity needed. The red wines do have a fine aroma and good flavor, and, with food, the dry finish is hardly noticed and scarcely matters. They should be enjoyed reasonably soon, however. The 1989 whites are very concentrated, and, whereas they, too, might not last long—their balance isn't quite right either—they are at the moment wonderfully, generously, imposing.

Burgundy's 1990 vintage is presently being promoted strongly and for the usual reasons: it's a "big" vintage. The summer of 1990 was hot and dry in Burgundy. Many growers thought the grapes would never ripen because the vines were so stressed. Rain at the end of August helped matters considerably, but, even so, some grapes "ripened" only through dehydration.

A few growers compare their 1990s with their 1985s, others with their 1988s. Most say they have never seen a vintage quite like it. Certainly, the year imposes its own unmistakable characteristics: one can recognizes a 1990 even when it's impossible to identify either the grower or the *cru*. The growers swear the wines will not be like the 1976s (most of which are still impossibly hard), but if they've "never seen a vintage quite like it," how do they know? I was impressed by some of the 1990 reds at Domaine Daniel Rion, especially the Nuits-Saint Georges Vignes Rondes, and thought a Corton Clos du Roi '90 of Domaine Chandon de Briailles, though very tannic, had a concentration of flavor that would eventually win through. But I have reservations about this vintage.

The 1990 whites are massive but austere, and sometimes painfully intense. I did taste an impressive village Meursault in Matrot's cellar, and in the summer of 1993 I enjoyed one or two other, similar, village wines. But at the time, anyway, rather than 1990, I preferred, if given the choice, to drink 1991 white Burgundies—they had more charm and were easier to enjoy, even if they gave an impression that they might not last long. But I'd rather have drunk a 1989 than either.

The 1991 growing season, like that of 1990, was hot and dry, and the vines had comparable difficulty bringing their fruit to full maturity. Rain during the harvest came too late to do much good, though it was a factor in making the whites softer and more accessible than they might otherwise have been.

The rain probably did more good than harm to the reds, however. Certainly growers who rushed to get their crops in before it arrived often made wines that are both flavorless and harsh, but others who picked in the rain made some that are more than attractive. That's how I would describe the Corton Clos du Roi of Domaine Chandon de Briailles and even more so the Volnay Champans of Domaine Marquis d'Angerville. Jacques d'Angerville attributes the success of the wine to his very small yield that year from vines that are particularly old. But the Champans, rich and concentrated, is far from being typical of the year. Most of the 1991s are short at best.

Though growers complained of rain again during the 1992 vintage, in the Côte de Beaune, at least, most of the crop was in before the big storm on September 16th (or that's what we're told). In the Côte de Nuits, growers assess their wines as having more substance than the 1982s but less than their 1985s. To talk of either of these two vintages in relation to 1992 is already encouraging.

I found it difficult to judge the vintage in the spring of 1993. New wine, still in barrel, is exuberantly and sometimes misleadingly fruity. But whatever shortcomings the 1992s eventually might prove to have, for the moment I like them very much. Even if the fruit does diminish when the wines go into bottle, they will still have flavor enough. Both firm and supple, the 1992s show every sign of early development—and that, as far as I am concerned, is all to the good.

Among the 1992 reds I tasted from barrel in May 1993, I particularly liked the Pommard Rugiens of Domaine de Courcel, the Nuits-Saint Georges Les Vaucrains of Domaine Henri Gouges, the Vosne-Romanée Beaumonts of Domaine Jean Grivot, the Musigny of the Domaine Comte de Vogüe, the Latricières-Chambertin of Domaine Rossignol-Trapet, and the Bonnes-Mares of Domaine Georges Roumier. The 1992s re-tasted on a quick visit in the fall of 1994 continued to show well, and although they have had a mixed reception from the critics (naturally: they don't lend themselves to those absurd and overblown tasting notes), I look forward to drinking them over the next few years.

The 1992 whites lack nothing. Again, one can easily be led astray by their exuberance; but they have a richness not found in the 1991s, an elegance missing from the 1990s, and better structure than the 1989s. They could, in fact, turn out to be very special, and though I can't guarantee the kind of transcendental experience that Monsieur Poupon had in mind, I am convinced we shall enjoy them very much.

A MATTER OF TASTE

O NE EVENING IN THE SPRING OF 1994, FRIENDS IN SONOMA COUNTY—AN INFORMAL GROUP OF WINEMAKERS—ASKED ME TO JOIN THEM FOR ONE OF THEIR REGULAR MONTHLY TASTINGS. There'd be a few Syrah wines from California and elsewhere, they said. In the event, only the winemaker responsible for assembling the nine wines knew that five of them were from California, three from France and one from Australia. The rest of us settled down, each with his notepad and pen and semicircle of tasting glasses, and watched him pour from bottles concealed in brown paper bags.

There was no need to discuss what we were looking for: everyone there had his personal criteria for judging a wine and his own idea of what a Syrah should be. We gave the wines our attention for more than half an hour, then each of us in turn ranked them from first to ninth while making some brief observations which—in theory, anyway—were intended to justify our preferences. A fellow with a sharp pencil quickly converted our individual choices into a "group preference."

Ranking wines, even when they are few, is never easy. It becomes more difficult when the wines are of widely diverse origin with styles affected by different traditions and intentions. Though we hadn't been told beforehand, we eventually learned that the wines we were tasting ranged in price from $6 to $65 a bottle. It's as reasonable to assume that a $65 wine would have been handled in ways that would ensure development over many years in bottle as it is to expect a $6 wine to be ready for early drinking, with all the soft contours and attractively forward fruit that that implies. An experienced taster can be expected to gauge a winemaker's intention and judge his wine accordingly. But assuming that those responsible for the $6 and $65 bottles had attained their respective objectives faultlessly, which of the two would we, should we, *prefer*?

The answer is obviously subjective. Ranking wines in order of preference tells us as much about the taster as the wine. A "group preference"—a numerical merging of individuals' selections—would therefore seem to make little sense. Members of a group can concur in an opinion on a wine; they can arrive at a consensus through discussion; but when they drop their ten individual preferences into a common basket, the ranking order of those in favor of forward, fruity wines, say, could simply cancel out the choice of those who look for structure, tannin and a potential for aging. We are left with meaningless data.

If everyone disliked a wine, we could draw a clear conclusion, as we could if everyone named the same wine as a first choice. But that rarely happens. On the contrary, a natural caution takes over, particularly among those trained to taste, when one wine stands out among others. The more it holds the attention, whether for style or quality, the more one wonders about it. Maybe it's the risk involved, the potential embarrassment of being called on to defend an unorthodox choice, that usually leads us either to reject such a wine firmly and to rank it lower, perhaps, than it deserves or, conversely, to take up its cause, with almost defiant bravura, and give it first place. Anyone who has ever been present at a group tasting will have met the phenomenon of "the wine you either love or hate": it's commonplace for a wine thought best by some members of a group to be rated last, or near last, by the others.

Tasting wine, incidentally, should not be confused with drinking wine. In tasting one is trying quite deliberately to judge the parts as well as the whole, even though one of the signs of quality in a wine is that its components fit together so seamlessly that taking them apart is, in fact, very difficult. In drinking, the integrity of a wine is paramount: it should flow naturally, harmoniously and convincingly from initial aroma to the taste that lingers after the wine itself has been swallowed.

Even those with extensive knowledge of painting technique recognize that there is something seriously wrong if they are drawn to the mechanics of a picture rather than the picture itself. It's the same with wine. It's not just that one shouldn't be able to "read" too easily the tannin, the acidity, the this and the that; the wine should be so satisfyingly complete that there should be no desire to do so.

For years Americans have been encouraged to think they must dissect a wine to enjoy it—checking on the "middle palate" and the impact of oak, consciously trying to gauge the level of alcohol and the measure of acidity, seeking out the tannins (ripe or unripe?)—and then quote from a shopping list of spices and berries in response to every fleeting strand of aroma and flavor.

This deconstruction approach to wine probably began in the 1970s, when California's new wineries, releasing their first wines, sent winemakers on tour to explain and promote them. Because many of these new-fledged vintners were young and fresh from wine school, their carefully restricted vocabulary obliged them to give scientific, as opposed to hedonic, appraisals of their wines. They had been prepared as scientists, and objective precision was fundamental to their training. But most of those they were speaking to were expecting to drink wine for pleasure rather than technical satisfaction.

With their enthusiasm for pH and "skin-contact" the winemakers seemed, at first, to be revealing the ultimate mysteries of wine and in no time at all wine writers, following their lead, were tossing out references to degrees brix and fermentation temperatures and naming all the forests of France from which the wood for barrels is culled. Meanwhile, consumers, enrolled in wine appreciation classes, were scorching their tongues with samples specially doctored to demonstrate indelibly what "acid" and "tannin" and "volatile acidity" meant.

As a result we soon had a princess-and-pea syndrome at dinner parties, where there seemed always to be someone determined to detect a fault in the wine everyone else, until then, had been enjoying. If he (it was always a man, never a woman) could dip into technical language to say what he thought was wrong ("This wine is sour" just wouldn't do), his success was immeasurable. There also appeared a jollier but no less disconcerting type who could look others in the eye and, without apparent embarrassment, say things like "This wine's a blockbuster," or "Gobs of fruit in this wine: you'll love it." It soon seemed inappropriate, even frivolous, to use ordinary words to express one's pleasure in wine. There are many who would, on occasion, be tempted to say, "My, this wine is delicious," were they not afraid of feeling foolish, untutored or unsophisticated. But most of the time, what more need be said?

As far as our evening in Sonoma County was concerned, though, the answer to that question would be "quite a bit." The wines that settled into our mid-preferences, I noticed, were essentially those that aroused the least controversy. They included, to general surprise when the bottles were finally unwrapped, the two most distinguished (and expensive) wines on the table—a Gentaz-Dervieux Côte-Rôtie 1990 and a Chapoutier Hermitage 1990—giving some vindication to those who hesitate when faced with stylistic extremes. These two wines—tasted, by bad luck or poor planning, sixth and seventh after two particularly robust California wines and the one from Australia—were too restrained for the company they were obliged to keep, raising yet again the point that comparative tastings can give dangerously distorted results. Both of them, made to be aged rather than opened so soon, had depth rather than exuberance, finesse rather than swagger, potential rather than impact. It had been to their credit, in fact, that there was nothing in particular to call attention to them.

I can't say that I had done specially well by them despite the generous praise in my notes. (This seems to be a universal trait: there was a perverse tendency among the winemakers to reserve their most articulate criticism for the wines they claimed to like most.) I'd stuck my neck out—alone—in giving first place to a 1990 California Syrah under Sean Thackrey's Orion label. Almost everyone else pronounced it their least favorite. On the other hand, my almost least favorite, a 1990 California Syrah from Qupé (a small winery in Santa Barbara County for which I have much respect), was greatly admired by the winemakers, and despite the dragging disadvantage of my low vote, it placed third in the group's assembled result.

The discrepancy of opinion on those two wines alone gave me food for thought. The Orion, a dense, ruby-colored wine, had the most distinctive and the most intense aroma of all nine wines; it had a smell of cassis found only in Syrah from old and low-yielding vines. Though I've tasted earlier vintages of Orion Syrah and know that Thackrey gets his fruit from a patch of old Syrah in Napa Valley, I hadn't even been certain this particular wine was from California. It was powerful but exceptionally velvety except for an unexpectedly astringent finish that shouldn't have been there. That's probably what the winemakers found unacceptable. Sean Thackrey, a San Francisco art dealer, had no formal training as a winemaker, and his wine was dramatically outside the norms established by the others we were tasting. I cheered it on, despite its slightly harsh finish; the others condemned it.

The Qupé was more massive and presented a classic assemblage of all those components a California winemaker would want to see in a Syrah. One could tick them off: bright fruit on nose and palate; substantial but correct tannins; the right measure of oak; alcohol and acidity in textbook measure. In short, it was a first-rate example of impeccable winemaking. But the ingredients hadn't really come together. Because each element seemed separate from the whole, each was easily identified, leaving me with the impression of an exercise in wine-making rather than a wine. The engineering was too obvious: I couldn't see the painting for the mechanics. It's possible, of course, that the winemakers tasting with me liked the Qupé Syrah for exactly that reason. They could admire with ease its sound workmanship.

But, meaningless or not, which wine came first in the "group preference"? Well, of course it was the $6 bottle, a 1992 Rosemount Shiraz from Australia: an inevitable—as well as poetically just—result. The reason for its success is simple: it was made to be liked. The Australians use impeccable winemaking to further, rather than obstruct, the notion of wine as pleasure, never forgetting that wine-making is a means to an end.

It's doubtful whether the all-conquering youthful charm of this particular Shiraz (the name used for Syrah in Australia), a wine almost two years younger than the others, will endure. It's also true that Australian wines in general often betray a lack of depth, of subtlety, and of grace. But their joyful vigor is instantly engaging. We shared an enthusiasm for this wine in part because the winemakers present could applaud the fault-free winemaking. (One criticism of Australian wines is that they can be boringly squeaky clean, a result of the Australian "show" system where the slightest technical fault means automatic disqualification for one of the awards that drive the country's wine industry). I could tip back my chair and enjoy the wine's gaiety without having to search for a single adjective.

PORT: YEARS OF GRACE

I N 1993 A MAJORITY OF PORT SHIPPERS—THE TRADE TERM FOR FIRMS PRODUCING AND EXPORTING PORT WINE FROM PORTUGAL—DECLARED (OFFERED FOR SALE) A 1991 VINTAGE, THE FIRST SUCH BROAD CONSENSUS SINCE THE 1985. But neither Taylor Fladgate, considered by many to be the leading producer of vintage Port (the firm's wines, even when still immature, consistently fetch the highest auction prices at any rate), nor its associated house, Fonseca, was among them. A year later, Taylor Fladgate and Fonseca, contrary to the position taken by almost every other shipper, declared a 1992 vintage instead. Which suits me very well: I happen to have grandchildren born in each of those two years for whom I must provide an appropriate cellar.

Vintage Port is not just the Port produced in a particular year—as is, say, a vintage Burgundy. It is a blend of specially selected Ports, deemed to be of the highest quality, reflecting both the style of the vintage and, more importantly, the style established over many years by the particular shipper. Sometimes the crop, though excellent, simply does not allow a shipper to prepare a vintage Port that will conform to the style of the house. This is usually the reason some firms declare in one year and some in another. Vintage Ports are always aged for two years in wood and then should be further aged in bottle for at least ten to fifteen years. Most are at their best at twenty to twenty-five years and can continue to give pleasure long after that—which is why they are so appropriate for laying down for one's children or grandchildren.

On average, barely three percent of Portugal's annual Port production is set aside by shippers for bottling as vintage Port, though the proportion can be much higher for some individual firms. Nevertheless, it's vintage Port that lends the trade glamour. And the quality of a shipper's vintage Port, above all else, establishes the firm's reputation, giving its brands recognition and credibility.

A Port shipper rarely declares a vintage more than two or three times in a decade, and then only as the culmination of much thought, tasting, consultation and planning. Each vintage Port declared, after all, will be seen and discussed in the world's auction rooms for at least the lifetime of those making the decisions. One way or another, it will continue over many years to contribute substantially to the image and business prospects of the house.

A firm's partners declare their intention of bottling a vintage Port about eighteen months or so after the harvest. During that time they will have ample opportunity to consider all the ramifications of their decision. The partners must be sure there will be enough wine of the necessary quality to make an impact on the market but also must weigh the effect on other blends when a considerable volume of high-quality wine is reserved for this one Port.

Perhaps the most important reason for waiting a year and a half before declaring their intention is to see what the following crop brings. No shipper likes to declare two vintages successively if this can possibly be avoided. One will inevitably eclipse the other and raise doubts about both. That is why, no matter how good the wine in hand, the partners will want to be sure that the following harvest will not produce wines of even higher quality.

When the decision is finally made to go ahead, possible blending combinations of the lots selected are presented to the partners for their consideration and final choice. How does the process begin? "It's structure we're after," is how Nicholas Heath of Taylor Fladgate put it to me when I tasted the newly declared 1992 with him at the company's premises in Vila Nova de Gaia, the hub of the Port trade across the river Douro from Oporto, Portugal. "That's why we find that a wine potentially suitable for vintage Port will reveal itself first in the mouth rather than the nose. At that early stage, fruity aromas can be ephemeral.

"We want a dense, concentrated wine, one with the capacity to age. Usually it will show a certain austerity. We must be careful not to tolerate the slightest fault, whatever balancing advantages there might be: however slight, a flaw can intensify over the years in bottle. And the blend itself must be compatible with the established house style. In our case that is rarely a problem because we

138

are consistent in using grapes from our own vineyards for our vintage Port.

"In fact, the style of our vintage Port is very much connected with the styles inherent in the wines of Vargellas and Terra Feita [two of the Taylor Fladgate estates many miles farther up the Douro in an area formally demarcated for the production of Port]. Normally, at least a third of the wine in our final vintage blend will have come from Vargellas. We think it's important to own the vineyards that define our vintage Port if we are to maintain consistency of style.

"It's different for our Tawnies [Port aged in cask rather than in bottle]. For them, one blends by introducing various strands over the years as the wine develops in wood, like the Nile delta in reverse. But even then we must always think ahead, confident from the start about what we intend to do with each lot of wine. When a wine is aged in wood, it's easier to adjust for the unexpected. The point about vintage Port is that once decisions have been made and the wine is in bottle, second thoughts are too late."

What is true for Taylor Fladgate is true for other Port shippers, by and large. The game of "guessing the Port" that used to be popular at London wine-trade lunches was based on remembering and recognizing the style associated with each house. Though obviously in part a result of winemaking decisions—such as how much sweetness to allow in the finished wine—that style is in essence a reflection of the estate, or *quinta*, where a key proportion of the grapes were grown. Certain vineyards on the north bank of the Douro, for instance, face due south and their grapes develop very ripe tannins. Any vintage Port in which they are used is likely to have a deep flavor suggestive of chocolate as opposed to the more openly vibrant, fruitier quality of a Port produced with grapes from the opposite side of the Douro. (Cálem's vintage Port, based on the vineyards of the firm's Quinta da Foz at Pinhão on the north side of the river, shows the chocolate characteristic particularly well.)

Other associations of this kind between shipper and *quinta* include Graham and Malvedos, Dow and Bomfin, Croft and Roêda, Warre and Cavadinha, Cockburn Smithes and Tua, Sandeman and Vau, Ramos-Pinto and Bom Retiro. Graham's style is rich; Dow's is a little drier and, though usually quite mild, develops an aroma of old, polished leather as it ages; Smith, Woodhouse (the firm owns no *quinta* but draws its grapes for vintage Port from a leased vineyard on the river Torto on the south side of the Douro) is fruity-sweet; Cockburn's, usually drier than other vintage Ports, is always elegantly refined rather than bold (the 1991, though, is meatier than normal), which is why the firm sometimes declares vintages at variance with its peers. Warre's, from vineyards at Cavadinha high on a mountain, is both aromatic and concentrated; and Taylor Fladgate's is always sumptuous—one of the reasons for its success, I suppose—a big wine with deep and long-lasting flavor, impeccably crafted and exquisitely balanced. The question of style might have been what prompted Taylor Fladgate to declare 1992 rather than 1991. The 1991 Ports have the bones and 1992 the flesh. At any rate, after developing a liking for the Ports of a particular shipper, one learns to spot its style with little difficulty.

The shippers' lodges—their offices and warehouses—have been clustered since the seventeenth century in the rather ramshackle little town of Vila Nova de Gaia, perched on a steep hill and stitched together by a web of narrow, twisting, cobbled lanes that become watercourses after every storm (there are many). Port itself, however, is produced from vineyards on a stretch of the Douro valley between the Serra do Marão, a range of mountains about forty miles upriver from Oporto, and the Spanish border, a hundred miles farther on. The mountains act as a weather barrier: to the east of them the amount of rainfall drops sharply, and the summers are hot.

Perhaps because the Serra do Marão was for so long an obstacle to access, there is still a remote, even bleak, atmosphere in the Douro. It is hard country. From time immemorial, and with only the most primitive tools, those who lived there on the precipitous hills created ledges stacked one above the other for hundreds of vertical feet, supporting vines that cling to each curve and follow each contour. That's why, in the Douro, the growers count by numbers of vines rather than acres or hectares.

There is almost no soil on those hills except for dust and grit created by the growers bashing at the schistose rocks. In my pursuit of wine I've met all kinds of soils and many geological terms, but nowhere else have I heard vineyard soil described as "anthropic" (man-made) and seen what that means. "In this place," wrote Miguel Torga, a Portuguese poet, "man with his bare hands wrings wine from a stone." And that's about right. In fact, the Douro wine region, a vast topographical sculpture, is soon to be taken into the protection of the United Nations' program charged with preserving the world's cultural heritage. Even if seen by relatively few—the tourist is still not well provided for "up the Douro"—it is a landscape shaped by a determination to generate life where otherwise there would have been none at all.

The mix of grape varieties in any vineyard will affect the wine's character. The choice of what is planted is usually a response to the imperatives of the site as much as anything else. Old vines are valued, and their age is one of the factors taken into account in the complicated points system used by the Douro region's authorities to grade vineyards (growers' scores determine how much wine they may produce). In newer vineyards each variety is planted in a separate block so that it can be given the particular attention it needs. But in older vineyards the varieties are jumbled together almost haphazardly because, as each usually flowers and ripens at a slightly different time, freak weather (a frost, hail, or violent rain) on one particular hillside would damage only those in a vulnerable phase and the loss would rarely be total.

Of the many varieties of black grapes traditionally used for Port (the production of white Port is marginal and is seldom taken seriously), five now predominate, thanks to varietal trials conducted over many years by Port shipper Adriano Ramos-Pinto, which published the results and made them available to all interested parties some years ago. The same five varieties were recommended by the World Bank in establishing its guidelines for a recent program aimed at improving agricultural development in the upper Douro, one of Portugal's poorest regions.

Among the five, Touriga Nacional is the variety most representative of old-style Port (though contrary to popular belief, it is not the most widely planted). This grape gives Port its intense color and a solid, tannic base; its scale; and sometimes, depending where grown, alcohol and a rich sweetness. Touriga Francesa, Nacional's currently favored counterpart, adds an engagingly spicy-sweet fruitiness to a Port's aroma and lends a suave elegance to the structure.

141

These two are usually supported by Tinta Roriz (said to be identical to the Tempranillo variety of Rioja in Spain), which contributes acidity and freshness and is therefore specially important for Ports destined to be wood-aged; and also by Tinta Barroca, a variety that ripens early, has good color, and brings to the blend a fleshy, fruity exuberance particularly welcome in vintage Port. Roriz and Barroca balance each other, their proportions in any vineyard dependent on the site: In a warmer vineyard Barroca is prone to overripening, and in a cool one Roriz can be a shade too reserved, but given opposite conditions, each does remarkably well. Tinto Cão (cão means dog) is found in most vineyards in small amounts. This variety, though weak in sugar, brings to a wine color, delicacy and aroma. Its unique spiciness is more easily missed when lacking than described when present.

Vineyard holdings in the Douro are very small—a vertical acre or two. Less than two percent of the Douro's growers are able to produce more than fifty pipes of wine a year. (A pipe, the traditional Port cask, holds about 140 gallons and is used as a standard measure.) More than eighty percent produce fewer than ten. Most of the Douro's growers, of whom there are many thousands, sell their grapes to the shippers, either as fruit or as wine. So the shippers' own vineyards—usually of considerable size and always equipped to make wine—are hardly representative of the Douro as a whole. But they are centers of activity that link the region with Vila Nova de Gaia and the world beyond.

A number of the *quintas*, both shippers' estates and independent ones, produce a *quinta* vintage Port, in some ways the Douro's equivalent of a Bordeaux château's wine. James Symington, of the family that owns a whole clutch of Port shippers—including Dow, Graham, Warre and Gould Campbell—told me that the Symington Group's purchase, a few years ago, of the distinguished Quinta do Vesúvio was part of a plan to market the wine in exactly that fashion. "We won't have to declare a vintage," he said, "because we shall sell the Port, with a vintage, every year—just as a Bordeaux château does. Each year's wine will be distinctive, I've no doubt, and some buyers will prefer one and some another."

The most famous of all *quinta* wines have for long been those of Quinta do Noval. Being an estate with a lodge in Vila Nova de Gaia, Noval has reversed the usual shipper-*quinta* relationship. With few other exceptions, the *quinta* vintage Ports offered until quite recently were those made from the fruit of a shipper's principal estate in years when it was not needed for the shipper's own vintage Port. Usually the vintages declared at such a *quinta* would therefore follow a pattern complementing the shipper's own. For example, Taylor Fladgate declared in 1970, 1975, and 1977, and Taylor Fladgate's Quinta de Vargellas released vintage Ports in 1972, 1974, 1976, and 1978. Clearly, the fruit did not have the appropriate quality in 1971, 1973, and 1979 to be used for either. Interestingly enough, the 1991 vintage Port declared by Quinta de Vargellas (because Taylor Fladgate, of course, had opted for the 1992) has been generally received by trade and critics as one of the best of the 1991s, which leads one to assume that Taylor Fladgate would have made an outstanding shipper's vintage Port in 1991 had the partners not decided that their 1992 would be even better.

Not all shippers declare vintage Ports at their *quintas*. Ramos-Pinto produces fine, single *quinta* Tawnies from its estates (a ten-year-old Tawny at Quinta da Ervamoira and a rich fruit-and-nut twenty-year-old at Quinta do Bom Retiro), whereas other shippers reserve their *quinta* wines, when not needed for their vintage Ports, for various special bottlings—a late-bottled vintage (more about that later) or a reserve blend of some kind.

Those *quintas* not owned by a shipper are only now beginning to bottle and declare their own vintage Ports. Before May of 1986 they were prevented by law from selling wine outside Portugal except through one of the shippers with lodges in Vila Nova da Gaia, a policy that virtually compelled them to sell their crop as grapes or as bulk wine. (That's partly why Quinta do Noval had established its own lodge downriver.) Now the independent *quintas* may bottle and sell their wines overseas directly. Among those already active are both Quinta do Côtto, whose proprietor, Miguel Champalimaud, fought for the change in law, and Quinta do Infantado, which recently introduced its wines in the United States.

Visiting the *quintas*, one quickly senses the keen interest of the owners in the potential of producing and selling their wine in this way. The *quinta* Ports I tasted had a more highly developed character than most of the shippers' Ports I'm familiar with. Among the reasons for this could be the greater age of the vines at

143

many of these *quintas*, the manner of winemaking, the self-imposed limitations on blending—these are, by definition, estate wines—or simply the time before bottling the wine spends in the Douro rather than in the cooler, damper lodges of Vila Nova da Gaia. At any rate, many independent owners will be watching the progress of Côtto, Infantado and Vesúvio (though Vesúvio, of course, will have the marketing clout of the Symington Group behind it) as well as La Rosa and one or two others. The trend is clear: I expect that in years to come we shall see more vintage Ports under the labels of individual estates, whether independent or shipper-owned.

Two categories of aging, in bottle and in wood, define Port. The results of one and the other are quite distinct, though some Ports are now made to combine attributes of both. Bottle-aged Ports—of which traditional vintage Port, whether from a shipper or a *quinta*, is the purest example—keep their deep color into full maturity and are usually redolent of fruit until such time as they become redolent of nothing much at all. Robust yet subtle, powerful yet velvety, a vintage Port will still be vigorous when a wood-aged Port of the same age has become autumnal.

Wood-aged Ports, on the other hand, exposed frequently and deliberately to air as they are regularly racked (transferred) from one barrel to another, soon soften in color to a rosy topaz from which all red tones will, in the end, disappear, leaving an amber-colored wine almost indistinguishable from a Sherry. But before then, its early fruitiness gradually acquires a mature patina of flavor in which one can find suggestions of hazelnut praline and peach compote. The wine becomes harmoniously silky, and eventually looks as it smells as it tastes. (I refer to properly wood-aged Tawny, of course; a suspiciously inexpensive Tawny Port is usually a blend of young red and white Ports and is rather pointless. A wood-aged Tawny usually carries an indication of the average age of the wines in the blend. It needs no further aging in bottle.)

I've noticed that wood-aged Ports are generally approached differently from bottle-aged Ports. When we drink a bottle-aged Port, especially the vintage Port of a prestigious shipper, we are always looking ahead, no matter what its age, wondering where it will go. "How much longer, do you think?" we ask each other.

And if there is any hint that the wine might have already seen its best, we drink it with a certain sense of regret for what is past.

Its past, however, is the chief attraction of a wood-aged Port. We approach it as we would an interesting character, a personality shaped by life's experience. It provokes reflection rather than speculation. Perhaps that's why a wood-aged Port comforts in a way that a vintage Port never can, no matter how impressive. After a simple dinner, give me a glass of a well-aged Tawny Port and a walnut or two and I am content.

As a Tawny Port ages, it is often refreshed in the course of the slow blending process with wines that are slightly younger to keep the color from fading too quickly, to retain more fruit flavor lingering in the background, and generally to maintain the wine's balance. If there were no adjustment, the wine would sometimes wear thin and show its corners. Because cared for in this way, old Tawnies are not usually sold with a vintage. The law allows them, instead, to be labeled with a statement of average age in steps of ten years: ten, twenty, thirty or forty. Coaxed along properly, even a forty-year-old Tawny can be astonishing. But some Tawny Ports are simply left to age, and that, for wine no less than people, guarantees nothing. I find most wood-aged Tawnies at their best between ten and twenty years. The regulations do not provide for a fifteen-year-old Tawny Port, and while there are shippers' Tawnies not quite developed at ten, others are already showing too much elbow at twenty. One must experiment a little to find the wine that suits.

As well as the poetic advantage of drinking old Tawny Port, there's a practical one: having been well exposed to oxygen in the course of aging, a Tawny can sit in a decanter (or its own bottle—as old Tawnies don't throw a deposit) for several weeks after being opened. So the man or woman who likes just a glass from time to time (as I do) will get more satisfaction from a bottle of old Tawny consumed at leisure than from a bottle of vintage Port that, sheltered for years from oxygen, must be decanted and drunk up once the cork is drawn. It's yet another way in which wood-aged and bottle-aged divide: one seems to be just right for a quiet *tête-à-tête*, the other for a broader conviviality.

A few houses keep their Tawnies aging as single vintage wines, though that doesn't make them vintage Ports (which are always bottle-aged). Tawny Port sold with a vintage is described as *colheita*. It must have been aged in wood for a minimum of seven years. Two shippers, Cálem and Niepoort, make a specialty of them. It's no accident that the British (or once British) shippers are not interested in *colheitas*. The British shippers, who were encouraged by their government to establish the Port trade in the eighteenth century as a political move to damage the French economy, had begun as agents and traders selling wool and salt cod in Portugal. They bought young wine to send back to England for bottling and aging there in order to bring cash to the Portuguese who could then use it to pay for the wool and fish. The British shippers had no interest in holding long-term stocks of wine in Vila Nova de Gaia.

Though wood-aged, *colheitas* are racked with greater discretion, usually less often, than other Tawnies. The aim is to conserve freshness and fruit even as the wine acquires its mature, wood-related patina. Cálem's 1986 *colheita*, the firm's current release, is exceptionally lively yet is already the color of old, terra-cotta roof tiles and has a refinement of flavor no bottle-aged Port could match.

Niepoort's *colheitas* are equally remarkable. But then Niepoort is a remarkable firm. Its powerful vintage Ports are consistently underrated, though always among the very best. This is probably because Niepoort trades mostly in the Netherlands, Belgium and Germany rather than Britain and reputations for vintage Port are still made on the London market. But the fact that Niepoort's is known in the trade as the Port shippers' Port says it all.

Niepoort is distinguished in yet another way: the aging of Ports of a single vintage in glass jars that vary in size from eight to eleven liters (something over two gallons). The firm has a big collection of these jars, made, for the most part, in the eighteenth century and housed on racks in a great rambling maze known as the *garrafeira*—hence the name given to this special kind of Port. The jars are used and reused; after thirty years or more in the *garrafeira* a wine is usually—but not always—decanted into bottles for further aging. Though neither wood-aged nor blended across vintages, a *garrafeira* Port may not be called vintage Port because it is not bottled, in the conventional sense, after two years in wood. But just as there are angels and then archangels, there are vintage Ports and *garrafeiras*. Last spring I tasted with Dirk van der Niepoort a 1952 Port that had been aged in the *garrafeira* from 1955 until it was bottled in 1984. It was magnificent.

Late-bottled vintage Port is a cousin of vintage Port. It spends from four to six years in wood, rather than the regulatory two, to bring it forward so that it can be enjoyed while still young. Pains are taken to protect the wine, while in wood, from the shading of hue and the development of wood-aged aromas actually encouraged in a *colheita*.

Modern late-bottled vintage Ports are almost always filtered at the time of bottling to prevent the formation of the crusty deposit that attaches itself to the inside of a bottle of vintage Port. They then need not be decanted, nor even handled with the degree of care conventional vintage Port demands and are therefore useful for restaurants that want to serve by the glass a Port that somehow incorporates the magic word "vintage" on the label. I have to admit to finding these filtered late-bottled wines dull for the most part. Even the best of them have neither the fine subtlety of a wood-aged Port nor the bravura of a true bottle-aged vintage Port.

A very few late-bottled vintage Ports—so few that I can think only of Niepoort's and Warre's—are not filtered. They are sometimes referred to as "traditional" late-bottled vintage Ports, and if allowed to spend four or five years in bottle, can give much of the satisfaction of vintage Port without as long a wait. These Ports will throw a light crust, of course, but decanting them is nothing like the mystery or the chore some people make of it. And even if it were, the small rituals of Port are part of the pleasure.

147

SANTA CRUZ

I HAD NEVER BEFORE BEEN ASKED, BEFORE SITTING DOWN TO DINNER, TO SIGN A RELEASE
ABSOLVING MY HOSTS FROM RESPONSIBILITY FOR ANY SUBSEQUENT "DISCOMFORT OR
DISTRESS." But then it was the first time I had been invited to the annual feast of
the Fungus Federation of Santa Cruz, held that year at India Joze restaurant on
Center Street where local chefs had gathered to show what they could do with
Dentinum repandum and *Pleurotus ostreatus*.

As might be appropriate in Santa Cruz, a sort of Berkeley-by-the-Sea,
India Joze, an airy cafe popular with everyone for miles around, usually specializes
in what I can only call Third World cuisines: a North Indian version of scrambled
eggs, for instance; falafel; Armenian chicken breasts marinated in paprika yogurt;
local snapper prepared *à la turque*; Balinese chicken; Greek prawns; tofu Malaysian
style with a hot bean sauce; Coptic chickpeas; and for Carnival Night, an
all-Brazilian menu (with samba lessons). Given the weakness of the dollar, I
suppose it was inevitable that their eclectic menu should now extend to classic
American folk dishes like eggs benedict and hash browns.

For the Fungus Feast, however, we began with chicken wings stuffed
with morels and ginger, crab and horn-of-plenty mushroom canapés, and oyster
mushrooms quickly fried in a light beer batter. No distress so far, and none likely
with David Bruce's California Blanc de Blanc Sparkling Wine. A salad of marinated
hedgehog, chanterelle and oyster mushrooms with fennel and slivers of Parmesan
led us to a cream soup of *shiitake* and morels, by which time we were ready for a
choice of 1986 Monterey Chardonnay from Bonny Doon or 1986 Mendocino
Sauvignon Blanc from Obester.

Dishes of chicken braised with *boletes* and red bell peppers arrived, along
with a steaming couscous studded with more chanterelles. Doubtless as a special

gesture to the spirit of India Joze, there was also a quickie world tour in the form of "Turkish style, wok-braised vegetables with tomato and fresh rosemary." Ahlgren's 1984 Cabernet Sauvignon from the Bates Ranch near Gilroy and 1983 Cronin Pinot Noir from Ventana Vineyards in Monterey County were offered with the chicken. Guests could drink either or both.

Dessert was a *Linzertorte* with candy cap mushrooms. In my innocence, I assumed candy cap to mean mushrooms of the genus *Confectioneris* and was amazed to discover the existence of a comparatively sweet fungus, *Lactarius Fragilis*. A 1986 Monterey Muscat Canelli from Devlin Wine Cellars brought the evening to a fine conclusion.

Perhaps it was an effect of the mushrooms or of the music, which drifted amiably all evening from a neighboring room, but guests at the crowded tables seemed to be a much jollier lot than the wine buffs I usually consort with. Mycologists, to their credit, simply reached for their wine as part of the evening's pleasure. They weren't overly zealous about mushrooms, either. I couldn't imagine anyone at my table proposing a comparative tasting to judge the *Craterellus cornucopioides*. In fact, no one at the Fungus Feast judged anything. They didn't sniff at the *Lentinus edodes* or suggest the *Cantharellus cibarius* might be over the hill. They ate everything and enjoyed themselves, swapping recipes and good humored stories, lapsing into the obscurely elliptical talk common to wine gatherings only when pressed to reveal the *exact* glade where they found such plump chanterelles.

Those with sharp eyes will have noticed that none of the wines offered by the Santa Cruz wineries represented at the dinner were made with grapes actually grown in Santa Cruz. The next morning, after a sound sleep disturbed by neither discomfort nor distress (nor, for those who are wondering, by psychedelic dreams), I set off to talk to some Santa Cruz winemakers to find out why.

Santa Cruz, on the Pacific coast about eighty miles south of San Francisco, is at the northern end of a bay that sweeps to the Monterey peninsula. It is a pretty town that has preferred, in recent years, to hide itself in the blur that most visitors see between San Francisco and Carmel. Nevertheless, its boardwalk is an inherited concession to tourists, and its old pier (known as the Wharf), swarming with shops and restaurants perched over the water, rivals the commercial enterprise of a medieval bridge.

Behind and above the town, roads twist into hills covered by magnificent redwoods that have replaced, for the most part, virgin forest logged when the area was first settled. But there is little agriculture, and none is encouraged. The county supervisors pursue a no-growth policy that, by rare coincidence, is supported both by the environmentalist student vote of Santa Cruz's large University of California campus and by Silicon Valley executives, who, fond of the trees that screen their houses, have no wish to see them exchanged for noisome tractors and Quonset huts. In any case forested hillside land is not only expensive to buy but costly to develop and cultivate. It is difficult to make grape growing pay.

Not surprisingly, then, even though the federally defined Santa Cruz Mountains Viticultural Area is extensive, spreading beyond the county to include the east flank of the mountains in Santa Clara, where barriers are less political than they are economic, and north along the ridge to embrace the high ground of San Mateo, barely three hundred of its acres are planted with vines presently bearing grapes. Of those, Santa Cruz County itself has forty-four acres of black grapes—mostly Pinot Noir—and sixty-nine acres of white: a mere hundred and three acres in all. In comparison, Monterey, a county adjacent to Santa Cruz, has more than twenty-eight thousand acres of vines.

Ironically, and some might say tragically, California's most distinguished wines were, in the past, grown in Santa Cruz Mountain vineyards; but it is now a struggle for Santa Cruz wineries even to promote themselves collectively because a Santa Cruz address counts for little on labels boldly qualified with appellations like Mendocino, Sonoma, and Monterey, the sources for most of their grapes.

Santa Cruz wineries are small. Except for Bargetto, a winery founded in time for Prohibition but revived in 1933, they are mostly businesses begun with the enthusiasm of expensive hobbies over the last twenty years or so. Two or three acres of vines, an extension to the garage, and some basic equipment are enough to produce the three or four hundred cases of wine that can be sold without need of employees, let alone a marketing plan. A few wineries still operate on that scale, selling through a limited mail-order list and at the premises on Saturday afternoons. Others, having grown to a few thousand cases, are in a double bind. While needing to establish a Santa Cruz identity to distinguish their products in a market awash with California wine, they are unable to find an adequate supply of Santa Cruz grapes—County or Mountain—to do so.

Desperate for grapes, Bargetto started to use local plums and apricots to make wines back in the 1960s and is now proud of its reputation for fruit wines (and pleased with the cash flow they generate). But it's nervous that with fruit wines still making up a good part of its business, the quality of its Santa Cruz Mountain Cabernet Sauvignon and other varietal wines could be overlooked or obscured.

David Bruce, whose wines were once known for their idiosyncratic style, is now so mainstream that, with a production of roughly 40,000 cases, his has become the largest winery in Santa Cruz County. But he makes no secret of being obliged to buy the bulk of his Chardonnay and Cabernet Sauvignon grapes from Sonoma County, selling the wines made from them with a catchall California appellation. Bill Frick has now relocated his winery to Sonoma County because of the difficulty of obtaining Santa Cruz grapes. Chuck Devlin grew up on the property south of Santa Cruz where he has his winery and hopes, one day, to have 20 acres of vineyard there. For the present, however, and although he is able to buy the Chardonnay he needs in Santa Cruz County, both the Zinfandel that provides the bulk of his business and the Merlot that has won him most acclaim are grown outside the area. Silver Mountain's Jerold O'Brien, a retired Air Force pilot, had hoped to be self-sufficient in grapes when he bought seventeen acres on the Santa Cruz ridge. The lot was an abandoned orchard that had been a vineyard before Prohibition, but he was nevertheless obliged to provide an environmental study of the impact of his proposal on flora and fauna. Delays lasted three years. He was eventually able to build his winery and plant his vineyard, but he ran out of money before his vines were bearing and so, for the time being he, too, has been obliged to buy grapes from growers elsewhere.

Some wineries, such as Bonny Doon and Roudon-Smith, have managed to grow or find at least enough grapes in Santa Cruz to establish the local character

151

of their wineries even if they must then supplement them with grapes bought elsewhere. Both are particularly imaginative, even in their quest for alien grapes. Bonny Doon Vineyard's Randall Grahm, California's only winemaking literary philosopher, has reached as far as the Willamette Valley in Oregon to find Pinot Noir. He has scoured California to find the needed proportions of Syrah, Cinsault, Grenache and Mourvèdre to reproduce, in his *Cigare Volant* wine, the quality and style of a Châteauneuf-du-Pape. ("It has a bouquet of ultraviolets," claimed Grahm in one of his tongue-in-cheek newsletters.) When I arrived to chat with him he was crushing a batch of frozen Muscat Canelli grapes for ice wine.

Ice wine in Santa Cruz? It is perfectly possible if the winery assists nature by putting the freshly picked grapes into a freezer and leaving them there until calm returns after the rest of the harvest is fermented and racked. "We can then make ice wine in a civilized way," Grahm explained. "None of that getting up at four o'clock in the morning before the sun gets on the grapes and thaws them. We pull one press load a day from the freezer and give it all our attention."

The Bureau of Alcohol, Tobacco and Firearms had disallowed Grahm's attempt to label an earlier batch of his ice wine *Vin de Glace*, but they have since seen the appropriateness of *Vin de Glacière*. Ever resourceful, Grahm is one of the few who usually manages to find a way through this thicket of regulation for the sake of regulation.

Understanding the need for focus, and recognizing the difficulty Santa Cruz wineries have in using a local geographic identity for the purpose, Grahm pursued instead an interest in wines made from grapes associated with the Rhône Valley. Apart from his *Cigare Volant* (a "flying cigar" is what the French call a flying saucer: the commune of Châteauneuf-du-Pape once passed a *Cigare Volant* ordinance forbidding such vehicles to land on local vineyards), Grahm makes a deliciously fruity Grenache each year under the name *Clos de Gilroy* that out-nouveaus most Beaujolais. He has planted the elusive Viognier, and makes a Marsanne-Roussanne blend (a formula, if you like, for Hermitage Blanc) under the name *Le Sophiste: Cuvée Philosophique*. And now he has extended his Mediterranean interests across the Alps into Italy, and is in the forefront of those producing California wines from long-neglected Italian vine varieties.

Bob Roudon and Jim Smith's winery is hidden among redwoods and rhododendrons in a setting that would make convinced environmentalists of the EPA. Through a network of contacts, these two manage to find small batches of Santa Cruz grapes. "Every so often someone with a house and a few acres will come up with the idea of a small vineyard. So, although it is true that most of the county opposes vines, every year a few people discreetly plant an acre or two. Plantings on such a modest scale usually go without remark." Roudon and Smith have also been creative with a Rhône variety. "I found this vineyard of Petite Sirah in San Luis Obispo," Bob Roudon told me. "The vines were about ten years old then, back in 1978. The fruit has got better all the time. I tried blending a little Chardonnay—just five or ten percent, depending on the year—to give some finesse. We've built quite a clientele for it."

Blending a few white grapes with black for red wine is still a current practice in some Rhône areas (and elsewhere; remember the touch of white grapes in Chianti). Until the nineteenth century it was a practice almost universal in France, and for the same end that Roudon and Smith add Chardonnay to their Petite Sirah: finesse. Roudon-Smith's Petite Sirah, aged for a while in American oak, has both elegance of structure and length of flavor. I am not surprised it is the winery's biggest seller.

153

I made my last call at the Santa Cruz Mountain Vineyard itself. Its thirteen acres of Pinot Noir and single acre of Chardonnay are planted on a choice section of the old Jarvis vineyard, established on Vine Hill in 1863. In those days, there were said to have been several thousand acres of vines in the Santa Cruz Mountains. Ken Burnap dry-farms his vines, uses only gravity in his hillside cellar (I watched while a cellarman gently raised one barrel on a forklift and siphoned the contents over to another barrel.) For fermentation he relies strictly on the ambient yeast that arrives with the grapes from the vineyard, for his pressed pomace is returned there to build an indigenous yeast population. His wines have character; but whether that character is stamped on them by this gritty, mountain terrain or imposed by the vigor of Ken Burnap's personality is hard to say.

I drove back to San Francisco over the Hecker Pass into Santa Clara County because I wanted to see the southern extension of the Santa Cruz

Mountain Viticultural Area, one of the few sections where vineyards, like those of the Bates Ranch, have been expanding. It was depressing, even there, though, to find myself almost immediately in the spreading community of Morgan Hill and, soon afterward, lost in the concrete sprawl of San Jose. I'm not sure about the future of Santa Cruz fungus, but I could see why Santa Cruz wineries, poised between preservers of manzanita scrub and builders of shopping malls, will need all the ingenuity and tenacity in the world to survive.

154

WINE ON WINE

I<small>T WAS A DELICIOUSLY UNCOMPLICATED DINNER AT THE HOME OF</small> L<small>ONDON FRIENDS:</small> <small>MUSSEL SOUP, BOILED BEEF WITH YOUNG CARROTS AND PARSNIPS, SALAD, AND SOME</small> E<small>NGLISH</small> <small>AND</small> I<small>RISH CHEESES.</small> We drank a glass of champagne before sitting down to a 1982 Meursault Genevrières. Then a duo of red wines made from Bordeaux grape varieties—Coleraine '85, from Te Mata Estate in New Zealand's Hawkes Bay, and a Dominus '85, from the Napanook Vineyard at Rutherford in Napa Valley (I rarely see either of these wines, and had never before had an opportunity to taste them together)—led to two Pauillacs, a 1961 Château Grand-Puy-Lacoste and Château Latour of the same year. Finally, with a plain almond cake, we had a disconcertingly unfamiliar sweet white wine that turned out to be a late-picked and slightly botrytized 1991 Chardonnay from Mâcon-Clessé. Our hosts had smiled discreetly as their guests—all of us professionally involved with wine in one way or another—tripped over themselves trying to guess what it might be. None of us came close.

Not that we'd shone at guessing the other wines. Almost inevitably, when one of us would take a really strong stand about what a wine could not possibly be—part of the process of arriving at a wine's identity, after all, is to close off options—he or she would regret having spoken. Once we'd decided the two Pauillac wines were about thirty years old (having been told they were of the same vintage), one of us lost no time in eliminating what turned out to be the correct year, and another, when we'd concluded they were Médoc rather than Graves or Saint-Emilion, in saying, "Well, at least they're not Pauillacs, that's for sure."

Fortunately, with hindsight, it was easier to guess why those particular four wines had been brought together. The Coleraine had probably been chosen as a compliment to John Buck, Te Mata's owner, who was visiting from New Zealand, and I expect the Dominus was to help me feel at home, as I'd arrived only a few

155

days before from California. But neither wine was presented as a mere courtesy; each was also a foil for the other (the tight and slightly angular New Zealand wine in bright contrast to the more somber Dominus), and both helped us appreciate more fully the 1961 Pauillacs that appeared with the cheese—they, too, having been chosen to set each other off as well as for our delight.

It's customary to use a young (or at least younger) wine to bring out the complexity of an older one, and the ploy works—provided, of course, that the one is neither so youthfully vigorous nor so massive as to make the other seem weary or flimsy rather than delicate and polished. It might have been less risky for our hosts to use other red Bordeaux to show off those 1961s: a couple of 1984s, for example, might have made an interesting though perhaps not very agreeable introduction to the older wines. In both 1961 and 1984 a wet spring caused the Merlot vines, ever capricious, to drop their blossom rather than set fruit, so the Médoc production in both years was almost pure Cabernet Sauvignon instead of the usual Bordeaux mix of grape varieties. But in 1961 a glorious summer followed that wet spring and it gave one of the great vintages of the last fifty years, whereas in 1984 a cold, wet September scotched the grapes' final ripening, leaving them low in sugar and tough with unripe tannins.

Our hosts, taking seriously their responsibility for our happiness while under their roof, had spared us that particular exercise, electing to take a chance instead. But not too much of a chance: the two 1985s (both, remember, produced from traditional Bordeaux grape varieties) had enough in common with the two Pauillacs to point up their greater maturity, while, to my surprise and pleasure, throwing into relief their distinctively French measure and harmony. So clear was the distinction between the two pairs of wines, in fact, that the Pauillacs seemed at first more similar to each other than was really the case. Only when New Zealand and California had ceased to linger, figuratively, on our palates, were we able to focus our attention on the older wines for themselves alone and notice how the silky restraint of the Grand-Puy-Lacoste underlined the almost opulent breadth of the Latour, which in turn allowed us to appreciate more fully the Grand-Puy-Lacoste's subtle charm.

It's difficult to put even two wines together, let alone four, free of all hazard: no wine can be relied on to perform exactly as expected. The longer it's been in bottle, the more likely it is to have deviated from the accepted norm for that growth of that year. "One cannot talk of wines, only of bottles," is an old saying we sometimes dismiss too quickly as folklore.

Each of the four wines served to us in London would have tasted different in a changed context because our perception of any wine is always affected by others. If one is very tannic, another will seem less so, allowing us to notice in the latter a quality we might otherwise have missed. A wine that's aromatic but a little thin will be remarked on for its fragrance rather than its lack of body if it's preceded by a glass of something light and fairly neutral. With this in mind, we begin to understand how we can use one wine to enhance another by emphasizing its advantages.

The key to a full appreciation of any wine is to choose a suitable foil. That's more important than embarking on a quest for the holy grail of the perfect food match. There is no perfect food match when wine is a meal's focus, but within the abundance of possibilities the simplest—such as our boiled beef in London— is most often the best and the least distracting. (Simple should not mean penitential, however. A few years ago, when I was a guest at a wine luncheon in a restored monastery in the Loire valley, our host had the genial idea of serving us the meal fourteenth-century monks assembled in that same refectory might have eaten: raw fava beans as an appetizer, then plain boiled tripe followed by cheese curds. He had gone to great trouble to have wheat roughly milled so that we could eat—or choke on—bread that resembled chaff cakes. Spiritually and physically, it must have done us a world of good; but the exceptional wines he had chosen for us, though not really diminished by the truly depressing food, were certainly not enhanced by it either.)

Ideally, the first of two wines should establish a frame of reference for the second, even introduce, if possible and need be, any stylistic imperfection that might divert attention from the qualities of the older, finer wine that follows. For example, suppose one wanted to show off a 1979 Château Pichon-Longueville, Comtesse de Lalande. The 1979s (of which this was one of the best) were aromatic and elegant rather than massive. I could precede the 1979 with a more

157

modest Médoc wine—from Listrac, say, or Moulis, or even the château's own second wine, Réserve de la Comtesse—from a vintage like 1987, a year in which the wines were agreeably balanced but lacked concentration. The 1987 would establish a base from which the 1979 would soar.

If I were concerned, however, that the 1979 might now lack sufficient power to hold center stage with a main course, even something as low-key as a leg of lamb, I could serve it after the main course—as is more often the case with the finest wine offered at dinner at any of the great Bordeaux châteaux. In that case it would provide a graceful epilogue to some livelier wine, but one with less finesse, served before it. Because of its place in the order of things, that wine would have to have more character than a 1987, and I would probably choose a 1988 of a good *cru bourgeois* like Chasse-Spleen or Sociando-Mallet. The 1988s have a density that remains somewhat unyielding, and, because they are still quite brisk, I would probably prefer to serve this wine with a rack of lamb or even duck breast—in any case, a slightly richer meat—before bringing on the 1979. For the relationship between the two wines to work, I must not get carried away and decide on a 1988 that is *too* distinguished. If I were to show Château Pichon-Longueville, Comtesse de Lalande's own 1988, for instance, it would overwhelm the 1979 rather than confirm its stature.

Any wine—a Bordeaux, a mature Chianti, a California Cabernet Sauvignon—can be improved for having been properly introduced in this manner. I remember how a 1967 Léoville-Barton was used several years ago at a dinner in San Francisco to prepare the way for a fading Langoa-Barton '37. The 1967 was softly agreeable—just substantial enough yet with little to catch on to. Its very quiescence, however, allowed us to enjoy the flavor and bouquet of that 1937 (which none of us is ever likely to taste again), when most other wines would have made it seem feeble at best.

Even the most sumptuous wine needs a setting to be enjoyed to the full. On one of the few occasions when I tasted the 1961 Pétrus, Jean-Pierre Moueix, the château's coproprietor, served before it his extraordinary 1962 Trotanoy to emphasize—if indeed emphasis were needed—how even more extraordinary the Pétrus was.

When selecting a wine to precede a California Cabernet Sauvignon, it's wiser to take the Pétrus rather than the Langoa-Barton approach. California Cabernet Sauvignons remain vigorous for longer than their French counterparts and therefore rarely need specially gentle introductions. What would one use if they did? Even young Cabernet Sauvignons from California's less successful years are rarely as retiring as Bordeaux wines of vintages like 1980 and 1987, and so they cannot be relied on to perform in the same way. I have found that a young, not-too-muscular, and fairly low-profile Merlot—Kenwood Vineyards' Sonoma County '90, for example, or Hanna Winery's Alexander Valley '90—provides better preparation for a fine, mature California Cabernet Sauvignon like Heitz Cellars' Bella Oaks '81, Beaulieu Vineyards' Georges de Latour Private Reserve '70, or Joseph Phelps' superb '75 (all legendary wines) than practically any young Cabernet Sauvignon would do.

Alternatively, California Cabernet Francs, growing in number, are usually svelte enough for the purpose, provided they're not too aromatically varietal (which would raise irrelevant expectations). One of the best I've tasted is the elegantly discreet 1991 Moon Mountain Vineyard Cabernet Franc from the Carmenet Vineyard in Sonoma Valley. That wine would be a worthy prelude to any mature California Cabernet Sauvignon. But then, on second thoughts, perhaps not all of them. It really is so fine, it could make quite a few I can think of seem as rough as grizzly bears.

CHARDONNAY:
TWIGS, BUDS AND CLONES

AT THE LAST COUNT THERE WERE MORE THAN SIXTY-FIVE THOUSAND ACRES OF CHARDONNAY VINES IN CALIFORNIA. That is almost three times the acreage in Burgundy, Chardonnay's home. The rising flow of California Chardonnay has coincided with a change in the way the state's wineries are handling this popular varietal. They are turning away from the chunky oak-and-fruit style that served, brashly enough, for a decade or two, and, with Burgundian tradition as their example and restraint as their new watchword, they are placing greater emphasis on balance and texture. But because, in the flood of brands and labels, they need more than ever to be distinctive, no matter how discreetly, subtle differences among Chardonnay's varietal clones and selections are now matters of serious concern. In Healdsburg and St. Helena, where wise heads once talked late into the night on the relative merits of light-toasted Vosges oak barrels and heavy-toasted Allier, conversation is now larded with references to Rued and See's and Old Wente.

For years I have been puzzled by references to Chardonnay clones. Occasionally, when curiosity got the better of me, I searched for information on the Curtis clone, the Spring Mountain clone, the Martini clone, and all the rest. There was nothing on Chardonnay clones in print, not the smallest reference to them even in Winkler's *General Viticulture*, the standard California teaching text.

Just when I had more or less given up trying to make sense of them in favor of the less abstruse tangles of East European politics, I received from Simi Winery a newsletter with a neatly drawn plan of a test vineyard they have planted on Diamond Mountain, above Napa Valley. It showed alternating rows of seven different Chardonnay clones. In the accompanying text were two key sentences: "The concept of choosing a plant according to intended use is familiar to gardeners

who plant plum tomatoes for sauce and beefsteak tomatoes for sandwiches.…
For several years we have been working with selected Chardonnay clones to
determine if there are aromatic or flavor differences between them that might be
the basis for varying styles of Chardonnay wine."

Perhaps it's because every vine is propagated from sprouted bud wood—
a twig taken from another vine—and never from seed, that the term *clone*, from
the Greek word for twig, has come to be applied to vines so loosely. (In much of
California the bud wood is grafted, on a bench or in the vineyard, onto phylloxera-
resistant rootstock.) Professors Carole Meredith and Michael Mullin of the
Department of Viticulture and Enology of the University of California at Davis
define a clone as a distinct subtype within a wine-grape variety. In their
"Romancing the Clone," a leaflet published by the university in cooperation with
the U.S. Department of Agriculture, they explain:

> Differences between these subtypes are genetic differences—they are
> stable and they are maintained through propagation. These differences are
> thought to arise as the result of mutations, very small changes in the DNA, the
> genetic blueprint in each cell that governs every process and structure that makes
> up the vine. Such changes are natural and normal and occur from time to time in
> all cells of all organisms. If such a change takes place in a grapevine cell that is
> destined to give rise to a bud, then the shoot that eventually develops from that
> bud will be genetically different from the rest of the vine. (This is called a bud
> sport.) Cuttings or buds taken from that shoot for propagation will give rise to
> entire vines that are now slightly different from the original vine but are identical
> to each other. A new clone is born.

161

A mass selection of Chardonnay, on the other hand, is the result of a
mass of bud-wood cuttings taken from a great number of vines throughout a vineyard that were in turn propagated from a similar mass of bud wood cut in another vineyard. If each time there is a deliberate effort to seek out and take bud wood
from vines with specific attributes, whether yield, aroma, or some other quality,
such repeated selections of selections, even when taken from a large number of
vines, can eventually lead to some common characteristics. But no matter how
homogeneous such a collection of vines might then be, they do not constitute a

clone. And because the individual vines do not share a single genetic origin, the reaction of each to common cultivation methods in a shared environment is likely at times to be surprisingly different.

I called Diane Kenworthy, Simi's viticulturalist, about that newsletter. It had seemed to offer hope, at last, of practical information on the subject. She told me the winery had planted three standard clones from the University of California at Davis and were testing them against others taken from commercial vineyards with both specific styles and distinguished records to see to what extent their qualities would be consistent when transferred. "We want to see if we can find anything among these clones better than what we already have," she said.

Four of the Simi clones were new, each propagated from a single vine chosen among the many similar or complementary vines within one of the specific and acknowledged Chardonnay selections. Diane Kenworthy was well aware that a clone propagated from just one vine of such a selection did not necessarily carry over all the selection's characteristics, "but we need a controlled experiment," she said.

One of the mass selections from which Simi has propagated a clone is popularly referred to as Spring Mountain. It is widely used in Sonoma County. Merry Edwards first brought it into the county when she was at Matanzas Creek, I was told. "The muscatlike strain in its aroma comes across as no more than a heightened fruitiness when it's used with restraint in a blend," said Diane Kenworthy. "The Rued selection—not one of those we are testing here—has an even more intense aroma, one we already know carries over wherever the selection is planted."

When I called Merry Edwards, now winemaker at Laurier Vineyards, Liparita Cellars and Pellegrini Family Wines, to ask where the Spring Mountain selection had come from, she told me she had taken cuttings from Spring Mountain Vineyard's old Wildwood Vineyard on Silverado Trail in Napa Valley. "I had gone there for cuttings of the Mount Eden Vineyards clone. I had understood there were Mount Eden vines there. But it was winter and difficult to see what was what. The vineyard manager must have misdirected me. I've been told that what I took is probably related to the *Chardonnay musqué* of Burgundy, and might even be the same vine. It certainly gives a very perfumed wine."

The Rued selection, named for Paul Rued's vineyard near Graton in the Russian River Valley, is also highly aromatic. "But it's supported by better texture and depth of flavor," Merry Edwards said. "I would never use Spring Mountain alone, but Rued gives a balanced wine of real interest."

Paul Rued has little light to shed on the origin of his vines. "We bought them from a nursery in Calistoga in 1971. There was quite a demand for Chardonnay at the time. This was what they had."

Whether or not either Rued or Spring Mountain owe their aroma to *Chardonnay musqué*, they exist as selections because growers have segregated cuttings from aromatic vines and propagated them. Larry Hyde, a grape grower in Carneros, the cool district by San Francisco Bay where Napa and Sonoma run together, found his aromatic vines through mass selections cut in the Long Vineyard in Napa Valley—a vineyard propagated from Stony Hill vines that lead us back to Wente, as we shall see. Sixty percent of his vineyard is planted with such vines. "Wineries rely on me for aromatic fruit," he told me.

I was ignorant of "the *Chardonnay musqué* of Burgundy." I eventually found a reference to this particularly aromatic subvariety of Chardonnay as a footnote in a French scientific directory of vines. Trying to trace it in California was even harder. Records of who had brought which variety, and when, were never very extensive, and many of those that did exist were destroyed during Prohibition, when the majority of wineries closed. Charles Wetmore, while president of the State Viticultural Commission, was responsible for some of the first Chardonnay to arrive in California in 1882, directly from Meursault in Burgundy. He had distributed its bud wood in the Livermore Valley, where he had established his own Cresta Blanca Winery. Some of that wood went to the Gier vineyard at Pleasanton.

Thirty years later, Ernest Wente persuaded his father to bring in some Chardonnay, along with other vinifera cuttings, from the vine nursery of the distinguished wine school at the University of Montpellier in the south of France. He also acquired Chardonnay cuttings from the Gier vineyard that were drawn from Wetmore's original importation from Meursault. It would therefore appear that the Wente vineyard, later to be a key source of Chardonnay in California, contained from the start at least these two distinct selections.

163

Paul Masson was said to have imported Chardonnay for his La Cresta Vineyard, in the Santa Cruz Mountains south of San Francisco, directly from Burgundy in 1896. The property passed to Martin Ray when he bought the Paul Masson company in 1936. Ray took cuttings from it for a new vineyard of his own nearby when he sold the company and La Cresta to Seagram in 1943. His widow, Eleanor McCrae, seems to think, on the other hand, that he might have imported his own fresh cuttings at that time—she mentions as the source Louis Latour's vineyard at Corton-Charlemagne—but the war makes it unlikely.

Others have suggested that the original Chardonnay at La Cresta had been supplied to Paul Masson by his father-in-law, Charles Lefranc, founder of Almaden, who had brought it to California in the 1870s. There are, indeed, several contemporary references to Chardonnay existing at that time in Almaden's Santa Clara County. But whatever its path to Martin Ray's vineyard, that strain of Chardonnay, now planted at Mount Eden Vineyards, has remained distinct, it is generally agreed, from the other Chardonnays that converged on, and later were to spread from, the Wente vineyard in Livermore Valley. The only commercially viable acreages of Chardonnay to survive Prohibition, according to an orthodox reading of California history, were those in Ernest Wente's and Paul Masson's vineyards.

To help me in my quest for the *Chardonnay musqué*, John Wetlaufer, a wine merchant and amateur historian in Calistoga, put me onto an old and out-of-print account of California vines by Professor Harold Olmo of the Department of Viticulture and Enology of the University of California at Davis, published by a now-defunct wine advisory board. In it, he made a brief reference to *Chardonnay musqué* imported by a Captain J. H. Drummond of Sonoma Valley in the 1870s. "It was probably lost," Olmo wrote, "during the vineyard removals of the Prohibition period."

I hunted for other references to Captain Drummond and found one only in several effusive paragraphs of Frona Eunice Wait's book *Wines and Vines of California*, published in 1889. She made no specific mention of the *Chardonnay musqué*, but did commend Captain Drummond for having "all that is rare in the fruit kingdom."

John Wetlaufer told me that Captain Drummond had been stepfatherin-law to Frederic Bioletti, the man responsible for the first attempts at clonal research at Davis prior to Prohibition. And Bioletti was himself mentor to Professor Olmo, the man who has since continued his work and who had written with such assurance of *Chardonnay musqué*'s presence in Drummond's vineyard.

Even in France, apparently, *Chardonnay musqué* is considered a rare oddity. If it had been planted in Drummond's vineyard, is it not likely that neighbors, for whom Drummond was always "demonstrating the advisability of fine varieties of grapes," according to Frona Eunice Waite, would have asked for, and been given, a little of its bud wood? And is it not probable that cuttings from their patches of vines—perhaps considered too insignificant to be pulled during Prohibition or counted afterwards—strayed into other Chardonnay vineyards, letting loose the muscat element now prevalent in the Rued and Spring Mountain selections?

Tracking with certainty any Chardonnay clone or selection would be difficult enough even if better records had been kept. The trail is further obscured, however, because of confusion on both sides of the Atlantic between Chardonnay and Pinot Blanc. Chardonnay has existed as a distinct variety in France for centuries, but it was always referred to under other names (and in some parts of France, still is) and was assumed to be identical with, or at least no more than a variant of, the Pinot Blanc with which it was often promiscuously planted. The Chardonnay name began to appear, spelled in a variety of ways, only in the mid-nineteenth century. From then it was used as if it were a synonym for Pinot Blanc.

Jean Lavalle's 1855 book, *Histoire et Statistique de la Vigne et des Grands Vins de la Côte d'Or*, is so highly regarded for its accuracy of observation that as recently as the 1930s it was used as the primary source for the definitions of controlled appellations in Burgundy. Yet even Lavalle, director of the Dijon Botanical Garden, refers to "*chardenet ou pinot blanc*" as if they were a single vine variety.

The experts now agree that Chardonnay is not a member of the Pinot family at all, though it is evident from past confusion that it has not been easy to distinguish one from the other. In California, where there was yet more muddle caused by the practice of referring to Chenin Blanc as White Pineau until the 1950s, the distinction between Chardonnay and Pinot Blanc was thought finally to have been settled until a recent finding that vines in the state formerly accepted as Pinot Blanc are in fact Melon de Bourgogne. Melon is more commonly known as the Muscadet grape and in France is used extensively to make a wine of that name in the low-lying vineyards south of Nantes at the mouth of the Loire.

This can only mean that true Pinot Blanc, certain to have reached these shores along with those early cuttings of Chardonnay, is probably still out there somewhere, like the *Chardonnay musqué*, misidentified and contributing to those surprises in the Chardonnay vineyards.

Alex Vyborny grows grapes in Sonoma County and manages vineyards for absentee owners there. He has worked extensively with the Spring Mountain selection and told me there were "several kinds," implying that it is inconsistent— as one might expect from a selection as opposed to a clone. He more or less dismissed it and said he preferred to work with See's clone, anyway.

See's clone takes its name fom what had been Charles See's vineyard in Napa Valley, now part of the Silverado Vineyards. Vyborny thought it had been propagated from cuttings taken there from Sterling Vineyards, where vines had been propagated from bud wood taken from the old Wente vineyard in Livermore Valley. See's sounded to me more like a mass selection than a clone, and Jack Stuart, the winemaker at Silverado Vineyards, agreed.

"The vines are inconsistent," he told me. "Grapes from some vines taste quite muscaty, but others not at all. Taken as a whole, though, fruit from the See vineyard brings a roundness to our wine and a touch of apricot or peach flavor. That vineyard is aging now and is in decline, suffering from leaf-roll. Perhaps because of that the fruit seems to be less aromatic than it was and could be less aromatic than the fruit of young vines that have been propagated elsewhere from our bud wood."

Sterling Vineyards had been far from the first to get bud wood from Wente. Fred and Eleanor McCrae had taken cuttings there long before, in 1948, for their new vineyard at Stony Hill, above Napa Valley.

"Herman Wente stood at the door of his house and said to us: 'There it is. Just go take what you want,' " Eleanor McCrea told me. "We knew nothing. There were no peas greener than we were. No one talked about clones in those days. We just went in and took cuttings from all over."

Others who subsequently took bud wood from the vines propagated by the McCreas at Stony Hill would refer to their own vines sometimes as Stony Hill selection, and sometimes, knowing where the Stony Hill vines had come from, as Wente.

Louis Martini was among those who referred to the cuttings he had taken from Stony Hill as "Wente." In 1951 or 1952 he had marked thirty vines that interested him. When they were dormant he had gone back to take cuttings from them, propagating twenty vines from each on a new Martini family property on Stanly Lane in Carneros. He allowed the Department of Viticulture and Enology at Davis to use his six hundred Chardonnay vines for trials.

"Davis would come over every year to measure them, take samples of the grapes, and make wine," Louis Martini recollected. In 1955 Professor Olmo made a selection from the "Wente" vines for the university's clonal propagation program.

Professor Olmo, who still has an office on the Davis campus of the University of California, told me that the Department of Viticulture and Enology released healthy bud wood from that selection before it had been through the hands of the plant pathologists. When the pathologists had indexed the bud wood—viticultural jargon meaning it was tested for plant viruses—but had not at that stage heat-treated it to ensure its being virus-free, it was rereleased.

Unfortunately, the pathologists worked with numerical references of their own, according to Professor Olmo, and the result is still confusion. The indexed material they released has been referred to by some as clone 2A, yet the viticulturalists say it should have carried a series of numbers in the sixties. It is astonishing, to say the least, that records even at the university should be so vague. But whether as one clone or as a series of them, this bud wood, too, was widely referred to as "Wente clone."

Both this original material available from Davis and the mass selections taken directly and indirectly from the original Wente vineyard are all dubbed indiscriminately now with the name "Old Wente clone." Not surprisingly, vines so called vary considerably. A characteristic they share, according to Bill Dyer, the winemaker at Sterling, is their "pumpkins and peas" look of large and small berries jumbled together in their bunches. But other characteristics—particularly those of flavor and aroma—have come to distinguish one group of these mass selections from another. Depending on the specific vines chosen for their bud wood, mass selections can differ markedly, even when taken from the same vineyard. When the characteristics of one mass selection are preferred to those of another, growers need rough-and-ready ways to indicate which is which, and new identities are created for them. Hence Rued, See's, and Spring Mountain.

Wente Brothers, not inappropriately, were the first to have, on their new property in Monterey County, a certified block of a heat-treated version of a Davis clone released by the university under the reference 108. That clone has now been redesignated as two separate ones, 4 and 5, to distinguish two different durations of heat treatment, according to some, and to designate two different vine sources, according to others. (I was beginning to learn why there was so little in print on the subject of clones. Academic angels had refrained from treading where inconsistency, contradiction, and incoherence lay in wait at every turn.)

In the late 1960s, millions of cuttings of cuttings of 108 bud wood were being used to plant much of the present Chardonnay vineyards of Napa Valley and most of those in the state of Washington. It was referred to colloquially as "the Wente clone," and "for a while," Eric Wente said recently, "we were making more money from its bud wood than from its grapes."

Later, bud wood of that same clone began to circulate from vineyards on the Curtis ranch north of Napa (the property of Bill Jaeger—a partner in Rutherford Hill Winery, whose mother had been born a Curtis—now renamed the Jaeger Ranch). That wood was referred to as the Curtis clone. For the record, it is synonymous with Davis clone 108, a.k.a. the Wente clone.

But whatever they call them, winemakers have sometimes been leery of these Davis clones, believing that their healthy yield capacity is at cross-purposes with quality. Yet Bob Dyer said he always got good quality from the the 108 clone planted on the hillsides of Sterling's famous Winery Lake Vineyard in Carneros, provided he controlled the crop. And although Merry Edwards thought that the Davis clones had been propagated to give healthy yields, she confirmed Dyer's observation. "If you let them, they tend to be highly productive of grapes with low-flavor intensity," she said. "But growers who hold down their crops to no more than three or four tons to the acre can get satisfactory quality from them."

The Mount Eden Vineyards Chardonnay strain—by now who can say whether it is a clone or a selection?—seems to be the only one that does not lead back to the Wente vineyard in Livermore Valley. There are still twelve acres of it at Mount Eden Vineyards, where some of the older vines, affected by phylloxera, have to be pulled. Small amounts of the strain might well have been mingled into other selections, but the only vineyards in California known to be planted with it exclusively, other than those at Mount Eden itself, are at Congress Springs and Cinnabar, both nearby in the Santa Cruz Mountains, and at Kistler Vineyards on the Sonoma side of the Mayacamas.

All who have worked with the strain enthuse over it, despite its lack of vigor, its virus, and its low yields. Merry Edwards, who knew it well from her three years as winemaker at Mount Eden, said that the tight, conical bunches of tiny berries give a wine that shows its complexity only after several months in barrel. She describes a Mount Eden Vineyards Chardonnay wine as richly textured, well rounded, and impeccably integrated.

Jeffrey Patterson, the present winemaker at Mount Eden, is struck by the change he finds in wine produced by Kistler from what are essentially the same vines, but in the different environment of the Mayacamas. "The Mount Eden Vineyard clone never gives an overtly fruity wine," he said, "but the wine of the Kistler Vineyard has orchard-fruit tones—apples and pears—quite distinct from ours."

David Ramey, a distinguished California enologist formerly associated with Chardonnay research and development at Simi Winery, and later winemaker at Chalk Hill Vineyards, describes the Mount Eden Vineyards strain as "classically Burgundian" and said, a few years ago, that the Kistler Vineyards Estate Chardonnay made from it was then "perhaps the best Chardonnay in California." (Ramey would be too modest to say so, but the 1987 Chardonnay he himself made at Matanzas Creek—he was winemaker there for a few years after Merry Edwards—wasn't bad either.)

Patterson's remarks point up the difference that site can play in moderating clonal distinctions. Dale Hampton, the leading grape grower in Santa Barbara

County, says site is everything. "Clones just change with the environment," he told me. "I can take one clone, put it in five different places, and get five different qualities from it."

Craig Williams, winemaker at Joseph Phelps Vineyards in Napa Valley, partly concurred. "The more I make wine," he said, "the more respect I have for differences of soil and environment, even though they were always played down [in California] before."

Questions of winemaking and site, selection and clone, are pointed up in the recent history of the Robert Young Vineyards in Alexander Valley. The vineyard first gained a reputation in the seventies when Richard Arrowood, wine-maker at Château St. Jean, began to release a succession of highly prized wines with labels that identified this vineyard as the source of the grapes. Encouraged by the success of Arrowood's wines, other winemakers bought grapes from Robert Young. A similarity in the wines they made was at first attributed to the vineyard itself, later to the selection of Chardonnay grown there, and eventually to the marriage of the two. Another explanation, of course, could have been that wine-makers drawn to buying grapes from the Robert Young Vineyards were those who, admiring the wines already made from them, would be likely to have adopted as their goal what they perceived as a "Robert Young" style and would therefore have been following similar winemaking procedures to achieve it.

Like so many others in the 1960s, the vineyard was planted with bud wood brought there from the old Wente vineyard. Robert Young's son, a recent graduate from the Department of Viticulture and Enology at Davis, made selec-tions of cuttings from their best vines a few years ago and took them to be tested for virus by the university's Foundation Plants Material Service. One selection showed virus-free, and from that one vine the Youngs have since propagated two blocks of vines that they have designated the "Robert Young clone." It is there-fore distinct, of course, from the general selection of their Robert Young Vineyards, and, like the transformation of wood from the early Wente selection in Louis Martini's vineyard into Davis clone 108, and the experimental lots on Simi's Diamond Mountain vineyard, it is a further example of a selection giving rise to a clone.

We shall see more of such transformations as growers, eager to take advantage of the concentrated flavor and distinction of older, non-heat-treated selections but anxious to avoid the drawbacks of virus-ridden vines, follow Robert Young's example. Selecting the best from the selections they have, they are checking for "clean" wood and beginning to propagate new clones.

The University of California, too, is conducting clonal tests in its experimental vineyards in Napa Valley. Fortunately, similar work has been conducted for more than twenty years by Raymond Bernard, regional director in Dijon of the Office National Interprofessionel des Vins. Some of the Chardonnay clones proved by him to be successful have been imported through the plant quarantine service of Oregon State University and are beginning to find their way into California. There is also rumor of a Burgundian clone on the loose in one or two vineyards in California, brought in from France by a less circuitous route. Whether we shall be better off with "controlled" clones than we are with the chance of our present random selections, who can say? We must just hope, though, that someone, somewhere, is keeping accurate notes on all this activity. Otherwise there will be scope for more conjecture in the year 2090. Watch this space.

HAUT-BRION: A MOST PARTICULAR TASTE

A LITTLE RISE OF GROUND, LIEING OPEN MOST TO THE WEST. It is noe thing but pure white sand, mixed with a little gravel. One would imagin it scarce fit to beare any thing..." John Locke's words are taken from his journal entry for May 14th, 1677. At that time, a philosopher's journey to view a vineyard at first hand and to write down his impression of it was as unlikely as the visit today of an eminent intellectual to ponder the significance of a cabbage patch. Locke's curiosity confirms a singular achievement of Arnaud de Pontac, the richest and most influential man in Bordeaux, first president of its Parliament (a configuration of law courts rather than a legislature), but best remembered as Château Haut-Brion's owner from 1649 until his death in 1681. During that time, Pontac raised the status of his wine estate from agricultural anonymity to one of fame and immense value.

Samuel Pepys, later to be Secretary of the Admiralty in London, had first noticed "a sort of French wine called Ho-Bryan which hath a good and most particular taste" in a London tavern in 1663, but Locke makes clear that what had been a novelty to Pepys had become, in a very few years, a wine so esteemed in England as to be almost an object of cult. Locke's journey to Haut-Brion and his report on what he saw there underline how identification of Pepys' Ho-Bryan wine with Arnaud de Pontac's vineyard at Château Haut-Brion helped bring that about. It is a wine-to-vineyard relationship we would take for granted today, but one that required new perception when wines were still as broadly anonymous as other agricultural products.

Pontac's great-grandfather, Jean de Pontac, a general trader descended from a pewtersmith, had acquired land at Haut-Brion in the village of Pessac outside Bordeaux through his marriage to Jeanne de Billion in 1525. In the course of a long life (he was still sound of mind and limb when he died at 101), he filled all those legal and administrative offices, for king and city, most likely to enrich and advance a man in a contentious age. While acquiring two further wives, fifteen children and the largest fortune in Bordeaux, he had found time to enlarge and embellish his property at Haut-Brion long before it came, through the usual chain of inheritance, into Arnaud de Pontac's hands.

Arnaud de Pontac paid close attention to the family estate at Haut-Brion. He introduced there the practice of regular racking from barrel to barrel, separating young wine from its coarse and mischievous early lees, and was among the first to realize that frequent "topping up" to compensate for evaporation allowed wine in cask to improve rather than spoil—simple usages that allowed him to reveal to the full the inherent advantages of his vineyard.

The general lack of such care in an absence of what we might consider basic cellar hygiene normally led wine to deteriorate so rapidly in the sixteenth century that new wine commanded a substantial premium over old. A buyer at that time concerned himself less with the fine points that preoccupy us today than with a wine's soundness and reliable drinkability.

Though this preference for new wine over old continued into the seventeenth century, there were by then, even among new wines, some more prized than others, the most highly regarded being those associated with powerful families, including the Pontacs, but with little attention paid, by buyer or seller, to specific vineyards. René Pijassou, of the University of Bordeaux, comments that consumers seemed to see a connection between a wine's quality and the financial strength and fame of its producer, a phenomenon not unknown today and one that might be justified by the care made possible by greater resources. The seeming lack of concern about vineyard of origin might have been no more than a worldly assumption that the families of the newly powerful administrative class would have their vineyards in privileged sites. But even if that were the case, there is no doubt that Arnaud de Pontac was the first to emphasize the relevance of his vineyard's unique *terroir* to the style and quality of his wine. And, in attaching Haut-Brion's quality and distinction firmly to the site where its grapes were grown, Arnaud de Pontac fathered a model, widely emulated, that is still responsible for Bordeaux's luster three centuries later.

Pontac realized, of course, that his wine would sell at a price to justify the pains he took only if it were distinguished from the general mass. But the urge both to raise quality and to sharpen distinction was itself a response to changed circumstances for Bordeaux wines in London. Despite having lost possession of Bordeaux two centuries before, England remained a vital, if not the principal, market for wine produced there. With the restoration of the English monarchy in 1660, Arnaud de Pontac and other Bordeaux winegrowers had probably looked for a strengthening of that market after years of puritan restraint. But even before the return of Charles II, chocolate and coffee had already made their appearance in London. Encouraged by the king's pleasure-loving court, and by those made rich from the country's mercantile success in winning leadership at sea from the Dutch, the purveyors of these novel and exotic luxuries proliferated and prospered in a city rebuilding itself after the Great Fire of 1666.

London society, euphoric and, to put it bluntly, energetically opportunist, found in coffeehouses not only a revival of political and literary vigor after Cromwell's "grim constraint of compulsory godliness," but the possibility of commercial and financial adventure; some of these meeting places evolved into the embryonic exchanges from which London's financial institutions have sprung, while others ripened into the city's great political and literary clubs. Is it any wonder that fashionable London was seduced from the simple pleasure of a pitcher of Bordeaux wine in a tavern?

To win them back, Pontac sent his son François-Auguste, together with the chef from his own Bordeaux mansion, to open London's first restaurant. It was elegant, expensive, and roaringly successful; and in that perfect setting the Pontacs presented their Haut-Brion wine to a clientele best able to appreciate it, to pay for it, and to further its cause.

Though he could have known little of marketing theory, and even less of its jargon, Arnaud de Pontac had used his wealth, political clout, and social connections to do more than reconstruct and reposition his product: he had transformed it into the very coinage of prestige.

Because Pontac's strategy was quickly adopted by others, he secured the future of the Bordeaux wine trade in providing for the success of Haut-Brion.

The war that erupted between England and France in 1688 was followed by almost two centuries of unrelieved hostility when punitive levels of duty imposed on all French wines, and sometimes their outright ban, restricted availability. Yet so thoroughly had the new style of wine initiated by Pontac captured London's fidelity, that while country squires made do and made merry with the cheaper Port urged on them by the government's new alliance with Portugal, there were always Englishmen willing to pay the high duty, and others prepared to resort to subterfuge, rather than be deprived of Bordeaux.

Americans, after 1776 no longer bound by English policies hostile to France, were free, of course, to do as they pleased with regard to Bordeaux. Thomas Jefferson, standing in 1787 where John Locke had stood a century before him, echoed the philosopher's words in his description of the vineyard at Château Haut-Brion as "sand, in which is near as much round gravel or small stone and a very little loam."

The *terroir* had not changed. But the world had turned with the success of the policies initiated by Arnaud de Pontac. Where once the price of last year's Bordeaux wine had dropped to barely a tenth as soon as wine of the new, and therefore more reliable, vintage was available, Jefferson reported a dramatic annual *increase* in the price of wine as it aged, and as demand responded to its quality.

Wines of the 1783 vintage of the great growths (which by then included Margaux, Lafite and Latour as well as Haut-Brion), he said, "sell now [in 1787] at 2,000 *livres* the tonneau; those of 1784, on account of the superior quality of that vintage, sell at 2,400; those of 1785, at 1,800; those of 1786, at 1,800 tho they sold at first for only 1,500." For comparison, wines of the 1783 vintage had first sold at 1,350 a tonneau, the 1784 at 1,300, and the 1785 at 1,100, while standard red wines of the region then sold for 200 to 300 *livres* a tonneau, a differential that has become only more marked in recent years.

On return to the United States from his tour as ambassador in Paris, Jefferson continued to order wines from Bordeaux, asking the U.S. Consul in Bordeaux in 1790, for example, to arrange a shipment of 85 cases of wine, some for himself and some for George Washington ("packed and marked G.W."). But,

GERALD ASHER

with other priorities and, no doubt, with other tastes, the young republic was not immediately an important customer for Bordeaux. Madeira had attracted lower duties in the English colonies, like Port in England, because of the Anglo-Portuguese alliance and an attachment to Madeira, thus established, stayed with Americans for many years, even when the Crown, and its use of import duties for political ends, had gone from the United States.

The Pontacs' heirs lost Haut-Brion along with their heads at the time of the French Revolution, and although it was eventually restored to their successors, the sustaining continuum had been broken. In 1801 it was sold to Talleyrand, Napoleon's foreign minister, who knew that diplomacy was built on a well-equipped kitchen and a well-stocked cellar. But he was rarely at Haut-Brion, and in selling it to a Paris banker in 1804, Talleyrand set in motion a chain of ownership that swung from banker to merchant. If Arnaud de Pontac had turned commercial instinct to the advantage of his estate, those who then gained control of Haut-Brion too often turned the estate to the advantage of their commercial instinct.

Jullien, in his *Topographie de Tous Les Vins Connus,* complained that Haut-Brion lost its reputation for some years because the vineyards were overfertilized—if true, it was doubtless to boost profitability by raising yields. "But the care of the new proprietor has improved it," he said, "and it has regained its place among the first growths with the 1825 vintage." He was referring, presumably, to Beyerman, a Dutch wine merchant established in Bordeaux, who had taken over the property in 1824.

The estate changed hands again in 1836, however, acquired by Eugène Larrieu, a retired banker, whose son, Amedée, was as devoted to restoring the grandeur of Haut-Brion as Arnaud de Pontac had been in first creating it. So far did he succeed that not only did Haut-Brion retain its rank of First Growth in the 1855 classification still binding today, but by the end of the century its wine could, and did, command prices above those of the other three First Growths—Margaux, Lafite and Latour. The 1899, particularly, opened at a price almost twenty percent above that of Margaux, and had a reputation that still reverberates. Charles Walter Berry of Berry, Bros and Rudd, the London wine merchants, tells in his book *In Search of Wine* of refusing to allow Christian Cruse to order for him a bottle of the

1899 at an impromptu lunch in Paris in 1934 simply because it was "one of the most famous and expensive wines to be bought." (His sense of decorum was rewarded: at a dinner party that same night he was served the 1899 Haut-Brion with a fresh, truffled *pâté de foie gras*. It was, he wrote, "a dream—I would like to be Rip Van Winkle, and take a bottle of this to bed with me.")

A few years ago, I, too, had an opportunity to taste the 1899 Haut-Brion at the climax of three days of tasting and drinking twenty-six vintages of white Haut-Brion ranging from 1985 to 1916 (the Château produces about a thousand cases of white wine a year from a small parcel of Sauvignon Blanc and Semillon vines) and forty-nine vintages of red. Marvin Overton, a Texas surgeon, rancher and wine lover, had organized this mammoth event as his own very original contribution to the 150th anniversary of the state.

He succeeded in proving that Haut-Brion Blanc can be as greatly enjoyed with catfish eaten at a bench in the shade of an open shed as with turbot in a private dining room at Taillevent; and that the red wines of Haut-Brion can be as much at ease as we were with barbecued pig and wild rice, cowboy stew, and make-your-own kebabs in a field full of blue bonnets and longhorn steer.

Above all, Overton succeeded in showing us, with the help of an illuminating commentary from Haut-Brion's director, Jean Delmas, how an Haut-Brion personality—precise, refined and intense, like the sound of a silver flute in the hands of a master—could be traced consistently through all those wines despite the vicissitudes of wars, changes of ownership, and the annual uncertainty of vintage.

Haut-Brion faltered early in this century when ownership passed to two godchildren of the last of the Larrieu family, and ended up as the retirement settlement of André Gibert, a director of the Société des Glacières of Paris. He took control before the 1923 vintage—"a pretty wine, one of the most beautiful of that very charming vintage," according to Maurice Healy, an Irish barrister devoted to the idea that Haut-Brion's name had somehow descended from a seventeenth-century compatriot. Perhaps that explains his serving a series of Haut-Brion vintages at a Saint Patrick's Day dinner in 1931, an occasion when his friend André Simon, founder of the Wine and Food Society, commented that the 1923 was "almost too ready," later qualifying his remark by adding, in his book *Tables of Content*, that "the same thing was said of the 1871s and 1875s; they were ready at a very early date and did last: in fact they are still lasting." The 1871s might indeed have lasted sixty years, but I have to report, with regret, that in 1986 the 1923 had not. The best I can say is that its strangely scented bouquet was not unpleasant.

Gibert's 1924 and 1926 were impressive, however, and have been praised over the years. André Simon, at that same Saint Patrick's Day dinner, had found the 1924 Haut-Brion preceding the 1923 "too green to drink with due respect" but said it showed great promise, and concluded that he would be "very much surprised if it does not turn out to be a very fine wine." (How agreeable to have lived at a time when experienced men refrained, even seven years after the vintage, from being dogmatic about a wine's future. Today, grapes are hardly picked before someone or other is telling us with insolent confidence how a wine will be ten, twenty and thirty years on.) Simon was right about the 1924. It was still superb when we tasted it at Overton's ranch, with the strength and richness of bouquet—vanilla and sealing wax—that I remembered from tasting it on one other occasion, in 1979. But the 1926, though equally forceful, was marred by the dry, hard finish which Edmund Penning-Rowsell, our most distinguished contemporary chronicler of Bordeaux, has described as "typical of that vintage."

Penning-Rowsell could find nothing kinder than "poor" to say about the 1928 Haut-Brion, and gave a head-shaking "not very good" to the 1929. The years must have tempered the 1929; I found it drying out, but fairly full and still deep of hue. Its fading bouquet of plums and violets had a nostalgic charm. Time had done little to help the 1928, however. It too was still big and dark, but its astringency was aggravated by an aftertaste others have described as medicinal but which was most likely mercaptan: an ineradicable smell and taste with sulfur component (that fact alone will help those unfamiliar with it to imagine its effect) most often caused by delay or lack of care in racking a young wine from its lees, an ironic footnote to Arnaud de Pontac's endeavors in this very matter almost three hundred years earlier.

The vintages that followed must have tested sorely whatever commitment André Gibert had to Haut-Brion. After visiting him at the close of 1934, Charles Walter Berry wrote that he wasn't much impressed with the 1933 and would risk saying nothing of the 1934 beyond "it may conceivably be an improvement on the previous vintage." Faint praise, perhaps, yet praise to some extent justified. Of the three vintages of the thirties at our giant tasting, the 1934 was the best, and it had worn better than many of which more had been expected. Nevertheless, Gibert had had enough, and when his offer of the estate as a gift to the city of Bordeaux had been refused, he sold Château Haut-Brion in 1935 to the American banker Clarence Dillon, whose family, still owning and controlling it today, has worked with the tenacity and intelligence of the Pontacs and the Larrieus to restore and extend its reputation.

The first result had to wait until the end of the war, but then the 1945 Haut-Brion was one of the most praised of a much-praised vintage. In Marvin Overton's barn it was still alive, full flavored, and superb. Other successful vintages followed, most especially the 1952 and 1953, the latter an epitome of Haut-Brion's "precise, refined and intense" personality. (Unusually and unfortunately, our bottle of 1953 in Texas was slightly oxidized, and the wine was overwhelmed by the 1952). Neither the 1955 nor the 1959 were as firmly structured as the 1952, but they shared both its scale and the whiff of sealing wax typical of Haut-Brion in its bigger years.

The sixties were a decade of transition at Haut-Brion. In 1960 the Château was the first to install stainless-steel fermenting tanks, the better to control the fundamental process of fermentation, and in 1961 Jean Bernard Delmas succeeded his father Georges as *régisseur*. The modification of style that then occurred was perhaps little more than adaptation to a series of difficult vintages, each of which presented varied problems of some magnitude. On the other hand, could the new tanks have made possible a noticeably leaner, tighter style? Or was it the result of a new philosophical direction given to, and supported by, the particularly able and perceptive new *régisseur*, a man who had been raised at Haut-Brion and understood its significance and potential?

Whatever the cause, from that time a new delicacy and restraint underlined Haut-Brion's precision, refinement and intensity. Though the new style was already obvious in the 1961, it could, and can still, be seen to even greater effect in the 1964—a disappointing year for many Bordeaux properties because of October rain on a late vintage, but a triumph for Haut-Brion.

Though weather conditions in 1972 and 1977 also proved difficult for Bordeaux, in other years of that decade—particularly 1971, 1975 and 1978—they allowed, and even imposed, a more robust, tannic style that has tended to continue, though more as fashion than necessity. It was obvious from the wines tasted at Marvin Overton's, however, that while respecting the more forceful characteristics imposed by those years, Haut-Brion has succeeded both in preserving the personality that evolved over centuries and in retaining its new, faultless elegance of style. The unity of these various strands can be seen most perfectly in the 1971: a seamless wine of impeccable balance that is all the Pontacs, the Larrieus, and the Dillons could have hoped for as justification of their efforts. The 1979, 1981 and, especially, the 1983 seem each to possess similar harmonies of quality.

To crown our last evening with the 1899, we had tasted backwards through the years, delighted that the 1921, the praises of which we had so often read, was still able to flatter with its light cherry color and fresh bouquet and that the 1907, though fading, had retained its Haut-Brion sealing wax hallmark after almost eighty years.

Finally, we came to Charles Walter Berry's dream wine, a wine that Hugh Johnson more recently compared to the pediment of the Parthenon. (It's never difficult to tell when wine fanciers are enthusiastic.) It was faded, of course, but surprisingly fresh and smelled of thyme. The flavor, too delicate to analyze, was astonishingly long. By then, as one might have expected, we were tired and exhilarated, so perhaps I only imagined hearing the voice of Arnaud de Pontac expressing satisfaction.

HERMITAGE AND CROZES-HERMITAGE

On the banks of the Rhône, after its junction with the Saône, and in the adjacent territories, several precious wines are produced: but although the vineyards in these departments may be regarded as among the most ancient in France... it is only in recent times that the merits of their choicest produce have become fully known.

THIS COULD HAVE BEEN WRITTEN YESTERDAY, SO NEW IS OUR REVIVED INTEREST IN WINES OF THE NORTHERN RHÔNE, BUT I'M QUOTING FROM ALEXANDER HENDERSON'S *HISTORY OF ANCIENT AND MODERN WINES*, PUBLISHED IN 1824. Hermitage and Côte-Rôtie—the principal wines Henderson is referring to—were then the rage of London, just as Côte-Rôtie had already been the rage of first-century Rome. Rome had discovered Côte-Rôtie when on business across the river at Vienne, a rich city that flourished in the early years of the empire as the center of its flax trade.

Pliny wrote that the wine of Vienne had a natural taste of pitch, just as some might now refer to a tarry taste in a red wine. Plutarch said it *was* "pitched," suggesting that the taste was not natural at all. It was left to Columella to explain, in *On Agriculture and Trees*, that this special taste of the wine of Vienne, admired above all others by his fellow Romans, came from the bark of a local tree, dried and powdered and added to the wine as a preservative. Evidently even ancient Rome was captivated by the taste of oak in French red wine and was prepared to pay dearly, as many still are today, for an extra dose of it.

Louis XIV of France held the wine of Hermitage in such esteem that he presented some to England's Charles II, his cousin, as a token of royal affection. It was a shrewd move on his part: the canal linking the Rhône valley with Bordeaux (opened for traffic in 1681) made the shipment of Rhône wines to northern Europe as easy as loading a barge. From that auspicious royal beginning Rhône wines found their way to other tables, including, in due course, that of Lord Hervey, Earl of Bristol, eighteenth-century England's arbiter of taste in all matters of wine.

With Lord Hervey's approval, the English took to Hermitage with enthusiasm. By the end of the eighteenth century London merchants were going so far as to blend it openly with the best of their Bordeaux wines, knowing that a dollop of Hermitage in the Lafite increased its appeal—and its value. At the time, advertisements for the wines of some of the great châteaux of Bordeaux listed two prices, the "Hermitaged" wine always being the more expensive.

Hermitage was even more popular in the nineteenth century. Its opulence suited Victorian London's confidence and robust taste in everything from well-aged game and solid mahogany to red-brick Gothic and muscular Empire building. Saintsbury's *Notes on a Cellar Book* was not published until 1920, but his much-quoted reference in it to Hermitage as "the *manliest* French wine I ever drank" is a reflection of that earlier cast of thinking.

The hill on which Hermitage is grown dominates the little town of Tain l'Hermitage, about an hour's drive south from Lyons on the Rhône's east bank. There seems at first to be an exception to the rule that in the northern and central Rhône fine wines are produced only on the granitic bluffs lining the west side of the river, as in Côte-Rôtie, for one, but also Condrieu, Saint-Joseph, Cornas and Saint-Péray. In fact, most of the Hermitage hill was formerly part of that opposite bank, until the Rhône changed its course. The hill is therefore an amalgam, its western side composed of the same rugged granite as Mount Pilat on the west bank of the Rhône and the eastern part a confusion of chalky clay and water-smoothed round stones from what was once the riverbed.

The red wine of Hermitage is made from Syrah grapes. John Busby—the man who took the first cuttings of Syrah vines from Hermitage to Australia in the 1830s (under the name of Shiraz, Syrah has become one of Australia's most widely planted red-wine grapes)—described Hermitage in his journal:

> The hill, though of considerable height, is not of great extent; the whole front which looks to the South may contain 300 acres, but of this, though the whole is under vines, the lower part is too rich to yield those of the best quality, and a part near the top is too cold to bring its produce to perfect maturity. Even of

the middle region, the whole extent does not produce the finest wines.... The gentleman whose property we were traversing pointed out to me the direction in which a belt of calcareous soil crossed the ordinary granitic soil of the mountain, and he said it requires the grapes of these different soils to be mixed, in order to produce the finest quality of Hermitage.

Busby had got to the heart of the matter. The mix of soils on the hill and a southern exposure across the Rhône—the river bends to regain its former course—do indeed give Hermitage its deep and lasting flavor. This combination of soil and sun also accounts for the scale of Hermitage wines, and for the boldness and vigor that prompted Saintsbury's remark. The longevity of all red wines made from the Syrah grape is well known, but nowhere is that quality more evident than in a bottle of Hermitage.

I tasted my first really mature Hermitage at a friend's dinner table in the late fifties. I no longer remember who had produced it, but it was a 1923, and like a vintage port, had thrown a crust against the side of the bottle rather than a loose sediment. The wine was still powerful after thirty-five years, its color dense, its flavor vibrant. Saintsbury probably tasted his manly 1846 Hermitage after it had spent nearly the same number of years in bottle, having bought a case and a half of it in 1878 for consumption at some leisure over the following decades.

In choosing the wine he may have been influenced by Henry Vizetelly, a fellow literary man and one of the most highly regarded judges of wine in late-nineteenth-century England. Just as Saintsbury is better known for his *Notes on a Cellar Book* than for his histories of English and French literature—though these are standard reference works—Vizetelly, too, is remembered for his books on wine rather than for his work as a journalist and publisher. Vizetelly's career was illustrious: it was he (as mentioned earlier) who first dared to publish in England (in English) the works of émile Zola, only to be charged and imprisoned under obscenity laws for his pains in doing so.

But long before that episode Vizetelly had described, in a widely read report on the 1873 Vienna Universal Exhibition, an 1808 Hermitage as "one of those unquestionably grand wines which [has] gone on improving in quality and perfume, and... retained much of its original richness of colour." Saintsbury would

183

have known of other astonishing examples of old Hermitage as well: one of the marvels of the Paris Exhibition of 1862 had been a bottle of 1760 Hermitage still in perfect condition, it was said, after more than a century.

Syrah, the black grape that gives Hermitage and other northern Rhône wines their lasting structure, is almost certainly descended from an indigenous forest vine, despite stories of its origin in far-off Syria or Persia. "Syrah," scholars tell us, refers neither to Syria nor to the city of Shiraz, as some claim, but is a corruption of Serine or Sereine, names still sometimes used for the grape by local growers. Serine, Sereine and Syrah are all based on *ser*, a root word in the ancestry of Indo-European languages meaning, appropriately, "long lasting."

But if Hermitage itself is long-lived, so are the myths that surround it. They include edifying stories of how the hill miraculously brought forth its first wine to assuage the thirst of medieval hermits who allegedly survived there on scraps of nature brought to them by wild birds and animals. (Only a cynic would suggest that scraps of nature found in the cooking pots of hermits living on the hill of Hermitage were likely to have been the wild birds and animals themselves: a partridge, perhaps, or a hare snatched while gamboling too close, having foolishly assumed any friar in a gray habit to be St. Francis himself.)

The most famous of the hermits, indeed the only one reliably documented, was the knight Gaspard de Stérimberg who retired to the hill in 1225 to a "hermitage" that eventually gave the place its name. But even he is enveloped in mystery. The popular image of him as an ascetic soldier piously beating his sword into a plowshare to make wine flow from barren rock to the greater glory of God is certainly appealing but unlikely to be true. Petitioning the crown for the gift of the hill of Saint Christopher (as it then was called), already covered with vineyards that for at least the previous thousand years had been reputed to produce the finest wine in France, was an unusual way for a man to seek a life of self-denial and penitence.

Far more likely was a mutual, if tacit, understanding that de Stérimberg was claiming his due for service rendered the French king in the fight against the Albigensians of the Languedoc—a military conquest disguised as a campaign against religious heresy. The "crusade" was successful in extending French royal power to the Mediterranean and to the Pyrenees. At any rate, de Stérimberg's name is the only reliably documented one to have come down to us, and is now further preserved in the white Hermitage called Chevalier de Stérimberg, made by the firm of Paul Jaboulet Aîné.

The mention of white Hermitage might come as a surprise to some because Hermitage is better known as a red wine. In fact, from a fourth to a third of the wine produced there annually is white, the exact proportion depending on the year's circumstances. It's made from Marsanne and Roussanne vines grown mostly on the eastern, chalkier, part of the hill. Of the two varieties, Marsanne is by far the more widely used; but Roussanne, having lost ground over many years, is gradually being replanted by growers who feel its benefits outweigh the disadvantages. Roussanne had fallen from favor because it both bears less fruit than Marsanne and is more trouble to grow in a region where weather can be unpredictably punishing. Marsanne used alone gives a rich, fat wine with the hazelnut and honey aromas typical of white Hermitage. Roussanne is never used alone, but when added to Marsanne it introduces an exotic flourish, a hint of orange and banana.

The large proportion of Roussanne in Jaboulet's Chevalier de Stérimberg—roughly forty percent—is what makes this wine captivatingly aromatic. Chante-Alouette, the white Hermitage of Jaboulet's rival, M. Chapoutier & Cie., is made from Marsanne alone. It has a richer texture, as one would expect, but is more subdued.

Other interesting white Hermitage wines include those of Gérard Chave, who brings a lift to his by using fifteen percent Roussanne (these percentages should always be taken as approximate, no matter how confidently growers bandy them about) and of Jean-Louis Grippat, who, like Chapoutier, prefers to stay with Marsanne alone. Grippat handles Marsanne with such skill, however, that his wine could serve, year after year, as a textbook example of how good this wine grape can be.

Busby had pointed out that a fine Hermitage is rarely the product of a single soil, no matter how prized the plot might be, but is more usually the result of an assembly of grapes grown on different sections of the hill. (For a red wine the grapes most often are Syrah alone, but occasionally there is a small admixture of white Marsanne to make the wine rounder.) So owners need to hold a diversity of small vineyards on the hill, even if that complicates their work. It's now almost impossible for small growers to spread themselves in this way unless they inherit or marry into land on the hill. Hermitage vineyards are jealously held and keenly sought after. Jaboulet and Chapoutier have an advantage because both houses have such extensive and well-dispersed vineyard holdings.

Although Jaboulet's primary red Hermitage, La Chapelle, and one of Chapoutier's, Monier de la Sizeranne (named for a former owner of one of the firm's prime vineyard sites), have long been considered among the appellation's best, both have fluctuated in quality over the last twenty years. For much of that time Chapoutier's wines were embarrassingly dull. The firm has made a strong recovery since 1988, when the present generation of the Chapoutier family, brothers Marc and Michel, took over. Perhaps lack of adequate competition from Chapoutier allowed Jaboulet to become complacent, but, if that were so, the changes at the rival house have been a spur to their reform.

Helped, it must be admitted, by the extraordinary success of recent vintages, both firms are presently producing red Hermitage wines as good as any of the past, and certainly of a standard Saintsbury would have admired. Their 1990s, by now mostly sold and laid away in private cellars, are massive, to be marvelled at some time in the next century. The 1991s, however, their flavor much more in evidence, are less tannic and will therefore be accessible sooner. My guess is that these friendlier wines will be enjoyable by the end of the decade even if, true to type, they then hold on for very much longer.

Jean-Louis Grippat makes a small amount of red Hermitage—his plot of Syrah on the hill is a mere handkerchief. But Gérard Chave has twenty-five widely dispersed acres of red-wine grapes there and in most years the wine he produces from them is probably the best Hermitage of all, although it might just be that the wine reflects the charm of the man himself. At any rate, no matter whose wine one might prefer, there never is and never can be enough Hermitage to go around. In the U.S., retailers have often sold their annual allocation before it arrives. Even when they haven't, bottles of Hermitage aren't allowed to sit long on a wine merchant's shelf. Those who want good Hermitage know they must seize each vintage when it is first released, for there is rarely a second chance of finding it.

One should have little difficulty, on the other hand, finding a bottle of Hermitage's cousin, Crozes-Hermitage. The vineyards producing it have been expanded from the mere 100 acres existing forty years ago to 2,550 acres today. Before World War II, Crozes-Hermitage came only from vineyards surrounding the village of Crozes, just to the north of Hermitage, to which it was a small and unimportant appendage. But when the Rhône wine appellations were revised in the 1950s Crozes-Hermitage was, in effect, created anew. The hundred acres at Crozes remain part of it, but the Crozes-Hermitage appellation we now know covers ten additional communities to the east and south of Tain l'Hermitage, where the soil, much of it clay-limestone and rolled stones, is a lot like those of the eastern part of Hermitage itself. Unlike Hermitage, however, the area is mostly flat.

In 1956, when Crozes-Hermitage was redefined as a region, it had more fruit trees than vines (cherry and apricot orchards had replaced vineyards there earlier in the century when phylloxera struck). But the introduction of this revised appellation encouraged some farmers to extend their vineyards and others to plant new ones. Expansion into wine grapes on any scale, however, didn't occur until the early sixties, when a wave of expatriates from former French Algeria, diligent farmers and expert grape growers, settled in the area.

At the time when Crozes-Hermitage was virtually synonymous with the village of Crozes, its production hovered around 8,000 cases a year. In 1966, the first year that vines planted by the French Algerians bore fruit, it jumped to a level of 130,000 cases. Taking both red and white wine together, the appellation's annual production is now roughly 500,000 cases.

Though, obviously, no longer the shy and rare little wine it once was, Crozes-Hermitage—both red and white—can be very good. Particularly in Lyons, the red serves as a meatier alternative to Beaujolais, even if Crozes-Hermitage sells at prices closer to the Beaujolais *crus*—Moulin-à-Vent, Fleurie, Juliénas. Until the late 1970s, most Crozes-Hermitage had been produced on behalf of the growers by the wine cooperative at Tain l'Hermitage. But as the region matured, growers, who at first had seen their grapes as just another crop, began to build for themselves small winemaking facilities and to produce their own wine. Often the change occurred when a son reached the age when he could join his father on the property, providing both a reason for adding value to the crop and the possibility of doing so. About a third of the crop, nevertheless, still goes to the cooperative, which does a passably good job with it.

Both Jaboulet and Chapoutier produce red and white Crozes-Hermitage. Jaboulet, with two important estates within the appellation, moved an important part of its wine-making operation to newly built premises at La Roche de Glun, south of Tain l'Hermitage, to be closer to the vineyards. One estate, *Les Jalets*, near the Rhône, produces a big red quaffing wine—in a way similar in style to a wine from the southern Rhône, despite being made from Syrah grapes.

From the other important Jaboulet estate, Domaine de Thalabert, a mature vineyard in a thickly pebbled area farther east, comes a wine with more distinction: the wines of Thalabert have brought Jaboulet numerous (and well-justified) accolades. They age well, and, although a few years in bottle cannot transform even the best Crozes-Hermitage into Hermitage, the Thalabert wines come close. (They cost more than other Crozes-Hermitage wines, too.) A mature Thalabert of a good year develops that medley of aromas sometimes described as old leather and sometimes as dried fruits, but which actually borrows something from each. Jaboulet's white Crozes-Hermitage, La Mule Blanche—made of equal parts of Roussane and Marsanne—is another success for the firm. The 1992, with its bouquet of honey and pears, will certainly claim devotees.

Chapoutier bottles both its red and its white Crozes-Hermitage under the label Les Meysonniers. Like its Chante-Alouette, this white is made solely of Marsanne and is therefore less aromatic than Jaboulet's. But it is fresh and firm when young and with a few years in bottle it acquires that admirable hazelnut quality typical of mature Marsanne wines. The red Les Meysonniers also needs two or three years in bottle to come together. It is a robust wine, and I am told, Chapoutier's fastest-selling brand.

To my taste, however, Alain Graillot, a newcomer to the area, is now producing the most exciting Crozes-Hermitage. His vines were among the first to be planted in the early sixties when the region was being resettled by those returning from Algeria, though Graillot himself acquired them only in the late eighties. Graillot, a Rhône valley native, had dreamed of becoming a winegrower during his years as a businessman traveling extensively in South America. Following a pattern more common in California than in France, he took the plunge and turned his life around, making his first wine in 1985 by buying the grapes from the vineyard he now owns.

Graillot is passionate about his wines, sometimes described as the most "expressive" of the appellation. They appeal to me because of their perfect balance, their consistently well-knit harmony, and their unexpected profundity (they are so forward, so open, so fruity that one doesn't hope to find *yet more*). I wonder what George Saintsbury would have had to say?

189

WASHINGTON STATE REDS:
MERLOT AND CABERNET SAUVIGNON

ONE OF AMERICA'S BEST BUT PERHAPS LEAST-KNOWN CABERNET SAUVIGNONS—
QUILCEDA CREEK—IS PRODUCED IN A CONVERTED GARAGE BEHIND ALEX GOLITZIN'S
SUBURBAN HOUSE NEAR SNOHOMISH, NORTH OF SEATTLE. Another—Woodward
Canyon—is produced in Lowden at the opposite end of the state, in what had
been a busy tool shop until Rick Small's winemaking overflowed the limited capacity of an adjacent shed and forced his family to find space elsewhere for their business of repairing broken plows and crippled farm tractors. In domestic basements;
in the outbuildings of remote farms; in the kind of small, rented industrial warehouses where enterprise is born all over America; as well as in the spacious tank
and barrel halls of Château Ste Michelle, the state's largest and best-heeled winery, a considerable number of outstanding Cabernet Sauvignon and Merlot wines
are now being produced. This is all the more astonishing when one realizes that
twenty-five years ago no more than twenty-one acres of Cabernet Sauvignon
vines—and no Merlot at all—were planted in the state of Washington.

Though there is still a great deal of map reading to be done—few growers
are yet entirely agreed on the characteristics to be expected from grapes grown on
this ridge as opposed to that—the quality and style of Washington's red wines are
largely matters of topography. The vineyards are mostly on the southerly slopes
of a series of east-west folds in the vast Columbia Basin—the Cascade Range on
one side, the Rockies on the other—with the advantage of a latitude more northerly
than California's (it is roughly Bordeaux's, actually), which adds an hour or two
of sunlight each day of the growing season. Behind the Cascades there is little of
the tempering influence of the Pacific, but most of the vineyards are at altitudes
that escape the extremes of eastern Washington's summer heat.

The additional hours of daylight ensure grapes with good sugar and ripe flavor, while moderated temperatures help preserve their fresh acidity. Thanks to the meager soils of the Columbia Basin—for millennia they had been virtually barren—growers can control the vigor that elsewhere so often leads to leafy excess and green, stemmy flavors in Merlot and Cabernet Sauvignon. As a result the wines are aromatic and richly textured, sometimes densely colored and tannic, with concentrated and lingering flavors suggesting apricot and plum—more like prune in a hot year like 1990—rather than the blackcurrant, mint, and eucalyptus so often associated with the Cabernet Sauvignons of California. Taste is subjective, of course, but however one might describe them, these red Washington wines come across with elegance and audacity.

In the last few years, while wine sales generally in the United States wavered, sales of Washington State wines more than doubled from roughly 2.5 million gallons in 1987 to more than 6 million in 1994. In all that time, and for long before, the state's Johannisberg Rieslings and Chardonnays have been particularly popular, both inside the state and out. In response to the expanding demand for white wines in the mid- to late-1970s, growers planted Johannisberg Riesling because it was thought to be the variety best adapted to eastern Washington's harsh winters. For a time, more of the state's acreage was devoted to Johannisberg Riesling than to any other grape, though Chardonnay, another winter-hardy variety, has now taken the lead.

The demand for white wines has greatly influenced many decisions over the past twenty years, but Washington growers and producers have also been drawn all along to the black grapes classically associated with Bordeaux, particularly Cabernet Sauvignon and Merlot. It was as if these varieties represented a yardstick against which a new wine region had to measure itself. Even before the magic wand of the so-called French Paradox had its effect (research here and in France revealed a few years ago that the French, who consume mountains of cheese, butter, cream, and *foie gras*, have a low mortality rate from cardiovascular disease, apparently explicable only in terms of their attachment to red wine), demand for Washington State red wines exceeded their availability. Even Château Ste Michelle is obliged to distribute its Merlot by strictly apportioned allocations.

The growers and producers are delighted. "Washington will always be known for its white wines," Mike Januik, Château Ste Michelle's winemaker, said to me recently, "but I think there's now even greater respect for our reds."

There have been vines in Washington for more than a century. Lambert Evans, a Civil War veteran, established the first vineyard of any consequence on Stretch Island in Puget Sound in the 1870s, using native American vines—labrusca—brought from the East Coast. But coastal Washington, for the most part, has always been too wet for grapes. The eastern half of the state, on the other hand, lying in the rain shadow of the Cascades, was mostly too dry. Its landscape and economy were changed early in this century, however, by irrigation programs that turned the region green with fields of grain, potatoes, and alfalfa. There are now fruit orchards—apples, cherries and peaches—hop gardens, and vineyards. The first vines in Yakima were again labrusca, but even before Prohibition the fruit was being shipped for making grape juice and jelly rather than wine.

Yakima farmers had preferred labrusca to vinifera, fearing that European wine-grape varieties would not survive their harsh winters. Once Prohibition was over, there were, however, a brave few who planted vinifera anyway, starting with William Bridgeman, one of Yakima valley's pioneers in irrigated agriculture. He established a vineyard and a winery in 1934, and despite dire predictions the vines didn't fail. But the winery did, alas; so the Bridgeman grapes disappeared into the blended and fortified wines that kept Washington's state-controlled distribution system going after Prohibition.

The Harlan family also planted vinifera in the Yakima valley, its grapes including, as of 1957, Washington's first block of Cabernet Sauvignon. Named for Otis Harlan, the vineyard still flourishes on the south slope of Rattlesnake Ridge, above the Yakima River. The family's Cabernet was a harbinger, though, that went unnoticed at first. "There was almost no interest in producing table wines in Washington. There weren't many people in the state who even owned a corkscrew," Otis Harlan told me recently. "Those of us who planted vinifera were clearly ahead of our time."

But the Harlans' time came soon enough. Interest in vinifera gathered momentum in Washington in the 1960s, a decade that saw a steady increase in table wine sales in most parts of the United States. A group of businessmen who had acquired American Wine Growers, a Washington company producing until then mostly fruit juices and labrusca wines, bought the original Bridgeman vinifera vineyard as well; they had doubtlessly been encouraged by experimental programs with vinifera at Washington State University. American Wine Growers released its first vinifera wines, among them a Cabernet Sauvignon, in 1967 and evolved into the highly visible Château Ste Michelle.

Another group—this one of amateur winemakers from the higher ranks of academia—was incorporated in 1962 under the name Associated Vintners and then acquired, in 1964, a five-acre vineyard of vinifera vines at Sunnyside, again in the Yakima Valley. By 1967 this group, too, was ready to release its first vinifera wines, which also included a Cabernet Sauvignon. Associated Vintners placed emphasis on Cabernet Sauvignon, buying, in 1969, the entire crop of the Harlans' Otis Vineyard and bottling it as a separate, single-vineyard Cabernet Sauvignon.

Associated Vintners was renamed Columbia Winery long ago now, but has continued to make an Otis Vineyard Cabernet Sauvignon every year. The first, the 1969, was a turning point for wine in Washington. The following vintages demonstrated that red wine from a single vineyard could be consistent and there-fore reasonably predictable. Consistency—predictability, in fact—is at the heart of any definition of a great wine, but this broader implication for Washington Cabernet Sauvignon was eclipsed by the dramatic consequences of the 1969 repeal of the state's protectionist tax structure.

Imposed after Prohibition, ostensibly to allow a Washington wine indus-try to develop free from "foreign" (namely, California) competition, the tax had actually done no more than encourage in-state wineries to produce large quantities of cheap, sweet, fortified wines. In 1968, the last year of the tax privilege, there had been only about four hundred acres of vinifera in all of Washington, and much of that was merely Muscat, Thompson Seedless, Alicante Bouschet and Palomino. Within three years of the law's repeal, there were close to twelve hundred acres of vinifera, including almost two hundred of Cabernet Sauvignon and more than thirty of Merlot. The acreage of vinifera was to go on increasing sharply even though (or perhaps because) many of the old wineries, except for the newborn Columbia and the reborn Château Ste Michelle, had by then disappeared.

The vinifera vineyards planted in the 1970s were scattered over a wide area. No one could say with certainty, after all, which locations were best suited for the purpose; and, even when technical data supported the planting of vines, there was no history to back them up. Advice given freely by Walter Clore, director of the viticultural research program at Washington State University, has turned out to have been pretty sound. Nonetheless, many growers had little to guide them except the basic principle of establishing a vineyard on a south-facing slope steep enough to allow cold winter air—more dense and therefore heavier—to drain away.

Seen on a map, the spread of Washington's vineyards seems to be strangely centrifugal until one remembers that a few hundred square miles at the heart of the Columbia Valley Viticultural Area are closed off for the Hanford Reservation, a nuclear site of the U.S. Department of Energy. The images of nuclear energy don't really jibe with the romance of vineyards and vintners, hence the Great White Space always left unidentified in the wine books, maps and brochures. But the site's physical presence cannot be wished away. It's because of Hanford that the Wahluke Slope seems so disconnected from the cluster of vineyards much farther south; without it Washington's vineyards would seem to be more compact and would therefore be easier to "read."

As things are, the officially designated Columbia Valley Viticultural Area (which incorporates both Yakima valley to the west and the Walla Walla valley to the southeast, though both are also recognized viticultural areas in their own right) is large and amorphous. To give some idea of scale, the Wahluke Slope, by no means at the northern limit of the Area, is roughly sixty miles from Canoe Ridge, the newest vineyard in the south. The rather isolated Red Willow Vineyards, far to the west in the upper Yakima valley, is about a hundred miles from Gordon Brothers' equally isolated vineyard far to the east on the Snake River. The greatest concentration of vineyards is found in a broad central band that stretches from the middle section of the Yakima valley between Wapato and Prosser to Sagemoor Vineyards, Balcom and Moe Vineyard, and other, smaller, vineyards dispersed over the Pasco Basin (sometimes, confusingly, called the Columbia Basin), above the confluence of the Columbia and Snake Rivers.

It is still too soon, many say, to categorize the varied vineyard locations. Yet every winemaker knows what he or she expects from where even if the characteristics of a particular vineyard are as much a reflection of vine age and cultivation practices as they are of soil and microclimate. And there are sufficient instances of several adjacent vineyards of different age and under different care producing similar fruit for conclusions to be drawn with regard to a probable link between style and location.

Grapes from the vineyards on Red Mountain—Kiona, Klipsun, Tapteal, and Ciel de Cheval, for instance—are generally accepted as giving powerful wines, well colored, intense and tannic, whereas Gordon Brothers Vineyard on the Snake River can be relied on for Cabernet Sauvignon with ripe, vivid fruit flavors. The Wahluke Slope is known for big, supple Cabernet Sauvignons and plump, fruity Merlots. Cold Creek, the inappropriately named vineyard estate developed north of the Rattlesnake Hills in the 1970s by Château Ste Michelle, gives big Merlots also, as well as an expansive Cabernet Sauvignon, both now bottled as single vineyard wines. Cabernet Sauvignon from Red Willow is intense and can be austere when young. But it ages well (I recently had the chance to taste a splendid 1981). The same variety grown in the Horse Heaven Hills south of the Yakima valley usually shows no more than medium tannins, and farther south towards Paterson, where Columbia Crest has its estate vineyard, the tannins are milder still.

Any wine made even partly with Cabernet Sauvignon grown on the old block of the Mercer Vineyard on Phinney Hill in the Horse Heaven Hills will, however, have a style all its own—a hint of violets in the aroma, intense flavor, graceful proportions—no matter who makes it. No one knows whether this is because the vineyard slopes eastward rather than towards the south or because Phinny Hill is what geologists call a "steptoe." Named for the man who first identified them, these strange, smooth mounds remain from formations that predate what is thought to have been the most powerful and extensive flood ever to have occurred in all of geological history, following an Ice Age melt. If Cabernet Sauvignon vineyard sites in Washington were one day to be classified, the Phinney Hill block of the Mercer Vineyard would quite probably head the list as the Lafite of Washington State. It's surely more than coincidence that three of the state's finest

Cabernet Sauvignons—Quilceda Creek, Woodward Canyon and Andrew Will—all include an important proportion of grapes grown in the Mercer Ranch vineyard.

Apart from Mercer Vineyard, the most reliably balanced Cabernet Sauvignon fruit is found on the south slope of Yakima's Rattlesnake Ridge, especially on that part of it known as the Roza plateau, site of the original irrigation program. Even there, however, styles vary slightly with altitude and depth of soil.

East of the Columbia, the Sagemoor vineyard is recognized not only for the balance of its Cabernet Sauvignon and Merlot but also for their structure. The grapes give firm, well-shaped wines. Cabernet Sauvignon and Merlot from the Balcom and Moe Vineyard and from Preston, farther into the Pasco Basin, are richer, thanks to slightly warmer temperatures, and have a more intense varietal character, perhaps because of the deeper, alluvial soils there.

Seven Hills Vineyard, within the Walla Walla viticultural area but across the Oregon state line, is known for the concentrated, cedary quality of its fruit. Its Cabernet Sauvignon and Merlot are among the region's best. Charbonneau Vineyard, between Walla Walla and the Snake River, also makes concentrated and highly perfumed Cabernet Sauvignon—concentration and intense aroma seem to be characteristic of the Walla Walla area in general—most of which goes, with the vineyard's Merlot, to Rick Small of Woodward Canyon Winery for his Charbonneau Red. And Canoe Ridge, an area perched above the Columbia River and developed only recently by Château Ste Michelle and the Chalone Group out of California, is now beginning to yield its first wines—well flavored and youthfully accessible, much as those from Columbia Crest's vineyards, only a few miles distant.

While some Washington winemakers emphasize single-vineyard wines, most prefer to blend, to bring together grapes with characteristics that complement each other—some Sagemoor, for example, to give structure to grapes from the Wahluke Slope, or Rattlesnake Ridge fruit to lend elegance to the power of Red Mountain. They blend to temper the balance of the finished wine, but as winemakers have different objectives, different styles in mind, blending also allows them to develop and maintain a winery identity.

The characteristics of certain regions, of specific vineyards, stamp a wine, however, and similarities among wines that include grapes from common vineyard sources are unmistakable. In fact, once familiar with the styles characteristic of the regions, one begins to form expectations of a wine just from being told its grape sources. As in other wine regions of the world, the higher the quality of the wine, the easier it is to recognize its origin; character and quality usually going together. The Quilceda Creek, Andrew Will, and Woodward Canyon trio present a case in point (interestingly, Andrew Will, like, Quilceda Creek, had been supporting its Mercer Ranch fruit with grapes from Red Mountain, and is now obtaining an additional, though limited, supply from Walla Walla, near Woodward Canyon).

Other producers of good Cabernet Sauvignon in which grape origins contribute boldly to the style of the wine include Barnard Griffin (Wahluke Slope and Pasco Basin), Bookwalter (Wahluke Slope and Sagemoor), Washington Hills (the winery's Apex blend is based on Wahluke Slope and Rattlesnake Ridge), and Covey Run (Rattlesnake Ridge and Red Mountain). Even without tasting, one knows that Wahluke Slope grapes must fatten the elegant Rattlesnake Ridge balance of the Apex Cabernet Sauvignon, while Red Mountain fruit will bring tannic strength to that of Covey Run. Hyatt Vineyards brings in grapes from the Roza plateau (balance, finesse) and from Red Mountain (tannin, power) to enrich the qualities (depth, concentration of flavor) of its own estate fruit grown at Zillah, in central Yakima valley. Gary Figgins, of Leonetti Cellars, one of the most celebrated of Washington's wine producers, relies on grapes from the Portteus vineyard at Zillah, and on grapes from Sagemoor, to add further density and structure, respectively, to the Cabernet Sauvignon he makes from Walla Walla grapes grown in the Pepper Bridge and Seven Hills vineyards.

Other producers, concerned more with what each region can contribute to a blend than with the preservation and balancing of regional characteristics, draw grapes from an even broader range of sources. Staton Hills, for example, while relying predominantly on Rattlesnake Ridge grapes, buys fruit from vineyards on Red Mountain, in the Horse Heaven Hills (including the Mercer Ranch), in the Pasco Basin and on the Wahluke Slope; and The Hogue Cellars, one of the state's most successful vintners, buys Cabernet Sauvignon and Merlot from just

197

about everywhere, including the Wahluke Slope, the Roza plateau, Red Mountain, Pasco Basin and both Sagemoor and Gordon Brothers vineyards.

Indications of origin are most obvious, needless to say, in single-vineyard wines. The Columbia Winery is unusual in producing not only the Otis Vineyard Cabernet Sauvignon but two others as well, one of them a Cabernet Sauvignon from Red Willow, a vineyard planted in the late 1960s and early 1970s (in which a proportion of Cabernet Franc has now introduced a more forward fragrance), and the other a Cabernet Sauvignon from Sagemoor vineyard, first planted in 1973. Sagemoor is an important vineyard source for many producers, but only Columbia vinifies grapes grown there as a single-vineyard wine.

Other single-vineyard wines include the Cabernet Sauvignon made by Hyatt Vineyards from a block of vines planted at River Bend, near Red Mountain, in 1961; Gordon Brothers' Merlot and Cabernet Sauvignon from vines planted by the family in 1980 on a hillside facing directly south to the Snake River; and the densely concentrated Cabernet Sauvignon made by Paul Portteus from vines on his family's vineyard at Zillah. In 1989 and 1990 Columbia Crest's Barrel Select Cabernet Sauvignon was a single-vineyard wine—from the Andrews Vineyard in the Horse Heaven Hills—but one knew this only from reading the back label. From the 1992 vintage on, Columbia Crest will be using grapes from their own estate vineyard in the Horse Heaven Hills.

Occasionally a wine made from grapes of a single vineyard carries no indication of the fact because there are years when it might incorporate grapes from other sources. Silver Lake Winery's 1992 Merlot, for example, was made entirely from grapes grown in the Thonney Vineyard on Rattlesnake Ridge, in accordance with a pattern established over many years. The 1990 Merlot, however, included grapes from the Boushey Vineyard, lower down the hill from Thonney, because in that rather hot year the Thonney Merlot, taken from old vines planted in meager, shallow soil, was too concentrated to be used alone. "It needed the softening effect of the Boushey fruit," Cheryl Jones, Silver Lake's winemaker, explained to me. (Some Boushey Merlot goes to Hyatt Vineyards, but much of it normally goes to Kay Simon and Clay Mackey of Chinook, who blend it with Merlot from another vineyard nearby. They give backbone to the tender Boushey style by adding a little Cabernet Sauvignon from Red Mountain, and intensify its aroma with a touch of Cabernet Franc from their own estate vineyard. Most Washington Cabernet Sauvignons and Merlots benefit, in fact, from a little admixture of the opposite variety.)

Yakima River Winery's reserve bottlings of Cabernet Sauvignon are made exclusively from fruit grown in the Tapteal Vineyard, the highest on Red Mountain. (The winery uses Tapteal grapes for its regular Cabernet Sauvignon, too, blended with fruit from the Crawfords Vineyard on the Roza plateau.) Preston Premium Wines makes an estate-bottled Merlot from its vineyards in the Pasco Basin, and Kiona Vineyards produces a Merlot from fruit grown on its own Red Mountain estate combined with fruit brought in from the Wahluke Slope and from the lower Yakima valley. "We buy additional fruit," Scott Williams, of Kiona Vineyards, told me, "to soften and lighten the character of Red Mountain and to give the wine a fresh berry aroma." Anyone specially interested in coming to grips with the character of a particular site could try comparing the Merlot and Cabernet Sauvignon produced by Latah Creek from vines in the same vineyard on the Wahluke Slope, or the same two varietal bottlings from the Gordon Brothers' vineyard on the Snake River. Or the Merlot and Cabernet Sauvignon wines made by Château Ste Michelle from grapes grown in their Cold Creek Vineyard.

Château Ste Michelle's expanded program of single-vineyard wines (previous offerings were sporadic) has been made possible by the special design of its new red-wine facility on Canoe Ridge. The presses, vats and tanks there have been designed to handle grapes in small lots. Starting with wines of the 1992 vintage released in 1995, Château Ste Michelle will offer every year a Merlot and a Cabernet Sauvignon from its Cold Creek Vineyard (as well as a Cabernet Franc, which, at present anyway, is available only at the winery's retail shop), as well as a Merlot from its Indian Wells vineyard on the Wahluke Slope.

It's specially fitting, somehow, that Château Ste Michelle should have made this move. It completes a circle begun in 1934 when William Bridgeman planted his vineyard in Yakima valley. If that was the first step on the road to Washington's present success with single-vineyard wines, it was also there and then that Château Ste Michelle, through American Wine Growers, can be said to have been born.

SAUTERNES: THE SWEET LIFE

O<small>N WHAT WAS ALREADY A PLEASANT ENOUGH DAY IN THE SPRING OF 1989, I</small> WALKED FROM MY APARTMENT ON SAN FRANCISCO'S RUSSIAN HILL DOWN TO AMELIO'S RESTAURANT TO TASTE SAUTERNES. Including four served with lunch, there were eighteen wines produced in various years from 1929 to 1986 by two first-growth properties: Château Rieussec and Château Lafaurie-Peyreguey. I couldn't remember when I had last had such an opportunity. For some reason, Sauternes are seldom offered for tasting, even in twos and threes.

In addition to Sauternes itself, four villages produce this traditionally plump, sweet wine: Fargues, Preignac, Bommes and Barsac. Together they make up the extreme end of the Graves, about twenty-five miles southeast of Bordeaux, up the Garonne River.

Wines made in this tiny region have long been distinguished from those of the rest of the Graves by being anything from mildly sweet to lusciously rich. There is a popular belief that the wines were dry until the mid-19th century, when the potential of *Botrytis cinerea*, the fungus known as "noble rot," was fully recognized. In fact, it is obvious from texts published long before that these wines were unequivocally sweet from at least the beginning of the 19th century and possibly earlier. André Jullien wrote in 1816, in his *Topographie de Tous les Vignobles Connus*, that "the grapes [for Sauternes] are not picked until they are touched by rot and their skin, having turned brown, sticks to the fingers. This means the vintage often lasts two months, especially in the growths which produce the wines of superior quality."

He does not suggest that there is anything new in this, and we can therefore assume that young Sauternes, at least, has tasted much as it does today for at least two hundred years. Other writers of the period refer to Sauternes wines being kept in cask for several years before bottling, however, and becoming less sweet in the process. What is more likely is that the wine would have seemed less sweet in becoming acrid with oxidation and bitter with excess wood tannins.

Botrytis cinerea, pourriture noble to the French, is a fungus that attacks the supple skin of fully ripe grapes when moistened by morning humidity. Hairlike filaments pierce the softened grape skin to draw sustenance, thereby allowing a rapid dehydration of the grape. Apart from concentrating sugar and mineral traces, botrytis provokes other changes, too: modification of the acids, a rich endowment of glycerol, and the formation of an antibiotic called botryticin that later will slow down fermentation to a point of helping arrest it and thus leave a considerable richness of unfermented grape sugar in the wine.

Semillon, one of the two principal white grape varieties used for Sauternes, accepts botrytis easily; but the fungus lives precariously on Sauvignon Blanc, a variety with more delicate tissue, where botrytis easily turns to destructive gray rot.

Botrytis does not infect a vineyard evenly, unfortunately, nor even individual bunches. It spots here and there, and spreads gradually. The only way to take best advantage of its presence is to pick over the same vineyard repeatedly, taking the crop berry by berry if necessary, selecting only those fully shrivelled to a suede-like texture. It is the severe loss of volume from dehydration and the immense labor costs of sending pickers back into the vineyards repeatedly over several weeks that make Sauternes such an expensive wine to produce. The business risks are considerable, too. In a dry year or one in which botrytis, for any number of reasons, does not adequately develop, the wine will be at best rather dull. Worse, rain after the botrytis has taken hold can rapidly turn it to rot of the most ignoble kind and so lead to a total loss of the crop.

Significantly, though the United Kingdom took much of Bordeaux's best red wine throughout the 19th century, the British obsession with Port as a dessert wine left little room for Sauternes. That is why, with Port in pride of place, Sauternes has figured so little in British wine literature. The British simply couldn't make up their minds what to do with it.

Saintsbury, in his Notes on a Cellar Book, writes of drinking Château d'Yquem with red mullet, and the cantankerous Charles Tovey, in *Wine and Wine Countries, A Record and Manual for Wine Merchants and Wine Consumers*, published in London in 1862, confirms that the British so misunderstood Sauternes that they seemed to value it the more, the less it had of those specific sweet qualities for which it was prized everywhere else.

And it *was* prized. For a time successful vintages of Sauternes fetched prices to match those of the most-prestigious classed growths of the Médoc. It is part of wine history, for instance, that Grand Duke Constantine of Russia paid more for a hundred cases of Château d'Yquem 1847 than had ever, until then, been paid for any Bordeaux wine, white or red. Yet Tovey, at roughly that same period, after acknowledging the special virtues of Château d'Yquem, goes on to say: "For England, however, we think that the peculiar sweetness which characterizes it, renders it less suitable to the general taste, which is rather in favour of dry wine. We, therefore, think it better to recommend to English consumers the best Barsac Wines, which are more alcoholic, have more body and flesh, taste drier, and offer all the requisite qualities of the climate of the country." He concludes with words in which one can almost hear him sniff at the absurd pretensions of a mere grand duke of Russia. "We might almost certainly affirm, that were it not for its name, Château Yquem Wine would very seldom be preferred to Latour Blanche, Coutet, or Climens, and particularly by English gentlemen." (Barsac wines, it should be said, are still thought to be less unctuously heavy, less rich than other Sauternes. They have a better balance of acidity.)

Tovey and his English gentlemen notwithstanding, demand elsewhere for these extraordinary, and extraordinarily expensive, dessert wines could not be met from their limited production. Thanks to Louis Pasteur's work on bacteria and yeast, however, any producer of white wine in Bordeaux knew, by the end of the 19th century, how to halt the fermentation process with a dose of sulfur dioxide. This left in the wine enough residual sugar to satisfy those who allowed themselves to believe that if Bordeaux's greatest white wines were sweet, then a sweet white Bordeaux must be great.

Shortages in the aftermath of phylloxera and of two world wars made consumers less particular in what they drank, so it took time for these mawkish wines to be rejected. But then, Sauternes, confused with its cheap imitations, was discarded along with them. Except for a short spell following World War II, when Sauternes was in such demand that many of the 1947 classed growths were sold at prices well above those asked for the classed growths of the Médoc, Sauternes became so unfashionable that its market virtually disappeared. Many growers there ripped out their Semillon and Sauvignon Blanc vines and replaced them with red varieties, preferring to produce humdrum but at least comparatively risk-free and saleable Bordeaux Rouge.

Numerous properties, neglected and badly in need of capital improvements, were sold—many of them to Bordeaux wine merchants who were in a position to place a certain quantity of Sauternes with their international clientele and some to foreign buyers who bought the properties less as agricultural investments than as desirable places to live. The newcomers liked the diffident charm of the Sauternes countryside.

The Médoc had burst on the world in the eighteenth century but had made money in the nineteenth. With rare exceptions the houses there—the *châteaux*—were erected with the opulent pomp of most of that century. Sauternes properties, on the other hand, scattered along narrow, twisting lanes leading nowhere in particular, had begun much earlier—sometimes in the thirteenth and fourteenth centuries—as fortified manors. Some, like Château de Malle and Château Suduiraut, were subsequently replaced by modestly scaled but exquisitely perfect seventeenth-century country houses. Elsewhere, creeper-clad towers and respectably decayed crenellations now adorn rather than defend houses as serene as dovecots. Yet others stand as plain and as chaste as Jane Austen parsonages, each presiding calmly over a courtyard indistinguishable from that of any other French farmhouse.

The wines of these revived properties began to recapture attention. Consumers came once again to realize that where sweetness in an ordinary wine might be the sum of all it could offer, in Sauternes it is merely the backdrop to a far greater complex of qualities. In fact, it is a mistake to make too much of a Sauternes' natural sweetness. That leads to overpowering it with rich desserts when its lusciousness is best brought out, in fact, by playing down the food that accompanies it.

Especially to be avoided are rich, creamy pastries. Unadorned fresh pineapple will make the wine itself taste richer and fuller, and so will minimally sweetened fruit served with vanilla yogurt instead of cream. An old Sauternes, like the 1937 Lafaurie-Peyreguey we tasted that morning, its sweetness faded to a patina of honey and praline, is best served with nothing more assertive than one of the plain whole-meal cookies the English call digestive biscuits. Jackie Robert, chef and coproprietor at Amelio's, had his own way of making sure that no creamy dessert would diminish the deliciousness of a magnum of Rieussec '67 served at the close of that lunch. To accompany pears poached in red wine he had prepared, instead of whipped cream, an artfully flavored mousse based on cooked, dried beans. (It had not been his intention, but the bean mousse caused such a sensation that it stole the show.)

The Sauternes proprietors, nervous at what was thought to be a lack of interest in desserts in a diet-stricken age, have pointed out, over the years, other ways in which Sauternes can be used. In France, where sweet aperitifs are common, a glass of young Sauternes is not considered out of place before a meal; and the marriages of Sauternes with *foie gras* at the beginning of a meal and with Roquefort—or any other creamy blue cheese—at the end are as traditional as lamb and Pauillac. An older Sauternes, one in which the sweetness is cracking a little and the flavor is nostalgic rather than vigorous, can be delicious with smoked fish—smoked salmon, smoked trout, or that newly rediscovered plebeian treat, smoked mackerel.

However, there is a problem in using Sauternes of any age as an opening wine or with a first course: It can wreck any red wine chosen to follow it, and a following dry white wine has no chance at all. I have noticed that Pierre Castéja, owner of Château Doisy-Védrines at Barsac, always inserts an intermediary course with an inconsequential red of a light vintage between a young Doisy-Védrines offered with *foie gras* and a more important red he might have chosen to accompany a filet of beef or a leg of lamb. Generally in Bordeaux, however, a cup of consommé will appear after Sauternes and *foie gras*, to give everyone a fresh start.

At our lunch and tasting in San Francisco I was impressed by the consistency of style in the wines of each property through the succession of vintages offered. The Lafaurie-Peyreguey showed the same somewhat angular firmness of structure from the 1929 to the 1986, while the Rieussec, in contrast, displayed throughout a characteristic fullness. I remembered, as I chatted with my hosts, how frequently I go to Bordeaux yet how seldom to Sauternes, and I resolved that on a visit to France planned for the following month I would spend a few days in Bordeaux and go nowhere but to Sauternes. There would be no side-tracking to the Médoc, I promised myself, not even for a peep at the new vintage.

And that is what I did, to be rewarded by tasting the 1988 Sauternes, the most thrilling vintage there since 1961; by tasting again the 1986s, distinguished but less voluptuous than the 1988s will be; and by the pleasure of confirming my earlier impressions of the 1983s—tender now, with expansive aromas of peach and hazelnut.

Sauternes classed growths, after years in a slump, are now selling at much the same prices as Médoc growths of comparable quality. Since the 1987 vintage, Lafaurie-Peyreguey has therefore been able to afford to put half the crop in new barrels each year. (Quality wine can command money but making it needs money too.) Michel Laporte, the estate manager, thinks half new wood is the right proportion: "I like the aroma of new wood, but I don't want it to dominate the wine." In his concern for fruit, Laporte told me, he starts each harvest by picking the Sauvignon Blanc in his vineyards before it can attract botrytis in order to allow the wine benefit of the full flavor of this varietal.

The *chais* (as the winery buildings attached to a Bordeaux vineyard are called) at Lafaurie-Peyreguey are air-conditioned, so Laporte can barrel-ferment the wines in a temperature-controlled environment. When the fermentation is over he draws the wines off the deposited mass of dead yeast, assembles them into one homogeneous *cuvée* and then returns them to their cleaned barrels to age. Having tried a modern horizontal press for a number of years, Laporte has returned to using a small, old-fashioned, hydraulic upright. But then each lot is small here: even in an average year pickers go through the vineyards five or six times, selecting only those berries in perfect condition. In 1988 there were seven separate pickings over the same blocks of vines.

205

At lunch we ate lamprey, the Gironde's rich, eel-like fish (eating a surfeit of which had brought King John of England to his unfortunate end), cooked in Sauternes and served with Lafaurie-Peyreguey 1984—a light, fragrant wine that caused few problems for the Clos des Jacobins 1979, a Saint-Emilion slipped in as a buffer before the Château Talbot 1978 that accompanied a traditional *entrecôte* steak *à la bordelaise* (smothered in minced shallots), served with a dish of *cèpes*. It was intended, obviously, that I should carry away a memory of how well Sauternes will fit with a rich fish, because no Sauternes was served with the dessert of strawberries.

Charles Chevallier, then technical director of Château Rieussec, told me that soil dictated the use of Muscadelle, a third variety of grape still sometimes used in Sauternes. Though few growers include it now, there is still a small lot of it at Rieussec. Its wine is usually of good strength, he told me, and because Muscadelle is a member of the Muscat family of vines, it extends the perfume of the wine when it is still young. The fruit of Muscadelle ripens quickly and attracts botrytis well. Otherwise, varietal proportions at Rieussec are eighty percent Semillon and eighteen percent Sauvignon Blanc.

Half of Chevallier's barrels are new each year now, he told me, more than was the case a few years ago. But the proportion of new barrels, as far as he is concerned, has less to do with the taste of new wood than with wine-making hygiene. "I like the note of vanilla new wood gives," he said, "that's all. But old barrels pick up maladies, inevitably, and it is best not to go on reusing them." He does not ferment his wine in barrel, preferring the greater control of fermenting in vats before racking the wine into barrel for aging.

By way of aperitif before dinner in a local restaurant, we tasted the wines of the 1975 and 1978 vintages: the 1978 light but mature, the 1975 dense and richly flavored. At table we continued ecumenically with a Puligny-Montrachet '86 with salmon, and Vieux Château Certan '70 both with the lamb and with the cheese that followed it. The Rieussec '75, especially, had left me with the impression of starting dinner with a Rossini overture.

The following morning I had an appointment with Patrick Eymery, estate manager of Château Rayne-Vigneau. I have a certain attachment to this property, though I had never before visited it. Many years ago, in the late fifties or early sixties, I bought a close-out lot of fifteen or twenty cases of half bottles of Rayne-Vigneau '23. For years it was the wine we served with a compote or a fruit tart once or twice a week at the end of office lunches. It is years now since I last tasted the 1923, and I am not sure if I would still recognize it. If I did, it would be at least as evocative for me as Proust's *madeleine* dipped in linden-flower tea.

I had heard that Rayne-Vigneau had been in the high-tech vanguard in recent years, and Eymery confirmed that he, unlike Michel Laporte, preferred to use pneumatic horizontal presses ("hydraulic presses need too much maintenance") and had been fermenting in stainless steel, though there were plans, he told me, to begin fermenting part of the crop in barrel in 1989. (He was already using barrels to age his wine, bringing in half new barrels every year as at Rieussec and Lafaurie-Peyreguey.)

Eymery had been among the first to work with Professor Serge Chauvet of Bordeaux's Institute of Enology on his new technique of *pressurage à froid*, also called cryoextraction—or, in plain English, pressing frozen grapes. The practice, somewhat controversial, is based on the fact that berries shrivelled by botrytis are too rich in sugar to freeze, while grapes not infected with botrytis will freeze "as hard as pebbles" if a bunch including both affected and unaffected grapes is held below zero centigrade for twenty-four hours. In a year when there is a risk that rain will destroy a crop already partly infected by botrytis and there is no time for selective berry picking, entire bunches can be cut swiftly, frozen overnight in trays, and then pressed the next morning. Only the juice of the botrytised or other overripe grapes will run from the press.

Eymery said he had experimented with *pressurage à froid* in 1986, "a year when we didn't really need it." But in 1987, he told me, growers who did not freeze their grapes before pressing had been obliged to declassify most of their crop. Among the properties that had used the technique were not only Rayne-Vigneau, but also Rieussec, Rabaud-Promis, La Tour Blanche and Yquem itself—much to the fury of the German gastronomic press, which doubtless saw the technique as an unfair challenge to *Eiswein*.

"Sauternes made this way," Charles Chevallier told me, "is not as good

207

as Sauternes made in the traditional way. But it is much better than it would be if one did nothing."

Before I tasted the 1988 Rayne-Vigneau, a magnificent wine—intensely flavored, luscious and powerful—Eymery was kind enough to let me taste the 1987. Its fruit lacked the intensity one might have expected in such a young wine, a fault that would have been much the same, however, given the difficulties of the year, even without *pressurage à froid*. But on the other hand, the wine had a balance and a sweetness it would otherwise have missed completely.

Appropriately, my short stay ended with a visit to Château d'Yquem, a royal possession that had been given in tenure to the Sauvage family in the late 16th century. They held it as tenants from father to son until Leon de Sauvage purchased it outright in 1711. Eventually it passed to Leon's great-granddaughter, Françoise-Josephine, the last of the Sauvage line, who, as a girl of seventeen, married in 1785 Comte Louis-Amédée de Lur-Saluces. Their descendants still own and run the property.

The 250 acres of vineyard, planted, like so many others, four to one in Semillon vines and Sauvignon Blanc, is an expanse of white grape varieties from which even a conservative winegrower would expect to produce more than twenty thousand cases of wine a year. But Yquem, drawing no more than a glass of wine from each vine, offers a mere five or six thousand cases annually. Rich and intensely flavored, it has become one of the world's most costly wines to produce. There was no Yquem in 1964, none in 1972, and none in 1974; in three other years of the past twenty the amount of Yquem bottled was respectively ten percent, twelve percent, and fifteen percent of a normal yield. It is not difficult to understand why the present owner, Alexandre de Lur-Saluces, is ready to try *pressurage à froid*.

Can any wine be worth such a gamble? Yquem, described as "the extravagance of perfection," smacks of privileged pleasure, even though a half bottle is within reach of anyone able to afford two good seats at a football game with the usual garnish of hot dogs and beer. The effect of Yquem extends beyond its own vineyards, however, and influences indirectly thousands who never have tasted it. For is it likely that other classed growths of Sauternes, let alone lesser wines of that region, and the sweet wines made in emulation of them around the world, would be as good as they are without Yquem's looming yardstick? High standards anywhere are always a stimulus to both expectation and performance.

Superbly illustrated and written in language made vivid by his training as a painter and long experience as a cook, Richard Olney's recent book on Yquem is equally a stimulus to expectation and performance. One chapter, though, offering vicariously the pleasures of menus past and the delights of dishes claimed to allow the idiosyncrasies of varied Yquem vintages to show at their best, I found perplexing. When the production is so scarce, why, for example, would anyone want to devise an entire dinner with each dish matched to a different vintage of Yquem, as though its production presented the same pressing need for consumption as a glut of zucchini? I am not convinced that Yquem would ever need such rococo food anyway. I have enjoyed young Yquem with *foie gras* and old with smoked salmon. But some of the combinations proposed, including suggestions from a squad of distinguished cooks who pour Yquem into their casseroles and sauté pans with the same free hand that Renaissance cooks once used to gild poultry, seem pointless except as gastronomic circus turns.

It is a rule at Yquem that no visitor is ever given the young wine to taste, a practice the more easily enforced because the château does not sell its wine until it is bottled—there are no sales *en primeur*, the custom with all other classed growth Bordeaux wines. But I was to meet Alexandre de Lur-Saluces for dinner that evening at Jean-Marie Amat's Restaurant St. James at Bouliac, presently the gastronomic temple of Bordeaux, and I wondered which vintage he would choose to show me. Given the extravagances of Olney's book I wondered whether he would offer it conventionally or in some surprising combination.

As soon as he sat down, Lur-Saluces said amiably that he was in a mood for champagne, and ordered a bottle with the tray of canapés that had appeared on the table. Mentally I crossed off Yquem as aperitif.

As he gave no other clue to his intentions, I chose from the menu very carefully, considering both courses ordered in terms of their suitability to accompany Yquem (yes, but will it be young, old?). To start I ordered eggplant with a coulis of tomato. I thought there would be an echo of sweetness in the tomato, but otherwise the dish would be mild enough to set off either a young or a mature Yquem. To follow it I ordered baked salmon on a bed of lentils. That would work, if it had to.

When he and his son had ordered he picked up the wine list and I waited expectantly. He asked for a bottle of Château Laville Haut-Brion 1979 to start—one of my favorite Graves, and not a bad choice to lead into a richer Sauternes with the main course. I admired his originality. But wait. Now he was ordering a 1979 Pomerol, Château Lacroix-St Georges, for our main courses. Well, it wasn't what I had been thinking of when I had chosen my salmon on a bed of lentils, but the lentils, according to the menu, were cooked with a little salt pork, so it would all work. Obviously, Lur-Saluces had decided to be conventional about Yquem and would use it as a dessert wine.

I relaxed and enjoyed my dinner while hearing about Lur-Saluces's recent trip to New York for the opening of the big French *L'Art de Vivre* exhibition at the Cooper-Hewitt Museum. We finished our Pomerol with a mouthful of cheese, and Lur-Saluces leaned forward. "What will you have for dessert?" he asked me. Aha! the test. He wouldn't catch me ordering one of those rich confections of Jean-Marie Amat, guaranteed to wreck any Yquem. I studied the menu carefully and told him I would like the plain *croustade* of figs. That would do it.

When he had ordered dessert for the three of us I waited to hear which vintage he would tell the waiter to bring. Instead he turned to me. "Will you have coffee with that?" he asked.

ZINFANDEL: CALIFORNIA'S OWN

THE TABLE IN MY KITCHEN IS SMALL AND ROUND; NO MORE THAN TWO, PERHAPS THREE, CAN EAT THERE TOGETHER COMFORTABLY, A LIMIT WHICH ALLOWS ME TO OPEN—FOR WHAT IS OFTEN AN IMPROMPTU MEAL—ONE OF THOSE BOTTLES WE ALL HOARD BUT WHICH COULD NEVER BE STRETCHED TO A DINNER PARTY. I share some of my best wines in the kitchen. But if asked to say which wine could always be counted on to fit its special, companionable atmosphere, I would choose a good Zinfandel.

The qualifier is important, because much Zinfandel, alas, is without interest. Twenty years ago, it would turn up as simple, dull red jug wine. Now it's more likely to be a simple, dull white (well, pink anyway). But during all that time, and particularly since the late sixties, there has been a thread of distinguished Zinfandels, almost all produced in wineries far from the mainstream, using fruit grown on what I can only describe as California's viticultural fringes.

For years these wines were hardly known beyond the circles of those who made a cult of them. But the secret's been out for quite a while now, and, as production has slowly increased, these handcrafted Zinfandels have become available to anyone prepared to take the trouble to look for them. Almost always from wineries that operate on a small scale, they range in price from as little as seven dollars a bottle, though most are from ten to fifteen, and a few of the more celebrated are now pushing twenty.

The potential for producing outstanding Zinfandel quality was always there, of course, even when there were few wines to provide confirmation of it. In his 1880s' book, *Grape Culture & Wine Making in California*—the standard text in California until well into this century—George Husmann said he had "yet to see the red wine of any variety [that he preferred] to the best samples of Zinfandel produced in this state." Some sixty years later, in 1941, when the California wine

211

industry was struggling to recover from the years of Prohibition, Frank Schoonmaker wrote in his classic work, *American Wines*, "[Zinfandel] deserves more respect than it generally gets... [it] reflects so obviously, in the quality of its wines, the soil on which it was grown...."

When Schoonmaker wrote that, few Americans gave much thought to the idea of a wine reflecting the soil on which it was grown. Accustomed to using the same name for a grape and for the wine made from it, Americans expected no more than that one should reflect the other. It was left to Europeans, who name their wines geographically rather than varietally, to concern themselves with a soil, with the climate that goes with it, and with a pattern of winemaking intended to enhance the two—or at least to resolve any incompatibility between them.

However, leaving aside such idiosyncrasies as White Zinfandel and Zinfandel Nouveau (no matter how successful commercially, they could hardly have been what Schoonmaker had had in mind), most California winemakers working seriously with Zinfandel would agree with Husmann that, when grown on appropriate sites and handled with the care given other varieties in California, Zinfandel can give red wine at least as fine as any in the state. They would also accept Schoonmaker's view that Zinfandel reflects its physical environment in ways that impose distinct variations on the wine from one region of California to another.

A year or two ago, tasting my way through some 150 California Zinfandels, almost all of them from the 1990 and 1991 vintages, I began grouping the wines by style to get an easier grasp of what I had before me. It quickly became clear that by doing so I was in fact also sorting them into regions of origin—wines from Dry Creek Valley here, Sonoma Valley there—though that had not been my intention.

In California, much is made of geography (witness the American Viticultural Areas, the officially delimited wine regions like Carneros or Stags Leap District or Sonoma Valley) when it suits a marketing strategy. Otherwise, little more than lip service is paid to the differences of style and taste imposed by location. Producers who buy grapes from various parts of the state know very well what these differences are—they base their buying decisions on them. But too often they then allow regional distinctions to disappear in the blending vat. Some of the Zinfandels on my table had obviously been made that way. Though not necessarily less attractive than the others, they were less focussed, less collected.

Most of the wines, however, were clearly marked by the regions from which they came. For example, the Zinfandels from Sonoma Valley were the hardest, the most tannic, and the most astringent. Those with a bright, crisp style—an edge of acidity, rather than tannin, coupled with the clear, forward berry-fruit aroma and flavor we most associate with California Zinfandel—were likely to be from Dry Creek Valley, Russian River valley or the Lytton Springs region, where the previous two areas meet. Wines from the upper part of Dry Creek Valley or from Alexander Valley, across a watershed, were more mellow, had a more complex—or at least a deeper—flavor, and were generally more plump.

Though no less bold, the fruit of Zinfandels from Amador County in the Sierra Foothills comes across as plum rather than berry, and sometimes as dried fruit rather than fresh, with hints of apricot and prune. Zinfandel grapes, known for their tendency to ripen irregularly within the bunch (some berries have already become raisins while others are barely ripe) accumulate sugar in a rush just before picking. So their alcohol, most often in the 13 and 14 percent range, is usually higher than the average for table wine in California. In Amador County Zinfandels, the alcohol can be particularly generous, and it is the headiness of these wines, combined with their spicy, dusky aromas and flavors, that makes them so richly and so appealingly exotic.

Napa Valley Zinfandels are the opposite: well structured, well-bred, and impeccably straight-backed. Though vigorous, they are restrained. They have perfect balance: nothing is to excess. Their aromas and flavors, persistent and at times quite powerful, have finesse and delicacy. Sometimes one can detect in them a touch of the cassis one associates with Cabernet Sauvignon. But then it's not unknown for the producers of Napa Zinfandels to add a little Cabernet Sauvignon to the blend, in proportions that the law allows, to give exactly this effect.

Zinfandels from the hillside vineyards above Napa Valley—from Howell Mountain, Stags Leap, and Atlas Peak on the east side of the valley and Spring Mountain and Mount Veeder on the west—have characteristically tighter flavors. Closed when the wine is young and then, as it develops, opening to an unexpected

213

(sometimes even medicinal) intensity, the flavors are nevertheless all of a piece with the wines' lean and forthright hillside style.

Such differences within a single region are not at all uncommon with Zinfandel; they are further confirmation of the way this variety adapts to and reflects every changed circumstance of growth. In Mendocino, there's an equally striking wide divide between the tense and concentrated Zinfandels produced from old vines planted by turn-of-the-century Italian immigrants who settled the exposed, high ridges between Anderson Valley and the Pacific and the subtly urbane wines from vineyards almost as old but planted in milder and better protected sites around Ukiah and in the adjacent McDowell and Redwood valleys.

Jed Steele of Steele Wines, a man who knows the vineyards on the Mendocino ridges better than anyone, says of them: "The vines there have never been irrigated and they yield very little. Even when the fruit is really ripe, the acid is always good. There is never a hint of the raisining common in late-picked Zinfandel elsewhere. That's why the flavor is so pure and seems to be etched into the wines despite their opulence." To see the difference between the two styles of Mendocino Zinfandel one need only compare the inherently wild qualities of a wine from the ridge with the supremely civilized Private Reserve Zinfandel from Lolonis Vineyard in Redwood Valley.

I found the Zinfandels from around Paso Robles, in San Luis Obispo County, the hardest to pin down, even allowing for the difference between wines made from the old, head-pruned hill vineyards west of the Salinas River and those made from recent plantings on what is known as the Estrella Bench to the river's east. They were supple and agreeable, but reserved—and therefore more easily recognized for what they weren't than for any particular shared characteristic. Even the more concentrated among them—those from the older vines on hill terraces west of the river—were amiable rather than assertive. Paul Draper, Ridge Vineyards' winemaker, told me that the very reticence of Paso Robles Zinfandel was a quality well appreciated in many markets. As far as Ridge wines were concerned, he said, Europeans in particular preferred the relative quiescence of the Paso Robles Zinfandel to the high vivacity of the Ridge Zinfandel from Lytton Springs.

Zinfandels from the Arroyo Grande at the opposite end of San Luis Obispo County (I know only of those from Saucelito Canyon Winery and Santa Barbara Winery) are remarkably engaging and sweetly harmonious—they've not a note out of place. In some ways they come close to the bright-berry style of Dry Creek Valley, but they are both more tightly woven and more supple. The intense fruitiness of these wines makes them irresistibly delicious.

Zinfandel is California's own grape but it's also California's mystery. Its history, both before and after its arrival in the state in the 1850s, has been continually revised in the light of both serious research and enlightened specu-lation. There seems little doubt that Zinfandel's name has come to us from the Zierfahnler grape by way of its Czech-language variant, *cinifadl*. The name was used for both white and black grapes grown in the nineteenth century in the vine-yards of a region that spilled across what is now the Austrian-Hungarian-Czech border. The black version—Blauer Zierfahnler—is thought to have been either the Kadarka grape or the Kékfrankos, both of Hungary. But that doesn't necessarily tell us anything much about California's Zinfandel because there is no certainty that its connection with the Blauer Zierfahnler goes further than the name.

Zinfandel came to California from nurseries in New England where vines of that name (or slight variants of it) were already being grown and offered for sale in the 1830s. But either there, or after its arrival in California, Zinfandel could have become confused with Black St. Peter's, a vine of similar appearance bearing similar grapes, developed from seed in eighteenth-century England (it's mentioned in William Speechley's *Treatise of the Culture of the Vine*, published in 1789). Black St. Peter's was introduced to California from East Coast nurseries at the same time as Zinfandel, and its wines started winning awards in California as soon as the first vines came into production. We know that cuttings of both Zinfandel and Black St. Peter's were sent in the late 1850s to General Mariano Guadalupe Vallejo, the last military commandant of what had been Mexican northern California, for his vineyard near the old Sonoma mission—a vineyard that was itself the source of cuttings for the establishment of many vineyards elsewhere in the county.

But no matter whether today's California Zinfandel is still the variety that arrived as such in the state or is Black St. Peter's with a change of name, we know

215

from genetic fingerprinting that it's related to the Primitivo di Gioia, a black grape grown in Apulia, the heel of Italy. For a while, after the Primitivo connection had been established, it was assumed that Zinfandel's mystery was solved and that one must have come from the other. But Primitivo was introduced into Italy only in the late nineteenth century, when the vines indigenous to Apulia had been destroyed by the vine pest phylloxera. That was long after Zinfandel had been brought to California. All that can be said with certainty is that Zinfandel and Primitivo are related and that they have a common connection, possibly a common ancestor, in the Plavác Mali, a grape grown on the Adriatic coast of Croatia. Croatia, of course, was part of the Austro-Hungarian Empire until 1919. And that, perhaps, brings us back full circle to the Zierfahnler.

The revival of California Zinfandel as a serious varietal wine began with the rediscovery of forgotten patches of old vines such as those on the Mendocino Ridge, most of them tucked away among hillside orchards. ("Rediscovery" might not be the appropriate word: when I used it once to Ken Deaver, a Zinfandel grower in Amador County, he stared at me and said, "We didn't know we'd been lost.") These old vineyards were always small because there was no point then in a man planting more vines than he could cultivate alone by hand. In any case, those who had planted vines had done so mostly to nourish their families. Wine was as intrinsic to the diet of most immigrant families settling on the land at that time as it had been in Europe, and they sold, more or less haphazardly, only the wine surplus to their needs. (In a recorded oral history of the Mendocino coast, Joe Scaramella, a former mayor of Point Arena, describes how, as a boy, he was given Zinfandel every day to take to school to moisten the otherwise dry bread that served as his lunch.)

Age gives an old Zinfandel vine many important advantages. Since most of them were grafted onto Saint-George rootstocks as a protection against phylloxera, they were also protected against climatic adversity. Once established, Saint-George roots deeply and extensively and rarely, if ever, needs to be irrigated. The Zinfandel vine it supported was always head-pruned—an old system of shaping and training a vine low to the ground in the form of a fistful of spread fingers with the support of neither stakes nor wires—with leaves and fruit open to sun and air to help the grapes ripen more easily. "It's interesting to look at what [growers] are doing today with leaf trimming, opening up the vine to let light onto the fruit," Michael Martini of the Louis M. Martini Winery recently told *Wines and Vines,* a trade publication. "That's exactly what happened naturally with a head-pruned vine."

The yield of old, head-pruned vines is limited, partly because of the age of the vines but also because it's more difficult to over-crop them, compared with vines supported on wires. For that very reason the regulations for some French controlled appellations stipulate that vines must be head-pruned and their shoots left unsupported.

Perhaps the most significant advantage of all, however, is that California's old Zinfandel vines are of a type giving small bunches of small berries that can be relied on to produce wine with character. Though cuttings from these old vines are once again being used for the propagation of new ones—anyone with an old vineyard is trying to extend, duplicate or preserve it—most of the Zinfandel vineyards established in recent years were planted with a clone selected and developed by the Department of Viticulture and Enology of the University of California at Davis. It's a clone that gives generous crops of large bunches of big berries—appropriate, perhaps, for White Zinfandel, but for little else.

Old vineyards have something more in their favor: a generous sprinkling of other black varieties—most commonly Petite Sirah, Carignane and Grenache—that the "little old winegrower" of yesteryear planted at random in his vineyard to add interest to his finished wine and, more importantly, to compensate for any possible lack of color, alcohol or finesse. A few years ago, Ridge Vineyards went through the vines it leases from the Trentadue family at Geyserville and found that the proportion of Zinfandel there was actually less than two thirds (the balance was made up of roughly even proportions of equally ancient Petite Sirah and Carignan vines). Having made remarkably successful wines from the vineyard exactly as planted for almost thirty years, Ridge Vineyards has chosen to continue as before, but it now sells the wine simply as Geyserville, with no varietal designation.

A few of the old vineyards had been abandoned, but most were still being cultivated for fruit to be used by the owners or sold to home winemakers or to the large producers who could always accept another ton or two for their big-volume blends. Jed Steele had started to make wine from old Mendocino Ridge Zinfandel vines at the Edmeades Vineyard & Winery in Anderson Valley in the early 1970s, but David Bennion and his partners at Ridge Vineyard had stumbled onto the possibilities of old Zinfandel vines almost ten years earlier. Colleagues at the Stanford Research Institute, they had bought their mature Cabernet Sauvignon vineyard on Monte Bello Ridge in the Santa Cruz Mountains, south of San Francisco in 1958. On their drives up and down the mountain they'd often stopped to buy Zinfandel made by their neighbors the Picchetti family. (The Picchettis had been making wine from their Zinfandel vineyard since 1877, selling it mostly at the winery gate.)

In his book *Angels' Visits,* an inquiry into California Zinfandel published in 1991, David Darlington describes what happened next. Darlington has a keen eye for the telling detail (and, although not evident in the following excerpt, a wicked skill in allowing the characters in his saga to skewer themselves on their own offhand remarks.) His book is one of the most entertaining (and informative) on wine to have appeared for many years. This is what he has to say:

> In October 1964 the [Ridge Vineyards] families were nearly finished with the Monte Bello harvest when they learned that the Picchettis were giving up the wine business—ordered by the county health officials to put in a concrete floor, the younger generation, insufficiently enamored with winemaking to comply, abandoned plans to pick their grapes. The '64 Monte Bello Cabernet crop had been short, so the Ridge owners leaped into the lurch. They harvested the Picchettis' Zinfandel (at twenty-four degrees Brix, a sugar level that the owners considered overripe) and fermented it according to their traditional methods. "It was so good right from the beginning," Dave Bennion recalled, "that when we needed a wine for dinner, I'd just go get some from the barrel and put it in a flask. Our Cabernet couldn't be quaffed that way. I saw right then that Zinfandel could be our bread and butter.

The next year Bennion arranged to buy more Zinfandel grapes from old vines in a Paso Robles vineyard that still supplies Ridge Vineyards to this day. He also agreed to help finance the restoration of the badly neglected Zinfandel vines in the Jimsomare vineyard, another property on Monte Bello Ridge. In 1966, Bennion contracted to purchase grapes from old Zinfandel vines in the Trentadue vineyard that is now the source of the winery's Geyserville *cuvée* mentioned above. All those early Ridge Vineyards Zinfandels were provocatively different from other wines then being made in California. Sometimes they were overbearingly clumsy, but they were always impressive. Ironically, by the time Ridge Vineyards had left that more or less experimental stage of winemaking behind them, others seemed to be taking Ridge's early wines as models for their own.

Those others did not include the late Joe Swan, a Western Airlines pilot, who had made a hobby of wine for years before a transfer from Los Angeles to San Francisco allowed him to buy a vineyard near the Russian River, planted in the old-timers' classic mix of Zinfandel, Petite Sirah and Carignan. He made his first Zinfandel in 1968, and the wines his Joseph Swan Vineyards continued to produce through the 1970s and 1980s are as much a part of California legend as the man himself.

Joel Peterson of Ravenswood—now perhaps the leader in California Zinfandel—served an apprenticeship of sorts with Joe Swan in the mid-1970s. Peterson had been raised with a broad knowledge of wine (he had sat in at his father's distinguished twice-weekly tasting group from the age of nine) and brought to winemaking a sophisticated palate, a scientific training as a biochemist, and a confident insouciance.

Acknowledging his debt to Swan, he told David Darlington, "[Swan] tended his fermenting wine as if it were a newborn child. He was so meticulous. He smelled every barrel in the winery, made sure everything was clean to his nose; he never rushed, never did anything unconsciously."

Peterson made his own first Zinfandel with Swan's equipment in 1976. His Zinfandels from the Dickerson Vineyard in Napa Valley and Old Hill Vineyard in Sonoma Valley are now among the finest wines—regardless of varietal— produced in California; few, at any price, are as thrilling as they. (On the day after my big Zinfandel tasting I passed up a chance to drink Leoville-Lascases 1970 with my lunch, preferring to have another go at the opened bottle of Dickerson Vineyard '91 instead.)

Peterson follows Swan's precepts: he chooses fruit from old, head-pruned vines with low yields and ferments it with its natural, indigenous yeast in old, open redwood fermenters that are wide rather than high; the mass of skins and pips that floats on the surface is then more shallow and easier to punch down for flavor and color extraction. "We let the fermentation get quite warm," he told me. "And, depending on the fruit and the year, we let the skins macerate when fermentation is finished, for anything from three to five weeks. For the size of our operation, we have a large cellar staff. That's important, too. You need to stay close to the wines. You just mustn't let them get away from you."

Ridge, Ravenswood and Rosenblum Cellars—the last a winery in Alameda, across the bay from San Francisco, founded and run by Kent Rosenblum as a sideline to his veterinary practice—are known among enthusiasts as the big Rs of Zinfandel. Of the three, Ridge Vineyards' Zinfandels have the most classic measure, Ravenwood's are flowingly romantic, and Rosenblum's are gorgeously, dramatically, florid. If Ridge Vineyards is the Bach of the Zinfandel world, Ravenswood is the Brahms and Rosenblum the Strauss. Johann, of course, not Richard.

220

PORTUGAL'S "GREEN" WHITES
(VINHOS VERDES)

A POSTCARD IN MY MAIL LAST YEAR WAS DECORATED WITH A SCENE OF AN EIGHTEENTH-CENTURY WINE HARVEST. While several men on rickety ladders leaned perilously to pick from a tangle of vines trailing from elm to poplar to olive tree, comely young women carried the gathered bunches in baskets towards what would then have passed for a crushing device: Clutching a staff for balance, one man was trampling the grapes as the baskets were emptied into his wide wooden tub. A couple of oxen harnessed to a flat cart were waiting to tow the crushed grapes away. If body language is anything to go by, I would say that all except the oxen were having a jolly time.

Vines hardly need encouragement to climb—the Romans planted them almost haphazardly to take advantage of any suitable stand of trees. An ancient autumn must have been spectacular with purple grapes and scarlet leaves twisted among tawny foliage. The poets of that time appreciated it, anyway, and were forever carrying on about "vines...clambering up high-storied elm." Pliny, the first-century naturalist, took a more prosaic view of the matter when he noted that vines grew so high up the poplars around Naples that "a hired picker expressly stipulates in his contract that he will be entitled to the cost of a funeral and a grave." (Ever committed to observing the condition of the world around him, Pliny met his own end on a beach near Pompei where he had insisted on landing to witness the eruption of Vesuvius in A.D. 79. He had given no thought to the risks he ran except to hold a small cushion over his head as he rushed into the hail of stones and lava. If he were being foolhardy, it must have been because he believed, in the circumstances, that burial would be provided in the nature of things. It was.)

I was reminded of that postcard and of those ancient poets last fall as I twisted in and out of the fog patches that bedevil the narrow roads crossing northern Portugal's mountains and marvelled at the profusion of red and yellow–leafed vines looped over the treetops. On all sides, color rippled from gigantic frames of poles, ropes and nets, and a gold and russet confusion of arbors encircled every tract of pasture and even the scraps of land where local fan-leafed cabbages grew at the tops of long, spindly stalks. Cabbages in Portugal always look vulnerably naked because the Portuguese pluck them a few leaves at a time. On country lanes in the early evening there will always be a man or woman walking home with a few cabbage leaves in hand to be shredded finely and then thrown into a hot broth thickened with potato and flavored with a slice of smoked sausage. Even more than salt cod, this cabbage soup is virtually the Portuguese national dish.

There are vines everywhere in northern Portugal. From a few miles south of the Douro north to the valley of the Minho—the river that forms the northern frontier with Spain—every hill and valley, town and village, Baroque church, Rococo palace, cottage, wood, garden, plot of maize, and potato field is draped with, enclosed by, wrapped in or smothered beneath vines that hang, festoon, and overflow in a way that would make Virgil, Martial, Catullus, yes, even Pliny and the rest of the gang—were they ever to return—feel absolutely at home. A small linguistic quirk says a great deal about northern Portugal. Elsewhere in the country, a vine is a *videira;* in this region, where vines and trees are indistinguishable, so rarely is one without the other, a vine is usually called an *uveira* (literally, a grape-tree).

Referred to misleadingly as the Minho (misleading because the river Minho forms only one of its borders), this is the territory of Portugal's "green wines," *vinhos verdes.* (In Portuguese the words are slurred to sound like "vinyosh verdsh.") Some suggest the name is simply an allusion to the lush greenness of a region warmer than Ireland but subject to just as many rain squalls. Others say it refers to grapes picked before they are fully ripe; but if that ever were the practice, it is certainly not so today. The most likely, and in any case the most relevant, explanation is that green is used here in the sense of youthfully fresh and tartly crisp. The liveliness of a *vinho verde* is part of its charm: it is one of the few wines in the world for which there is a minimum acidity imposed by law.

Red and white grapes were once used here together to make a kind of deep-colored, full-bodied rosé, a custom common just about everywhere in Europe. Now there are both red and white *vinhos verdes*, but while the reds are a local taste, the whites are sold worldwide. Most of those exported, however, are blended on a scale that eliminates much of the flavor and aromatic distinction specific to the region's grapes. As a substitute, a slightly teasing spritz and a hint of sweetness cover the natural bite of the wine's acidity, beguiling the palate rather than stimulating it.

Unhappy at the changes they had seen and fearful that the pressures of commercial competition in the larger European Union (Portugal joined in 1986) could make matters worse, the leading Minho wine estates—both large and small—came together in 1985 to form an association that would "affirm and encourage a policy of maintaining the quality and individuality of wines produced and bottled by the growers at their respective properties...." Every member of the Associação dos Produtores-Engarrafadores de Vinho Verde agrees to use only grapes grown on his or her own property, no matter how that might limit production, and to respect and enhance the individuality of those grape varieties permitted by the laws controlling the *vinho verde* demarcated area. Each undertakes to promote the characteristics of his or her own microclimate and of each successive vintage. They also agree to bottle their own wines (no freelance bottlers arriving with a truckload of equipment once a year), an undertaking with heavy financial consequences for a small estate. In short, they are determined to save the distinctions of *vinho verde* from being lost in the great, levelling, blending vats of the commercially successful brands that have dominated the region.

Half a dozen grape varieties are now used with some degree of regularity to make *vinho verde*. The presence and proportions of each depend partly on the stylistic intentions of the grower, but there are also restrictions within the Minho on what can be used where—in one case, the restriction is imposed by law; the others are created by the particular conditions with which a grower must contend. The varieties are Alvarinho, Loureiro, Pedernã, Trajadura, Azul and Avesso—this last a grape grown only in the area around the small town of Amarante in the extreme southeast of the region; it keeps its acidity well and gives a light, soft wine with a gentle aroma.

GERALD ASHER

The two counties adjacent to Monção, a river port on the Minho at the extreme north of the region, are reputed for wines made from the Alvarinho, a grape prohibited elsewhere in the *vinho verde* region. Its presence lends to the wines of Monção and Melgaço counties a distinctive and specific style, one that is rounder and more deep flavored than other *vinhos verdes*. When the varietal is used alone, its name appears on the label. But more often than not it is boosted with Trajadura, a variety found almost everywhere in the *vinho verde* zone because it yields abundantly, compensating for the shy yields of the other varieties. Unfortunately, Trajadura grapes have the disadvantage of losing their acidity quickly as they ripen, which is why the variety is seldom, if ever, used alone. But it contributes sugar, and therefore the power, to support other varieties and gives, when used with restraint, a wine of greater breadth and substance. Too much Trajadura makes a wine common, but a little will flesh it out.

The best of the Monção wines, and one thought by many to be the best *vinho verde* and possibly one of the best white wines of Portugal (it is certainly the country's most expensive), is a pure Alvarinho from the Palacio da Brejoeira, an imposing pile that can be seen through its great ceremonial wrought-iron gates on the road from Monção to Braga. There are prettier palaces in Portugal, but few are grander or more impeccably maintained.

Behind its sumptuous façade, dramatically reinforced by square towers at each end, the Palacio da Brejoeira is of a rare magnificence. A small, private theater on the ground floor is decorated with the extravagantly elaborate Rococo plasterwork that seems never to have been out of style in Portugal (one of the theater's stage backdrops is a view of the house itself). The main staircase, wide enough, I would guess, for half a dozen footmen marching abreast, is lit by huge gilded lamps suspended from floor standards that rise gracefully from each side before inclining to form an arch. The stairs lead to a bust of Don Manuel II, the last king of Portugal, set in a large rotunda winter garden where he seems to preside over the arrival of guests much as his predecessor Don João VI appears to supervise their reception in an adjacent ballroom where his portrait is contained within a gilded canopy—complete with hangings—as if he himself were enthroned there. The adjoining King's Bedroom is complete with slippers awaiting his use at the bedside. No, I was told, the slippers had not been left behind inadvertently. They had always been there in case they had been needed. The fact is that despite the extensive preparations to receive him royally, no king of Portugal ever actually visited Brejoeira.

It could be that the northern Portuguese had always been content to grow their vines up trees. There was the ancient model to guide them, after all, and then high vines, free of the long, damp grass encouraged by the frequent showers of summer, were less likely to suffer from molds and rot. I was also told that high vines discouraged thieves: even today, one needs quite a paraphernalia of ropes and baskets, not to mention ladders, to gather the grapes of an *uveira*.

But in the eighteenth century the Marquês de Pombal, the king's virtually omnipotent chief minister, concerned both with protecting the wine industry of the Douro and with encouraging the production of food for a growing population, forbade the planting of vineyards—as we know them—in the Minho, but had allowed farmers to plant vines on trees and arbors around the periphery of any land used to produce food.

The ingenious Portuguese made their fields even tinier than before to increase the mileage of their perimeters, and developed in the Minho a distinctive pattern of vine supports shaped like inverted Ls. The vines grew at the edges of the fields, but were projected over them by the arm of the vine support or *ramada*. Surrounded by such an arbor, a field no bigger than a drawing room to begin with would have precious little space left open directly to the sky. But the law would be respected.

That law continued in effect even after Pombal's fall from grace in 1777, and was once more rigorously enforced when the population of nineteenth-century Portugal again exceeded for a time the country's capacity to feed it. The restrictions eventually lapsed, however, and if *uveiras* and *ramadas* continue it is largely through habit and because they allow many small subsistence farmers to grow a few grapes for their domestic wine along with their corn and potatoes or around the edge of a field where they keep a sheep or two.

The first change towards a more rational vineyard was the introduction of the *cruzeita*, a system based on rows supported at intervals by a stout post crossed (hence *cruzeita*) with a wide bar near the top at right angles to the direction of the row. Each post might have attached to it one or more vines, which spread themselves over wires drawn down the rows and resting on its crossbars. The *cruzeita*, quickly smothered by the vines it supports, is really no more than an orderly variation of the ubiquitous vine arbor, the *ramada*. From *cruzeita*, though, growers have recently moved to the double cordon, a universal system of training a vine so that its trunk and two spread arms form a low *T* and provide a base for the year's fruit-bearing shoots, which are caught and supported by wires above them.

As with many recent changes in Portuguese viticulture, what was a gradual drift towards practices common elsewhere in Europe has been given urgent impetus by Portugal's entry into the Union. The old methods of cultivating grapes in the Minho, though still by far the most usual, are also the most labor intensive. A man working half a dozen acres to feed his family can choose to spend his weekends up ladders pruning vines if he wants. But if he relies on hired labor at a time when movement across European borders will become even more common, he will find that Portuguese workers will cost the same as any other in Europe, and he will not be able to afford to use them wastefully. Even the *cruzeita*—albeit an advance on the trees, poles and nets of yesteryear—will no longer be acceptable in an era when so much vineyard work can and must be mechanized. The loss of this rare survival of the ancient world is certainly to be regretted, but at least the change allows individual vines to produce less and overall yields to be reduced. Almost everyone is agreed that the smaller crops are giving better wines. For this, then, and perhaps for other reasons, the movement from *uveira* to *videira*, is likely to be irresistible and irreversible.

The forty-two acres of vineyard at Brejoeira, established in 1835, the year the house was built, show the extent of these changes in the growing of *vinho verde* in the last century or so. One will find there neither *uveira* nor *ramada*, nor are there poles and nets and strange constructions. There is still an extensive acreage planted in *cruzeita*, but new plantings are moving relentlessly in favor of the double-cordon.

Because Alvarinho is so finicky and shy bearing, even those entitled to use it in Monção and Melgaço counties rarely did, or did so more as a garnish to

Trajadura than as a principal variety. Even today, only seven estates offer Alvarinho unblended. But in Portugal the popularity of *vinho verde* as an aperitif, as a social wine, has grown greatly in recent years; and along with that popularity has grown a special demand for Alvarinho—perhaps driven by snobbery, perhaps just by that perversity that always makes us want what is least available. At any rate, the demand has raised prices for Alvarinho wines and grapes, encouraging more growers to plant them. It is a good thing for these local growers, anyway. The production of ordinary wine will bring them little return as trade develops within the European Union.

With Alvarinho they have reason to be optimistic. Apart from the potential for Portugal's quality wines in the rest of Europe, a market on their doorstep continues to grow as the small beach resorts of northern Portugal increasingly attract Portuguese from the light industrial textile towns in the Minho itself as well as a swelling number of tourists from Spain, just across the river. (Many Spaniards come to Monção just to eat at João Guterres's restaurant hidden in a grove of age-old chestnut trees fifteen hundred feet up on Monte do Faro. Partridge from the surrounding woods and salmon from the Minho river have helped establish Guterres's reputation. It doesn't hurt the business of local growers, either, that the full, soft style of Alvarinho goes perfectly with both.)

Because of Alvarinho, the *vinhos verdes* of Monção are not typical of *vinhos verdes* as a whole. Generally speaking, the best of the other *vinhos verdes* are based on Loureiro—a grape so aromatic (it reminds me of quince) that some clones are mistaken for muscats. But Loureiro is almost always supplemented by Pedernã, less aromatic but more reliably balanced, and, of course, by Trajadura, the workhorse grape. In fact, up to a point well short of a hundred percent, the higher the proportion of Loureiro in a *vinho verde* (an Alvarinho wine excepted, of course), the better the wine is likely to be. But there are nevertheless exceptions both ways. For instance, the *vinho verde* of Casa do Compostela of Vila Nova de Famalicão, which took top prize recently in Madrid as best wine from northwest Iberia, is predominantly Pedernã and relies but little on Loureiro, whereas the distinguished wine of the Quinta do Tamariz is pure Loureiro.

There is another twist, though, to the way in which a grower can use these traditional grapes to balance and support each other. The closer his vine-yard is to the Douro, the less convenient is it for him to grow Trajadura. The river valley's humidity spreads rot quickly among this variety's thin-skinned grapes as they ripen. So the farther south one goes, the more will one find yields supple-mented by Azal rather than Trajadura. Azal is also moderately prolific but much lighter than Trajadura; it holds its acidity better, and has a flavor reminiscent of grapefruit. As a result, and contrary to what one might expect, *vinhos verdes* become lighter and more, not less, fragrant the further south one goes and the closer one gets to the Douro.

If percentages of grape varieties were the beginning and end of *vinhos verdes'* shades of style and flavor, one could distinguish this from that quite simply with the numerical jargon that is already taking over most communication on the subject of wine. But the determination that has driven Manuel Gonçalves, a highly successful businessman, to devote so much of his time, energy and money to perfecting his Casa do Compostela winery is quite different from the passion that drives Antonio José da Costa Leme and his two enologist sons who must work their terraced *cruzeita* vineyards by hand to produce a wine sold almost entirely in the region where it is grown. Yet the wine of the Da Costa Leme family is deli-cious enough, indeed extraordinary enough, with its aroma and flavor of honey and lemon, to be worth a detour or even a special journey, as the Michelin guide likes to say. The same proportions of the same grapes cultivated with the same care will still give an infinite variety of wines depending not only on the vineyard site but on the growers' own convictions.

As one might expect, an estate-grown and bottled *vinho verde* will sell for more than a wine that comes from an umpteen-bottles-a-second production line—which is not to say that one is always better or the other necessarily worse. But nuance, delicacy, flavor, harmony and balance have a price too often resented, alas, in today's market place. A few of these charming wines find their way to our shores where sometimes they sell too slowly for their own good. (An old *vinho verde* is rarely the better for its age.) Anyone traveling in Portugal should take whatever opportunity presents itself to try any estate-bottled *vinho verde* of recent vintage offered from beyond the usual publicized high-volume brands. A bottle of São Claudio or of Casa do Compostela, of Terras da Corga or of Quinta da Cabanales, of Solar das Bourças, of Quinta do Tamariz, of the exquisite Casa de Sezim, of Casa de Penela, of Quinta de Aldriz, of the remarkable Quinta de Miogo or of any one of the more than thirty estates that now support the aims and adhere to the standards of the *vinho verde* association is unlikely to change the direction of anyone's life. It might not bring to mind some immortal line by Virgil or one of Martial's witticisms. But it will most surely brighten the day.

229

CALIFORNIA SAUVIGNON BLANC:
A CINDERELLA STORY

Despite the shortages and the many things that simply weren't there—no cream, no lemons, few eggs, little meat, four ounces of cheese a week, and nothing but ersatz coffee—we were astonishingly well fed in wartime England. What particularly amazes me, looking back at my boyhood, was the choice we had of fresh, unrationed, and relatively cheap fish. The men of the North Sea and Atlantic fishing fleets were our unsung heroes. The hazards faced by fishermen today are nothing compared with the then-constant danger of meeting a torpedo from blockading submarines; but whiting and hake, haddock and cod, herring and plaice glistened on fishmongers' slabs every morning.

Habits formed young stay with us, and I often eat fish, particularly when I am on my own. For me it's a sort of comfort food. It's also quick, and I am what you would call a plain cook. I season the fish, wrap it in foil together with a few shreds of scallion and fresh ginger, and pop it on the steamer for ten or fifteen minutes while I shake together a sauce of lemon juice and olive oil and pour myself a glass of wine. A few green beans or a bunch of spinach if I feel energetic, a salad perhaps, a slice of light rye pumpernickel and the table is ready.

Lately it has become very modish to drink red wine with grilled fish, particularly with tuna and swordfish. I expect that's what the fishermen around the Mediterranean always did drink, red wine being more common there than white. A friend who lives in a village near Marseille serves her own rather stubborn red wine with the excellent *bouillabaisse* she makes for special occasions (in a huge iron pot suspended over a wood fire set on the paving stones of the courtyard behind her house). To her, red wine and *bouillabaisse* go together naturally, and when she sees others hesitate she explains that everything is possible with garlic. "*L'ail permet tout*," she says, with a demure but saucy shrug.

My own tastes, though, are more conventional. I am the man for whom the "white-wine-with-fish" rule was written, and I prefer one with a little weight, some character, and a good acidity. California Chardonnays, it seems to me, are at their best with the expanded flavors of grilled fish; but even my simple steamed bass or halibut would support one if I could be bothered to make a hollandaise. In the great Paris fish restaurants, a classic dish—now rarely met because critics desperate for copy constantly push for complicated novelty (calamari dredged in cumin, that sort of thing)—was plain steamed turbot served with a hollandaise and a few new potatoes. It is the perfect foil for any really grand, mature white Burgundy.

I don't remember consciously deciding in favor of Sauvignon Blanc for my fish evenings at home, but I gravitated toward them and have been ringing the changes among them for some time now. There have been more than a few disappointments, but as one vintage has succeeded another the odds in favor of my being satisfied, even enthusiastic, have lengthened dramatically.

It took a while. Only three or four years ago, at a seminar in Healdsburg in Sonoma County, Zelma Long, president of Simi Winery, described the variety as California's Cinderella, hoping there would be a place for her at the ball. "When consumers are ready," Ms. Long had assured us, "they'll find a large group of wines that have evolved and are evolving."

The evolving has been one of the problems. A theme for Sauvignon Blanc could well have been that old Billie Holiday song: One Never Knows, Does One? Nothing about Sauvignon Blanc was predictable except for the high likelihood of finding that green stemminess always referred to, politely but euphemistically, as herbaceous. The trouble was that Sauvignon Blancs without that particular characteristic often tasted of nothing much, and on occasion it was clear that a winemaker had just given up on the variety and had so loaded the wine with oak that nothing else mattered.

I had the impression in those earlier days that few growers or winemakers had much feeling for Sauvignon Blanc, so rarely did I meet a wine that offered more than a hint of what the variety could offer. Surprisingly, given the state's reputation of allowing each to his own, winemakers in California have never been what one might call existential. They are reluctant to let a wine be itself. An unestablished variety is pushed to resemble some other currently in vogue. For years it had been assumed that California could not produce good Pinot Noir when the greatest obstacle (one must admit, there were others) was the error of handling Pinot Noir as if it were no more than Cabernet Sauvignon of a different flavor. Wines that should be velvety, scented and instantly appealing were packed with tannin—often from chopped stalks, if you please—for the sake of a longevity totally irrelevant to this variety. In much the same way, Sauvignon Blanc's own character escaped many of California's winemakers because they expected it to behave like a poor relation of Chardonnay. In fact, that was how one and all referred to it—"poor man's Chardonnay," a phrase unlikely to make friends and influence drinkers in the show-off eighties. No wonder Prince Charming never called.

Sauvignon Blanc, indigenous to France, was introduced to California in the last quarter of the 19th century. To most of us, its usual association is with Bordeaux, where it is used with Semillon to make the dry white wines of Graves and the sweet wines of Sauternes, among others. But its origins are thought to lie in the upper Loire Valley in the center of France, where it is used in its purest varietal form for the fragrant, dry wines of Sancerre and Pouilly-Fumé.

No one in France is confused by the stark contrasts among the various wines there based on Sauvignon Blanc because the French identify their wines by geographic origin rather than grape variety. So even those who might drink both Sancerre and Graves regularly probably give little thought to the possibility of a connection between the two.

But in California, the diversity of wines under the Sauvignon Blanc name has been very confusing. No other varietal offers such broad differences of style and flavor. True, the difficulties would be fewer if California producers, like the French, had some way (geographic or otherwise) to suggest what style of wine was in the bottle. Many American consumers, already bothered by the chances they take when buying any wine, have been particularly dismayed by Sauvignon Blanc's uncertainties.

The extent of the frustration was clear that day in Healdsburg as soon as the Sauvignon Blanc seminar was opened to the floor. The panel, a group of Sonoma County growers and winemakers, all of them with considerable experience of the variety, flunked the first question.

"How should a Sauvignon Blanc taste?" a participant wanted to know, addressing Larry Levin, the winemaker at Dry Creek Vineyard. The question went straight to the heart of the matter, but the answer was pure Humpty Dumpty. "Sauvignon Blanc should taste like Sauvignon Blanc," Levin replied solemnly. "It's a varietal wine."

What did that mean? What was the norm for Sauvignon Blanc? Should it be grassy, as most of them then were, or figgy? Should it smell of pineapple? Or melon? Should it be flat, or sharp? Why were some overpoweringly herbaceous? How could a consumer know what he would find in the bottle he was thinking of buying?

Why were there two names? If both Sauvignon Blanc and Fumé Blanc are made from the same grape, why do wineries in California not help consumers by applying one or the other systematically to help identify two styles of wine rather than apply them arbitrarily?

The name Fumé Blanc was first applied to California Sauvignon Blanc by the then-recently established Robert Mondavi Winery in the late sixties. There had been so few Chardonnay vines in California at the start of that decade that the state wasn't bothering to list the variety separately in the annual grape acreage reports. But even in those days there were nearly two thousand acres of Sauvignon Blanc. Only a handful of wineries were using the fruit to make varietal wines, however, and rarely were any of them particularly memorable. With the possible exception of a wine from Wente Bros., those that weren't characterless and sweet were characterless and dry. Sauvignon Blanc was not a variety that generated enthusiasm, though that was equally true, at the time, of most California white wines.

Robert Mondavi could hardly afford to ignore Sauvignon Blanc at a time when varietal grapes of any kind were still in limited supply, but he had to distinguish the wine he made from those already on the market. He chose to call it Fumé Blanc, a name that made direct allusion to the fresh, dry Sauvignon Blanc wines produced on the Loire—wines he had preferred to take as his model over those of Bordeaux. We forget, so far have matters now improved, that in the sixties even Bordeaux's Graves and Sauternes were pretty dull.

Mondavi established his right to describe Sauvignon Blanc as Fumé Blanc by insisting that he was merely using a regional French synonym (he was playing a little with Blanc-Fumé-de-Pouilly, the official alternative name for Pouilly-Fumé) and could therefore hardly prevent others from using the name too. And, of course, they did. But the success of Robert Mondavi's Fumé Blanc did more than generate a new marketing term for California wineries. It restored Sauvignon Blanc's respectability.

The boost was worldwide. In New Zealand, growers who followed his example reserved the name Fumé Blanc, by common consent, for wines that had been aged in oak. Though that's the reverse of what one might have expected, given the style of Loire Sauvignon Blancs compared with those of Bordeaux, they were adhering faithfully to what Mondavi himself was doing. The important point, in any case, was that their applying the name with consistency had as much value for the consumer as applying it appropriately. The New Zealander knew roughly what to expect when he bought a bottle of Fumé Blanc as opposed to Sauvignon Blanc.

Unfortunately, there was no such agreement among wineries in California. Nor is there likely to be, unless some wineries are willing either to substitute one name for the other or to modify their style to suit the name they prefer to use. The question is less pressing than it was. Sauvignon Blanc, the varietal name scorned thirty years ago, has reclaimed the fashionable high ground and is now more widely used than Fumé Blanc; and the styles of Sauvignon Blanc have become less extreme with the years. (In New Zealand, too, there is less consistency than there was in the use of the two names—most wineries now preferring to use Sauvignon Blanc in any case.)

The question of the variety's style was thrown open to the Sonoma County panel. Levin, together with Glenn Proctor, the viticulturalist at Glen Ellen, took pains to explain the extent to which it was set not in the winery but in the vineyard, something that was specially true of the bothersome herbaceousness.

That herbaceousness had become so specifically identified with California Sauvignon Blanc that even those who didn't particularly like it were nevertheless pleased to recognize it (how could they not?), believing it to be a step toward connoisseurship of some kind.

Researchers in Australia, where there seems to have been some concern at the lack of herbaceousness in their Sauvignon Blanc wines, have recently found that this aroma and flavor, almost always aggressively obvious when it is present at all, is based on the merest trace of a compound identified as 2-methoxy-3-isobutylpyrazine. (No one need remember that; it won't be asked in a trivia game.)

To nonscientists, however, neither the compound's sci-fi name nor its complicated molecular structure (neatly illustrated in the research report by those hexagonal stick drawings beloved of chemists) is as riveting as the Australians' discovery that our threshold of recognition of this compound, the concentration at which our noses can detect it, is just two parts per trillion. To put such a number in perspective, Malcolm Allen of the Riverina-Murray Institute of Higher Education, the report's author, explained that "two parts per trillion is equivalent to five single grape berries out of an entire year's crop of California wine grapes." Some Sauvignon Blancs have as much as thirty parts per trillion of this compound, a mere bunch of grapes out of a whole harvest, but at fifteen times the threshold it's no wonder we are so overwhelmed by the wines' herbaceousness.

Some members of the panel had brought along charts illustrating the connection between specific styles of Sauvignon Blanc, including herbaceousness, and the vineyard factors associated with them. Reviewing the spectrum of familiar Sauvignon Blanc characteristics—ranging from "pungent" and bell pepper through herbal to flinty, straw-perfumed, pineapple and fig—one began to sympathize with Larry Levin's dilemma: which of these should he have identified as Sauvignon Blanc's norm?

All other things being equal, we were told, climate and soil established style: vegetative, herbaceous, and grassy aromas and flavors were associated with the coolest growing conditions and fruit flavors with the warmest. Whereas deep, fertile soils likely to encourage vines to put out vigorously dense leaf canopies tended to yield vegetative, herbaceous wines, vineyards on gravelly, sandy soils—where vines were less vigorous and leaf coverage lighter—could be expected to give those wines on the fruitier end of the scale.

Density of leaf coverage, though not itself the primary cause of herbaceousness, clearly plays a role in its intensity. Pending the more fundamental solutions being introduced as vineyards are replanted (they include choosing slightly warmer sites for Sauvignon Blanc, grafting the vines onto devigorating rootstocks, and trellissing for an open-leaf canopy), growers can do little to change the nature of their vines. As Diane Kenworthy, Simi Winery's viticulturalist puts it, "A vine expresses itself and its environment. We can only nudge it in the direction we want it to go."

To some extent, however, growers can influence the development of the fruit by summer pruning—thinning the leaves to let in more sunlight. In making sure that no leaf grows in the shadow of another and that ripening bunches are exposed to leaf-filtered light, growers can reduce potential herbaceousness to an agreeable grassiness or even to no more than the hint of fresh peach that makes a young Sancerre so particularly welcome. In the right circumstances, they can eliminate it altogether, though there are some who say that herbaceousness is indeed part of Sauvignon Blanc's character and, within limits, should be respected. Either way, the problems with Sauvignon Blanc have certainly given added weight to the old axiom that winemaking begins in the vineyard.

Though no one disagrees that the styles of Sauvignon Blanc in California are expressions of vineyard site and methods of cultivation, there has been some interest lately in a clone referred to as Sauvignon Musqué, said to give "fruitier" grapes with no hint of herbaceousness no matter where or how they are grown.

The original cuttings of Sauvignon Musqué came from a depleted stock of plant material at the University of California, Davis, for which there is now no adequate record of origin though much has been written on the subject. After propagation by a grape grower in Monterey County, the clone was confirmed to be Sauvignon Blanc by Pierre Galet (the reigning authority on vine identity at the Ecole Nationale Supérieure Agronomique in Monpellier, France) when he was visiting California a few years ago, but the state grape-reporting service is presently listing it as a separate variety. (The figures it gives, however, substantially underestimate the quantity of fruit already being produced.) Whether as a Sauvignon Blanc clone or a separate variety, Sauvignon Musqué has now spread to Carneros, to Sonoma, and to Napa Valley.

Sauvignon Musqué is an important component of the Sauvignon Blancs made by Spottswoode, and of those made by Kenwood, too. Both buy grapes from

Larry Hyde, a Carneros grower who specializes in what one might call wayward clones. Kenwood has a couple of rows of its own and Mike Lee, Kenwood's winemaker, tells me he so prefers it to the generally available standard Sauvignon Blanc that he will use it when replanting.

Cain Cellars of Napa Valley has released two vintages of a pure Sauvignon Musqué *cuvée*. Unfortunately, the two wines—one of the 1989, the other of the 1990 vintage—are so different, one from the other, that no general conclusion can be drawn. (But that's typical of Sauvignon Blanc.)

Whatever the clone, wherever the site, and regardless of methods of cultivation, winemaking does at least modify the style of wine. Paul Hobbs, a former winemaker at Simi Winery, one of the panelists at Healdsburg, pointed out that barrel-aging, particularly, smooths the varietal's occasional angularity and gives it length by allowing an increased range of flavor to linger on the palate. What's more, a wine matured in wood for a few weeks or months, in contact with the fine, organic lees that fall from fermentation, will be rounder, less aggressive, and more thoroughly melded. These are the essential and most desirable attributes of any fine wine, and some older vintages of Sauvignon Blanc introduced to the seminar for tasting—especially a Dry Creek Vineyards '81 and a Murphy-Goode '85, both, as it happened, labelled Fumé Blanc—showed how Sauvignon Blancs appropriately prepared in this way, can develop in bottle, contrary to popular belief.

Many wineries now ferment as well as age their Sauvignon Blanc in barrel. Others, whether subsequently barrel-aging their wine or not, prefer the greater control possible with stainless steel. Some ferment part of their blend in each and assemble them before bottling.

There are other ways to bring complexity to a blend. Though a few wineries still make one hundred percent Sauvignon Blanc, most blend from ten to twenty percent Semillon into their wine to provide for a more stable aging. The flavor of Sauvignon Blanc tends to fade with age, whereas Semillon, if anything, becomes more interesting. At least one winery—Caymus—uses a small proportion of Chardonnay in its barrel-fermented Sauvignon Blanc rather than Semillon.

Allowing for the occasional wine that fits no category, the results, as far as I can judge, give us "wood" Sauvignon Blancs of the kind introduced by Robert

Mondavi, whose To Kalon Reserve Fumé Blanc is still one of the best examples; stainless steel wines, of which Flora Springs is a leading proponent; and the vast middle of the road in which attempts are made—some more successful than others—to bring together the herb and the melon, the zest and the roundness possible in Sauvignon Blanc.

Some of those who succeed particularly well on that middle road are Greenwood Ridge and Hidden Cellars, both of Mendocino County (Greenwood's wine is particularly light and melony; Hidden Cellars' is bolder, with more oak and lemon); Firestone Vineyards and Santa Barbara Winery, both of Santa Ynez Valley; St. Clement, Louis M. Martini, Silverado and Stag's Leap Wine Cellars of Napa Valley; Murphy-Goode (among my favorites), Dry Creek Vineyards, Quivira and Simi Winery of Sonoma County; and Buena Vista, using Lake County grapes.

On the stainless steel, peachy, softly herbaceous side I would place both Grgich Hills and Kenwood. Kenwood's wine is particularly delicious—as silky, as elegant, and as tender as Sauvignon Blanc anywhere. It is among the two or three best of the state.

Exceptional wines among the barrel-fermented, aged on the lees, group include one from Clos du Bois; the reserve, barrel-fermented wine from Dry Creek Vineyards, quite different in texture and flavor from the winery's standard Fumé Blanc; and the Livermore Valley Sauvignon Blanc from Ivan Tamás—soft, full and convincingly Graves-like.

However, if I had to choose just one from among many that I drink often, it would be a Sauvignon Blanc from Matanzas Creek. The winery's Sauvignon Blancs are impeccably crafted: delicious when young and superb as they mature. The 1990 has now all but disappeared, and might have a little too much bottle age by now anyway, but it was, at its peak, among the finest white wines produced in California. Seductively elegant and seamless to nose and palate, it was—if I might say so—a wine fit for a prince.

CELEBRATING OREGON'S PINOT NOIR

Of all the festivals, fairs, fetes, and other wine gatherings my work takes me to (yes, it's a hard life), the one I most enjoy is the International Pinot Noir Celebration, held every year since 1987 in McMinnville, Oregon, on the last full weekend of July. The setting—a redbrick college on a tree-shaded campus at the edge of a small rural town—is idyllic, of course, but it's the gaiety of the event and its lack of pretension that I find especially appealing. The basic message of McMinnville is that one drinks wine (and Pinot Noir in particular) for pleasure.

The celebrants, as I suppose one must call them, their numbers limited to a manageable 550, are usually a knowledgeable and jolly lot. They are wine drinkers rather than collectors and include a high proportion of literally down-to-earth growers from Europe and Australia as well as the United States. The Swiss and the New Zealanders are not as thick on the ground as the French and the Californians, but the *international* of the event's title is not vainglory. Places are much in demand, and the organizers begin each year's roster of guests with the waiting list from the year before.

One might think there has to be a limit to what can be said or learned about one grape variety, but every year changes of focus give a fresh perspective on the familiar and provide a look at something new. The tastings are, in any case, always instructive and enjoyable, the presentations well prepared and enlightening, and the prevailing shirtsleeve informality inclusive of all. There is ample opportunity to get to know the men and women who make the wines; everyone participates and has a good time.

And at the heart of this unabashedly hedonistic retreat are the memorable meals, which offer proof enough, if any be needed, that wine really does gladden the heart, loosen the tongue, and bring people together. Nick

Peirano, whose Nick's Italian Cafe put McMinnville on the gastronomic map, and Michael Wild of The Bay Wolf in Oakland, California, supply continuity in the kitchen from one year to another. They are usually responsible for the opening Friday lunch and help to organize the other meals.

On Saturday night there is always a salmon roast under a grove of ancient, lantern-lit trees. Spitted on stakes, Northwest Indian style, the fish cook over a great fire pit and are served with a cornucopia of Oregon's bounty: shell-fish, fruit, corn, and salads of all kinds. In its simple, delicious abundance, the salmon roast sets a tough standard for chefs who come from all over the United States and from France to prepare the other meals. In 1992, when I was last there, Gregg Higgins of Portland's Heathman Hotel met the challenge with a Friday night dinner of chilled soup based on toasted almonds and roast garlic, a terrine of pork rillettes and shiitake mushrooms wrapped in vine leaves and served with a focaccio of caramelized onions, grilled spiced leg of Oregon lamb with an Oregon version of ratatouille, a chipotle remoulade and blue corn meal Anadama bread, and, finally, sweet polenta fritters accompanied by a fruit compote and cinnamon ice cream.

Saturday's lunch was cooked by Thierry Guillot of the Michelin-starred Côte d'Or restaurant in Nuits-St Georges, who kept to much-loved French dishes impeccably prepared: *jambon persillé au Chardonnay*, the classic Burgundian dish of pressed ham set in a white wine jelly; filets of Atlantic red mullet on a potato purée whipped with a thread of olive oil and a touch of garlic (as far removed from traditional mashed potatoes as the Eiffel Tower from the St. Louis Arch) and a Burgundian *coq au vin*. He ended the meal with meltingly short pastry shells filled with sorbets and Oregon berries. No one goes hungry at the International Pinot Noir Celebration.

Wines are not matched to specific dishes. Any group of eight (seating is casually where-you-will) finds ready at table up to a dozen bottles of assorted red and white wines from wineries in Oregon, France, California, Australia, or from wherever else Pinot Noir and Chardonnay might grow. The wines are there to be tasted, to be drunk, or to be swapped for wines at other tables. No two tables have quite the same selection, and it's amazing how quickly word gets around that "the table over there" has a superb Pommard Epenots, say, or that another has a Saintsbury Pinot Noir, and how soon suitors appear with other bottles to swap for one's coveted Wild Horse Pinot Noir or Henry Estate Chardonnay. "What if I give you both of these for that one," is a common negotiating ploy. It's illuminating to see how quickly a market of relative values establishes itself.

Demand for the wines of "hot" Oregon producers is a reminder of the speed with which the state's growers have placed themselves center stage in the world of Pinot Noir. When Richard Sommer, an agronomy graduate of the University of California at Davis, established a Riesling vineyard in Oregon's Umpqua Valley in 1961, to be followed three years later by David Lett, a graduate of the Department of Viticulture and Enology at Davis, who pushed farther north to the Willamette Valley to plant Pinot Noir, they were regarded less as pioneers than as madmen. Lett, in particular, was warned by his professor, Maynard Amerine, that he would be frosted out every spring, rained out every autumn, and would get athlete's foot up to his knees.

But Sommer and Lett would certainly have known that wine grapes had been grown successfully in Oregon in the last century and that their risks were therefore to some extent limited. In fact, the first vine planted in the Willamette Valley had been an Isabella, a labrusca originally from the eastern United States, brought to Oregon in 1847 by Seth Lewelling, a settler from Iowa.

According to Thomas Pinney in his *History of Wine in America*, European vinifera vines were planted in the Willamette Valley in the 1860s, probably having spread there by way of the Umpqua Valley from the Rogue Valley, just north of the California border, where Peter Britt, a Swiss immigrant, had planted them in the 1850s. A vinifera vineyard established by the Doerner family in the Umpqua Valley in 1878 still exists (though probably not the original vines); its grapes are now sold to neighboring wineries, the family having closed its own wine-making facility as recently as 1965. But the first Doerner winemakers had not been alone. By the 1870s there were so many wine-grape growers in the state that prizes for wine made from both "American" and "foreign" varieties were offered regularly at the Oregon State Fair.

Prohibition most likely gave the Oregon wine industry its *coup de grâce*, but it had been in decline and had all but vanished long before that. The strongest markets for Oregon wines were the gold-mining settlements in the southwest of the state, and once the miners began to fade away, the vineyards faded with them. Jacksonville, a gold town in the Rogue Valley now protected in its entirety as a living national monument, has a population today of only a thousand or two, but at the turn of the century it supported fifteen thousand—as well as Peter Britt's Valley View Winery.

Unfortunately, when towns like Jacksonville lost their free-spending miners, Portland offered the growers scant alternative for the sale of their wines. Portland's timber and fishing industries had attracted northern European settlers, especially Scandinavians, who felt more comfortable with their own particular mix of hard liquor and piety. In Oregon, the sale of spirits is still limited to state-controlled stores, just as in Norway, and the rural population, especially, are less than enthusiastic about wine's renaissance in the state, despite the economic benefits it has brought to their counties. In McMinnville, an economically moribund town that is now—thanks to wine—flourishing, the police department raised objections when the town council voted to include a bunch of grapes in the municipal emblem.

Without some acquaintance with this viticultural past, it is tempting to shrug off Oregon's recent success as a passing phase, an accident of nature. But neither Richard Sommer nor David Lett was mad. The success of Lett's Eyrie Vineyards Pinot Noir '75 in the now notorious Gault-Millau competitive tasting in Paris in 1979, repeated in more rigorous conditions in Beaune in 1980 by a skeptical Robert Drouhin, was not a fluke.

Drouhin, dismayed that the Eyrie Vineyards Pinot Noir '75 had placed third in Paris among a range of wines that included several distinguished Burgundies, insisted that the result would have been quite otherwise had the competing Burgundies been of appropriate quality and the tasting conducted in a more closely controlled atmosphere. On January 8th, 1980, a jury composed of European professionals, assembled by Drouhin in the thousand-year-old Hall of Justice of the former dukes of Burgundy, tasted blind a dozen wines, including the Eyrie Vineyards Pinot Noir '75, six Drouhin burgundies—among them a 1961

Chambertin-Clos de Bèze, a 1978 Beaune Clos des Mouches, and a 1959 Chambolle-Musigny—and assorted Pinot Noirs from other countries. It was assumed that this tasting, meticulously conducted, would reverse the findings of that in Paris. But, although the wine with the highest combined score of 70.0 was Drouhin's 1959 Chambolle-Musigny, in second place by only 0.2 of a point was the Eyrie Vineyards Pinot Noir '75. The third wine, Drouhin's 1961 Chambertin Clos de Bèze, trailed well behind at third place with a combined score of only 66.5.

Today, one need only taste the Pinot Noir wines of Rex Hill, Domaine Drouhin (after those events of 1979 and 1980, Drouhin took to heart the old aphorism "If you can't beat them, join them), Ponzi Vineyards, Adelsheim, Yamhill Valley, Amity, Cameron, Henry Estate, Girardet, Callahan Ridge, Bridgeview, Knudsen Erath, Cooper Mountain, St. Innocent, and at least a dozen more to see that Oregon Pinot Noir does not have to be judged by standards different from those by which one would judge Pinot Noir produced anywhere else.

Which is not to say that Oregon Pinot Noir could, or should, pass for Burgundy. Though taking Burgundy's wines as their criterion, Oregon's wine-growers have said consistently that their Pinot Noirs do not have to taste like, or be mistaken for, those of Burgundy to be legitimate. Nor is it true to say that every Pinot Noir produced in Oregon is even worthy of comment. As production has increased, so the range of quality has widened.

And production has increased dramatically. The rush to plant Pinot Noir in Oregon after Lett's initial success in Paris and Beaune accelerated when Drouhin bought land in the Dundee Hills and announced plans for a winery there; it came close to fever pitch when Brian Croser of South Australia's distinguished Petaluma Winery announced plans for a sparkling wine facility at Newberg in the Willamette Valley with a partner no less renowned than the champagne house of Bollinger. Between 1979 and 1991, the acreage of Pinot Noir in the state grew from 212 acres to 2,131. Whereas ten years ago, annual sales of Oregon wines were 260,000 gallons, they have now increased to some 900,000, and in that same span of time what was a mere handful of wineries has blossomed into almost ninety.

This growth has been accompanied by much change. For a start, Oregon's wine reputation is now bankable. New wineries have had less difficulty in

243

attracting money; rarely are they so acutely and obviously underfinanced as those that went before. Money alone doesn't guarantee quality, but it helps provide space appropriate to the work; equipment to give the best possible technical support; and more, better, and newer barrels. Formerly, the rule was always make shift and make do, but now there is everything a winemaker could reasonably want.

There is discreet elegance besides: The Rex Hill winery, converted from the buildings of a hazelnut farm, has a charming bricked courtyard surrounded by an extensive rambling garden. Its reception area, complete with fine old rugs, has the odd piece or two of eighteenth-century English furniture. Argyle, Brian Croser's facility for making sparkling wine from Pinot Noir and Chardonnay by the classic Champagne method, uses the nineteenth-century frame house that once was Newberg's city hall as a decoratively picture-perfect setting for its tasting and reception rooms. And Domaine Drouhin—which expects to spend another five million dollars on top of the seven million already invested in its vineyard and winery—brought from France eight sea containers of specially-made tiles for the roof of a winery planned as much by the supervising landscape designer as the architect.

Other changes, in the vineyards and in the approach to winemaking, are sometimes simply the result of time passing but have profound consequences anyway. For example, now that vines planted in the 1970s and 1980s have matured, their grapes have a more concentrated flavor; vines planted in the last three or four years, though hardly yet bearing fruit, have included Pinot Noir clones brought in by Oregon State University from the French government experimental station at Dijon.

These new clones supplement the three on which most growers were previously obliged to rely. One of those three came from the Swiss viticultural station at Wadenswil near Zurich and was valued for the structure and delicacy it gave to wine. Another, drawn from the University of California's program at Davis, was originally brought to California from Pommard in Burgundy and was appreciated for the body and color it could contribute. The third is the Pinot Noir clone known in California—confusingly—as Gamay-Beaujolais, because of the fragrant wines it gives. For balance, most Oregon winemakers have tried to have access to all three of these clones and they have done well with them. The clones newly introduced from France extend their options further, however, and should help them produce wines of even greater depth in the future.

If research has shown that a mix of clones gives the best result for Pinot Noir, many believe that a variety of yeast strains for the fermentation makes a similar contribution. Some Oregon producers are experimenting with combinations of two and three different strains of selected yeasts, but others—including Drouhin, whose newly released wines are outstanding—rely on wild yeasts to get their fermentation going. "Wild yeasts are always a mix of many," says John Paul, the winemaker at Cameron Vineyard. "I encourage them along with two or three selected yeasts to add yet another layer to my wine."

Oregon growers have also had to concern themselves with cultivation techniques, though that has been the case from the very beginning of the present resurgence of grape growing. Those first growers soon realized that the state's climate wouldn't allow them to rely entirely on either French or California experience. As Dick Ponzi puts it, "In those early days, we were forever in seminars teaching each other as we learned—the importance of training our vines vertically, for instance, the better to expose the leaves to sunlight, as opposed to what they were doing in California, where leaf canopy gave shade to both plant and fruit. We have now learned that, like the Europeans, we must plant our vines more densely. We then need fewer bunches on each vine to get the same yields, and that allows us more leaves working for each grape."

All new vineyards in Oregon are being planted almost to the standard European density. Domaine Drouhin, for example, one of the largest of recent plantings, has a density of 3,000 vines to the acre against California's usual 650. Those who can't start over again have inserted vines between existing ones. Along with density, Oregon's growers have experimented with trellising to increase leaf area, and their innovations are now influencing the way wine grapes are grown elsewhere in the world. After all, what is of crucial importance in Oregon, close to the northern limit within which wine grapes will ripen, is usually at least beneficial to any vine no matter where it is grown.

The system developed by Scott Henry of Umpqua Valley, for instance, was praised and recommended by Richard Smart of New Zealand in his book *Sunlight into Wine* (Dr. Smart is presently the international wine industry's guru on trellising) and is now being introduced in vineyards all over the world with excellent results. Henry divides the vine's shoots, training some up and some down, to create for each vine a great sheet of leaf surface that acts like a solar panel.

Oregon growers are also more flexible in their expectations. The marginal climate of Oregon, and of Willamette Valley in particular, is what makes it possible to produce great wines there. But a marginal climate has a serious drawback, too: consistency from year to year cannot be guaranteed. Wine producers, having found that difficult to accept at first, are now much more sensitive to the style inherent in each year's fruit and are less preoccupied with forcing it to a predetermined end. Fruit from a cool year, for example, when body is sure to be light, is fermented at a low temperature likely to bring out as much fragrance as possible. In other years, fermentation can be warmer. Producers have also learned to avoid packing in tannin and extract, a practice based on the false notion that a wine unapproachable when young is sure to be better for it when aged. One need only compare the rather massive wines of 1983 and 1985, both successful vintages in Oregon, with the same wineries' elegant 1988s to see how far winemakers have come and how quickly.

Oregon winegrowers pay a price for their success with Pinot Noir and for their decision, taken through the Oregon Wine Advisory Board, to capitalize on it by projecting for the state a clear image that focuses on this one variety and, essentially, on the Willamette Valley. Other varieties produced in Oregon and other regions—even when they produce Pinot Noir—remain in the shadows. Pinot Gris is carried along by the success of Pinot Noir (three of the best Pinot Gris are from The Eyrie Vineyards, Ponzi and Rex Hill), but Chardonnay gets less attention than it deserves.

Oregon Chardonnays are mostly lighter and silkier than those of California, partly because of more restrained levels of alcohol but largely because of a higher acidity that encourages growers to rely on malolactic fermentation, the bacterial change that converts harsh malic acid into milder lactic acid. Malolactic fermentation affects more than the acidity of a wine, however; it draws all the wine's flavor components together in a way that has been compared to that of the final wash applied to a watercolor to bring the disparate hues into harmony.

The wines rely on subtle appeal rather than assertive aromas and flavors, though there are exceptions (such as Henry Estates', which are richly full-bodied). Consistently among the best of Oregon's Chardonnays are those produced by Tualatin from a vineyard tucked into an angle on a hillside that traps warm air rising from the Tualatin Valley floor. Other wineries offering good Chardonnay include Argyle, Rex Hill, Ponzi, The Eyrie Vineyard, Adelsheim (the winery gets such accolades for its Pinot Noir that its Chardonnay, a model for all Oregon, is often overlooked), Valley View Vineyards, Ashland and Weisinger's. Bridgeview, at an elevated and somewhat remote location in the Siskiyou Mountains close to the California border, offers a delicious barrel-select Chardonnay with something approaching a California style as well as another, very modestly priced Chardonnay with the mild fruit, nerve, and freshness of a good French Chablis.

We hear little of the state's remarkable Gewürztraminers and Rieslings, and even less of some better-than-creditable Cabernet Sauvignons and Merlots. Tualatin's Gewürztraminer has a following because of the winery's success with Chardonnay and because of its proximity to Portland, but the intensely flavored Gewürztraminers of Foris, Bridgeview, and Weisinger's, all in the Rogue Valley, are little known—if at all—outside the state and are not very familiar to consumers even within it. The Umpqua Valley Rieslings of Richard Sommer's Hillcrest, of Henry Estates, and of Callahan Ridge, particularly, are also superb.

I shall long remember a 1987 Callahan Ridge Riesling, a wine picked in relays, overripe berry by overripe berry and labelled *Vinum Aureolum*. I sipped it under a tree at the back of the winery after an *al fresco* lunch. As I sat there, Richard Mansfield, the man who had made it, wandered off into a strawberry patch to bring back a few sun-warmed berries to accompany it.

There are exceptional Rieslings being made at Valley View, too, in the Rogue Valley. But even more surprising are Valley View's Cabernet Sauvignons and Merlots, neither variety being as rare as one might expect in Oregon. Wines of similar, and perhaps even better, quality are also being produced at Ashland

Vineyards. In fact, the 1990 Merlot from Ashland is as concentrated, as well formed, and as fine as any other American Merlot I have tasted from that vintage.

Oregon's Chardonnays, Gewürztraminers, Rieslings, Cabernets and Merlots are at present obscured rather than illuminated by the success of its Pinot Noir. But perhaps, in time, we'll be celebrating them, too. After all, France makes a virtue of its diversity—Burgundy, Bordeaux, Alsace and Champagne are just the beginning there—and eventually Oregon will surely find a way to do the same.

248

ORVIETO: FAIR LILY OF UMBRIA

To those who grew up with them, Italian white wines of the old school—
blunt and throaty—are as reassuringly familiar as the pungent salami or the
fiercely aged pecorino cheese that accompanied them so convincingly. "We know
what we like and like what we know" is true even when what we know and like is
not necessarily appreciated by everyone else.

Indeed, urban and international taste today is for lighter, fresher, more
aromatic white wines. So Italian growers have been sending their sons to enology
schools and sprucing up their cellars with better presses, water-cooled stainless-
steel tanks and sterile bottling lines to make their wines that way. In the course
of a decade or two, the standards of making white wine in Italy leapt across
centuries. In this transformation, a few wines, inevitably, lost more than they
gained and are now indistinguishable from all the other brightly anonymous wines
served cold by the glass in restaurants from Milan to Osaka. But change, overall,
has brought new life to most Italian white wines. Orvieto, a distinctive wine from
Umbria, from vineyards about midway between Rome and Florence, is one of
those which have recaptured an identity and a market.

Once an Etruscan settlement, the hill city of Orvieto perches on a flat
rock a sheer thousand feet above sea level. Both the rock and the countryside it
dominates are of a chalky tufa similar to the broken terrain that supports the vineyards of Vouvray on the Loire, southwest of Paris. As at Vouvray, the soft tufa of
Orvieto has allowed local winegrowers to burrow with ease, and since earliest
times the hills have been riddled with their underground cellars, chambers
and galleries.

Watered by the Tiber and the Paglia (the two rivers become one just
before passing under a Roman bridge a few miles south of Orvieto), this part of

Umbria is green and fertile. The farmers produce wheat and fruit as well as wine, and graze their large, white Chianian beef cattle, peculiar to central Italy, on the high pasture. Despite the drama of the city itself, the valleys and hills that surround Orvieto are engaging rather than imposing, their roads shaded by umbrella pines and punctuated by stands of oak, chestnut and acacia. They look their best when splashed with color in spring and early summer: the hills gaudy with yellow broom, the fields with purple-red clover blossom, and the roadsides with scarlet poppies, blue lupines and pale mauve *cicercchio*, a favorite Italian wild flower, as fragile as a sweet pea. At that time of year, too, the village streets, on cool evenings, are intoxicatingly fragrant with old linden trees in bloom.

But despite its position astride the main *autostrada* from Milan to Rome, Umbria is reclusive—perhaps because it is the only one of Italy's administrative regions to have neither a seacoast nor a foreign frontier, or perhaps because centuries of direct papal government have left their mark. Friendly but watchful and used to keeping their own counsel, the people there are normally slow to take up the ideas and habits of others. At Orvieto, in particular, growers are still far from unanimous in their perception of the changes that have overtaken them.

Piero Antinori and his then technical director, Giacomo Tachis, were probably first to stir local growers with ideas brought from adjacent Tuscany. There, the firm of Antinori had already provoked its Chianti neighbors with a revisionist view of vine varieties. Having helped start the movement to integrate Cabernet Sauvignon into the customary range of Tuscan grapes, Antinori and Tachis brought cuttings of Chardonnay and Sauvignon Blanc to the firm's Castello della Sala property in Umbria to see what could be done with them alongside the established varieties of Orvieto.

In proportions dictated by custom and by law, those varieties are: Trebbiano (minimum 50 percent, maximum 65 percent), Verdello (minimum 15 percent, maximum 25 percent), and Grechetto, Drupeggio, and Malvasia (20 percent to 30 percent of these three combined, with Malvasia restricted to a maximum of 20 percent of the total volume of wine.)

Each of these five compulsory or permitted varieties has its supporters and its detractors. Many growers would like to further contain the role of Trebbiano, for example. Despite claims that it enhances aroma in the young wine, they maintain that it contributes only volume at the expense of quality. There is a further technical gloss to the battle over Trebbiano. Locally this grape bears the Umbrian name Procanico, but many credible Umbrian growers claim that Procanico is more than a local name for Trebbiano. They insist that the name identifies a Trebbiano strain peculiar to Umbria, a less prolific strain giving wine of superior quality. They maintain that in the recent rapid extension and replanting of the vineyards, encouraged by growing demand for the new style of Orvieto, the large-scale use of Tuscan Trebbiano (as opposed to authentic Procanico) has led to difficulty in controlling yields from this variety, to the detriment of Orvieto quality. (In little more than thirty years, from 1962 to 1993, annual sales of Orvieto—and therefore its average annual production—has swollen from 2.8 million bottles a year to over 19 million.)

Everyone agrees that Grechetto gives Orvieto its structure, texture and body, though some argue that it also contributes a rasp if not handled carefully. Drupeggio helps provide body and structure as well as brightening some of the early flavors. Verdello grapes bring finesse and subtlety, and are said to improve the balance of alcohol and acidity. Few have much to say for Malvasia, however. At best it is aromatic when the wine is young, adding another shade of flavor. But it ages badly. Malvasia in careless combination with roughly treated Grechetto was a surefire formula for those oxidized, slightly acrid wines of the past.

Far from rushing to turn the existing vineyards on their head, the Antinoris, who had acquired the Castello della Sala before World War II, began a restoration of the property and a renewal of its vineyards only when hostilities had ceased. They studied and worked with the grape varieties already there, seeking through experimental changes in cultivation and wine making to improve the estate's traditional wines. Their achievement can be seen in the recent vintages of their Orvieto Classico. A dry and lively wine, now surnamed Campogrande rather than Castello della Sala (less than 25 percent of the grapes used in the *cuvée* now come from their own Sala vineyards), it has a deliciously persistent flavor softly compounded of hazelnut, citrus and honey. (The term *Classico*, when attached to an Orvieto wine, is of geographic significance. Though it has a usually justified

251

connotation of superiority, it means the grapes were grown in the central heart-land of the region.)

Yet even when satisfied with the evolution of their Orvieto Classico, Antinori and Tachis were still confident that nontraditional "international" varieties would do equally well in Umbria. It has been said that by developing new styles of wine from them, alongside Orvieto, they hoped that world atten-tion, obsessively focussed on a handful of such star varieties, could be drawn to Umbria's potential for making other high-quality wines.

Even if that were the motivation, it is clear that Antinori and Tachis are natural iconoclasts. The wines closest to their hearts have always been those for which no models have existed and for which trial and error can offer no final answer—only an ever expanding horizon of possibilities. Working with Giacomo Tachis on the Campogrande *cuvée*, Renzo Cotarella, Antinori's manager at Castello della Sala, has helped revive dry Orvieto's former reputation. He has also sought to reproduce the sweeter *abbocato* wines for which Orvieto was once distinguished, using the same five traditional varieties, and, since 1987, has produced a truly rich wine, Muffato della Sala, from Sauvignon Blanc grapes concentrated by botrytis and blended, in proportions that have varied from year to year, with the region's traditional Grechetto. (*Muffa nobile* is the Italian term for botrytis, or noble rot, the suede-like fungus that concentrates a grape's sugar to produce the world's great dessert wines on the Rhine and in Sauternes.)

Above all, however, he has produced any number of experimental wines, in some of which Chardonnay, in others Sauvignon Blanc, has been used to extend the possibilities of one or more of the local varieties—or vice versa—in ways not tried before.

Antinori's Cervaro della Sala, for instance, now a pure Chardonnay, began as an oak-aged blend of Chardonnay and Grechetto. Antinori felt that Grechetto braced Cervaro as it braces Orvieto Classico and his Muffato della Sala, without blocking the wine's essentially generous Chardonnay character. These "new" wines change and evolve continually, however. Giacomo Tachis could give me no guarantee, for instance, that the crisply dry 1988 Borro della Sala I drank with him at lunch at Castello della Sala in the summer of 1989 was in its final version.

Sauvignon Blanc has been its common thread through successive vintages, but the proportion has gradually increased, perhaps as more grapes have become available. In its earliest version, labelled Castello della Sala, there was 35 percent Sauvignon Blanc, with Procanico making up the balance. In 1987, as Borro della Sala, there was 50 percent Sauvignon, a proportion increased to 70 percent in the 1988. The proportion of Sauvignon Blanc in the most recently tasted vintage, 1993, is 85 percent.

Dr. Luigi Barberani, a lawyer with a degree in agriculture, joined his family's estate winery fifteen years ago and took over its management completely in 1979. His vineyards, southeast of Orvieto, are several hundred feet above Lake Corbara, created in the 1950s when the Tiber was dammed. He, too, has been experimentally combining local with nontraditional varieties. His Pomaio is made from Sauvignon Blanc, Semillon and Grecchetto grapes grown together in a single vineyard.

"Fifty-five of our seventy-five acres of vineyard are planted with the five traditional Orvieto varieties," he told me. "The other twenty, planted a few years ago, have Sauvignon Blanc, Semillon and Chardonnay for white wine, and Cabernet Sauvignon, Cabernet Franc and Sangiovese for red.

"It was never my intention to make a pure Sauvignon Blanc or a pure Chardonnay from these new vines. I wanted to see what each of them could add, if anything, to varieties already here. I wanted to see if we could come up with wines that reflected the personality of our region and the character of our traditional varieties—but with something more.

"On the other hand, my approach has been more concerned with the particular vineyards than with the specific varieties grown in them," he continued. "On this estate the idea of a wine from a single, defined vineyard was as novel as the introduction of nontraditional varieties. Until twenty years ago the vines on our property, like those of our neighbors, were planted promiscuously among fruit trees, wheat and olives. It was the custom in Orvieto. There were few vineyards as such. We made our first move to plant vines separately, in vineyards, only in 1967.

"By ending the practice of mingling grapes with other crops, we could make wines from the classic Orvieto varieties—and from others—while discovering and respecting the distinctively varied characteristics of the individual vineyard sites of our estate. The Pomaio, for example, is a case in point, as is our Calcaia vineyard. Calcaia faces the lake, so *muffa nobile* attaches itself quite frequently to Trebbiano and Drupeggio grapes as they ripen there.

"In Orvieto, its presence doesn't always lead to a sweet wine," Barberani went on, "but it gives a richer texture and finer flavor to wine made from grapes affected by it. *Muffa* therefore accounts for Calciaia's characteristic style and we preserve it by fermenting the grapes and bottling the wine separately. We handle the grapes from our Castagnolo and Pulicchio vineyards in the same way, because each has an equally distinctive style worth preserving."

Wine from the Castagnolo vineyard, he told me, is always quite dry, with an aroma and flavor as much herbal as fruity. The Pulicchio vineyard gives dry and sometimes off-dry (*amabile*) wine, depending on the year. But even when *amabile*, it is fresh and lively, too, so that the residual sugar, barely detectable, gives roundness and fullness to the wine rather than sweetness. The Pulicchio wine has a riper quality than that from Castagnolo. Calcaia, despite the botrytis (there is usually a telltale, slightly honeyed aroma), has less residual sugar than Pulicchio. Yet it seems softer and fleshier.

When I last visited him, Barberani brought out two vintages of Pomaio, his Sauvignon Blanc–based vineyard blend. The 1987 was half Sauvignon Blanc and half Grechetto. It had an attractive, slightly fruity nose, and a flavor that reminded me neither of Sauvignon Blanc nor of Orvieto. It probably owed its austere structure to the high proportion of Grechetto—a higher proportion than there would ever be in an Orvieto Classico. I thought to myself, too, that Sauvignon Blanc had perhaps been less effective in fleshing it out than had Chardonnay in Antinori's Cervaro della Sala. As if reading my mind, Barberani offered me the 1988, explaining that he reduced the proportion of Grechetto in the next vintage, substituting Semillon for half of it.

I can't say how much of the difference had sprung from a basic contrast between the 1987 and 1988 vintages in Orvieto, but it was certainly true that the structure of this 1988 was firm where the 1987 had been quite bony. Though the 1988 was too young to have yet developed beyond the stage of superficial flavors of fermentation, the Semillon had not only brought a more gentle texture but had exchanged the rigidity of the 1987 for something more lighthearted.

Before leaving, I tasted from barrels Barberani's experimental 1988 Sangiovese and his 1988 Cabernet Sauvignon–Cabernet Franc blend. The Cabernet blend was agreeably balanced and had good varietal flavor: unexciting, perhaps, but attractive. The fruitier Sangiovese was much more boisterous. Barberani intends to combine them, allowing the Cabernets to smooth the Sangiovese, lending it subtlety, and the Sangiovese to invigorate the Cabernets.

I tasted just such a delicious Umbrian red table wine—subtle and vigorous, more robust that Chianti, but less refined than Brunello—later that same day at lunch on a terrace hanging over the vineyards of Decugnano dei Barbi. I had found my way to the Decugnano estate after so many false starts that I was convinced I was still on the wrong track even when I wasn't. Over and again I found myself muttering "Surely it can't be this far" as I drove along miles of unsurfaced road, in parts no more than a donkey trail, past lakes and over streams, through remote hamlets of a cottage or two, along ridges, down through valleys, and up a final hillside.

Claudio Barbi, now in his forties and an enologist like his father before him, is a wine merchant in Brescia in northern Italy who specializes in wines of Orvieto. He acquired this property in 1973, having for years bought wine from the previous owner. Of its hundred acres, almost half are planted with vines, all of them traditional Orvieto varieties except for a section of Chardonnay—the source of his small production of a champagne-method sparkling wine—and some Sangiovese and Montepulciano (confusingly, the name of a vine originally from the Abbruzzi as well as of a wine grown in Tuscany). Grapes of these last two had been used for the red wine we drank with our lunch: huge, grilled beefsteaks.

With hairsplitting attention to detail—from the handheld baskets in which unbroken bunches are brought to the press house to the way in which the most modern equipment has been chosen or constructed to fit existing stone farm buildings—Barbi produces six thousand cases of Orvieto a year at Decugnano. He is no fanatic, but he is as careful to avoid disturbing the way things look as he is sensitive to the local ecology (no pesticides, no herbicides, no nondegradable plastic bindings on the vines). The zeal with which he oversees his estate is no more than a symptom, however, of his concern for the preservation of Orvieto's viticultural tradition.

We had started lunch with a dish of pasta prepared by the farm manager's wife and a bottle of Barbi's 1988 Orvieto Secco, a wine of intense fragrance—steely dry and delicately tender at the same time—and ended it with a bowl of apricots and a mild young Pecorino, intended, no doubt, to show off a 1987 Orvieto Classico affected by *muffa nobile*. Barbi identifies his botrytised wine with the initials P.N. (presumbly for *pourriture noble*) in the rare years he is able to produce it. I didn't find it as luscious as the experimental wine I had tried from wood at the Castello della Sala, but it had a balanced sweetness and a fine flavor. We drank it, in appropriately contemplative silence, while listening to the distant call of a cuckoo.

Corrado Bottai of Le Velette is no less passionate than Guido Barbi on the subject of guarding viticultural tradition, even though he has just splurged on two new Bucher presses—"the Rolls-Royce of presses," he told me proudly—as part of the modernization of a family winery that has been the pride of Orvieto since the last century. (The labyrinthine tunnels extending from beneath the kitchen of the family house might easily have been started before the foundation of Rome.) Bottai argues forcefully that the quality and character of Orvieto are largely a matter of the varietal mix in the vineyard. In his own he holds down the proportion of Trebbiano to the minimum required by law. "Trebbiano," he said, repeating a theme I had heard all week, "is naturally prolific. In recent years it has benefited from all the new cultural practices with which we protect our crops. Nature used to take care of its tendency to overproduce, but now it is free to yield in superabundance. Unfortunately, the common use of Tuscan Trebbiano instead of Procanico has now aggravated the situation."

Though he has no strong opinion about Malvasia—"It's true, it does oxidize easily, but in small quantities it adds dimension"—he believes ardently in using as much Verdello, Grechetto and Drupeggio as the law allows. "These are the varieties on which the character of Orvieto has been built," he says, "and on which its future will depend."

"Seventy percent of our wine in Orvieto is made by cooperatives who pay their members on the basis of grape tonnage delivered, thereby divorcing them from a concern for the finished product. Involvement for these growers stops when they pick their grapes. How can they be expected to feel for the character of the wine? Yet Orvieto is not some sort of soft drink to be manufactured, swallowed, and forgotten. It should make an impression. It should be remembered."

Bottai has no quarrel with those who choose to experiment separately with varieties from other regions and from other countries, but he fears these alien varieties creeping into the composition of Orvieto Classico. To introduce such grapes into the composition of Orvieto Classico, he feels, or to banish any of those presently allowed by law and long custom, would neither improve nor protect Orvieto. "On the contrary," he said, "we would be abandoning it."

With his emphasis on Grechetto and Drupeggio, it will come as no surprise that his own wine, Le Velette, is a mouthful: perfumed, lively, balanced, firmly structured, long, and with more character than Henry VIII.

Lacking, perhaps, the nobility of Bottai's Orvieto Classico but echoing its scale and intensity, the wine from the Torre Sant'Andrea vineyard on the Vaselli family's estate is fatter and more generous than most others. The property is extensive (the Vaselli construction company built much of Italy's ingeniously engineered *autostrada* system). There are olive groves; orchards; fields of beets, grain and sunflowers; pasture; and acres of tomatoes and peppers as well as vineyards.

The special quality of the Sant'Andrea wine and the soil and exposure of its hillside vineyard site are inextricable one from the other, a reason for the grapes to be handled separately and differently from the rest of the crop grown on the estate. Riccardo Cotarella (brother of Renzo Cotarella of Castello della Sala), Vaselli's consultant winemaker, believes, however, that the distinctive style of the wine is largely the result of macerating the crushed grapes with their skins for twenty-four hours before fermentation.

By following this old Italian winemaking practice, Cotarella is now working in direct opposition to Italy's current fashion for separating juice from skins as quickly as possible, part of the technique of lightening a wine and leading it to a swiftly aromatic rather than a slowly evolving style.

257

But Cotarella looks for depth as well as delicacy of flavor, so he also keeps the wine in wood—for weeks rather than months—before bottling. He does so not to introduce wood flavor. (In fact, he is constantly afraid of smothering what he takes such trouble to preserve in the earlier stages of winemaking.) He does it because he believes that the qualities of a wine unify in wood in a way not possible in a steel or glass-lined tank. Those few weeks in wood, he told me, make possible a more subtle development once the wine is in bottle.

Vasselli is a single estate but Bigi, a subsidiary of the Italian Wine Group, is a colossus—the largest producer of Orvieto. It bottles roughly half the wine crop of the region, buying grapes and even wine from other producers, both large and small, in addition to handling the production of its own vineyards near Lake Corbara.

"Largest" and "colossus" are relative terms, of course, but Massimo Panattoni, Bigi's chief enologist, is not embarrassed by them. Size has its own advantages, he says. Efficiencies of scale allow him technical innovation denied others, and Bigi's sheer volume provides resources for laboratories equipped both for quality control and research, as well as support for projects in the vineyard and the winery every bit as imaginative as those of his smaller, more flexible neighbors.

Bigi's Vigneto Torricella, for example, a single-vineyard Orvieto Classico, much as the Torre Sant'Andrea at Vaselli, and Marrano, a Grechetto wine from Bigi's Vigneto Orzalume fermented in French oak barrels, are as stylishly distinctive as any made in the region. (Stylish or not, I shall be less than honest if I do not confess that initially, at least, I found the bouquet of Marrano—with its powerful toast and citrus notes—difficult to appreciate. I was told, though, that the company's customers in Germany and the United Kingdom clamor for it.)

Panattoni is unenthusiastic about the present fashion for white wines that seem to burst with fruit ("Those aromas and flavors vanish as quickly as they arrive. We want our simplest wine to hold its flavor and freshness"); but then, his well articulated views on just about everything are the opposite of what one might expect to hear from a giant in a region of small producers.

He speaks for yield control ("when a crop seems excessive we reduce it by cutting out some bunches to allow greater concentration to others") and against the industrial manipulation that has made modern wines boringly homogeneous. He believes balance in a wine is the result of good vineyard practices. "If a grape is healthy, its juice is balanced. Anything taken out or added will disturb its equilibrium, so that one change will eventually call for another, and another, and another. If we start in the vineyard by controlling yields to concentrate quality, we shall not need to manipulate the juice. Our technical skills should be directed to protecting it with the least interference possible." He limits the size of each of his fermenting tanks and allows the wine in each to develop its own characteristics.

He is less of a purist when it comes to producing his slightly sweet Orvieto *abboccato*. Skeptical of the claims some growers make of producing botrytised wines ("I think we see more grape dehydration than botrytis in this region," he told me), he arrests the fermentation of his own sweet wines by chilling the must, leaving in the wine a measure of unfermented grape sugar. In the more ordinary quality of *abboccato*, he simply adds grape concentrate.

Bigi has a few rows of Chardonnay, Riesling and Pinot Noir for experiments, and Panattoni told me he gets some interesting results from them. But he left me in no doubt where he stood on the integrity of Orvieto.

"This preoccupation with other varieties is all fashion and marketing," he said. "If we move away from our regional varieties—and specifically the Umbrian clones of those varieties—we shall end up making second-class versions of other people's wines."

On my last day in Orvieto I skipped lunch in favor of a glass of wine and a few slices of prosciutto of wild boar at the Cantina Foresi. I sat at a table in the sun, on the piazza by the Duomo, known since it was completed many centuries ago as the Golden Lily of Cathedrals. Grazia Foresi, the proprietor's wife, set down for me a glass of pale Orvieto Classico. Its enticingly fresh, almost herbal aroma wafted from the glass, and I told her how different it was from the rustic Orvieto I remembered from the past.

Squinting against the sunlight, she hesitated for a moment before asking: "You like the old-style Orvieto?"

In a nostalgic sense, I do. Faults and all. Just as I like reruns of old Anna Magnani movies. So I shrugged and said, "Sometimes."

In half a minute she had replaced the pale wine in front of me with another: it was a rich, burnt gold. She stood there, waiting for me to take my first swallow. I could smell the wine's rasp. It tugged at my memory even before it caught at my throat.

"It's the wine we keep for our local customers, for the old men," she said. "They enjoy their glass of Orvieto in the afternoon. And that's how they like it."

There was nothing to be said. I smiled.

260

A VINEYARD BY THE SEA:
THE NORTH FORK OF LONG ISLAND

In 1993 WINEGROWERS ON LONG ISLAND'S NORTH FORK HAD THE KIND OF SUMMER THAT THEIR CALIFORNIA COLLEAGUES TAKE FOR GRANTED: BRILLIANTLY SUNNY, COMFORTABLY WARM, AND WITH LESS THAN A HALF INCH OF RAIN FROM THE FIRST OF JUNE TO THE END OF AUGUST. Despite the last-minute scare of two or three days' heavy showers in September just as picking was getting under way, the grapes arrived at the wineries healthy and textbook ripe. In the vineyards and at the presses there was an air of exhilaration, a mood close to ecstatic.

By the time the following winter's cold had helped the new wines settle, it was clear that the 1993 reds were destined for success. They are fuller, fatter, and rounder than the wines of 1988, the region's previous best vintage. The 1993 weather made this possible, of course. But there was more to it than that. Maturing vines, methods of both cultivation and winemaking adopted and adapted over the previous few years, and increasing confidence among growers and winemakers in the unique character of North Fork wines came together in 1993 in ways that will be of lasting consequence for this newest of American wine regions.

A narrow but curiously shaped peninsula stretched between Long Island Sound and Peconic Bay, the North Fork was first settled in 1640 from the New Haven Colony across the water. Led by their minister, the Reverend John Youngs, a group of men originally from Southwold on the North Sea coast of England's Suffolk County, established Southold (not the way the English town's name was spelled, but certainly the way it was pronounced) soon after New Haven had acquired the territory. Until the Dutch were finally driven from New York in 1674, the peninsula and its adjacent islands—all under the authority of the Southold town Fathers—continued at intervals to answer to the jurisdiction of New Haven (later, to the union of the New Haven and Connecticut Colonies). The link was never totally severed, except politically: the North Fork today remains essentially a part of rural New England, having more in common with Cape Cod than with the rest of Long Island.

It's been more than twenty-two years since Louisa and Alex Hargrave planted a vineyard on what had been a potato field at Cutchogue, a village near Southold. They were not the first there to have planted European vines, *Vitis vinifera*, but they were the first to do so successfully.

The Hargraves were long preceded by Moses Fournier—known more familiarly as Moses the Frenchman—who planted *Vitis vinifera* at Cutchogue in the late seventeenth or early eighteenth century (accounts differ). Fournier recognized instinctively what we now know from scientific data: Southold, Cutchogue, and the surrounding midsection of the North Fork are peculiarly apt for growing grapes. The town is the sunniest in the state, with the same moderate annual rainfall as Bordeaux. And, because the expanses of water to its front and back temper both cold and heat, the chance of spring frost damage is limited and the risk of vine stress in summer greatly reduced. In fact, the North Fork's climate is at its most balanced at this peninsular midpoint. To the extreme east the strip of land becomes too narrow and the maritime influence too great for vines; to the west the effect of the mass of Long Island eventually outweighs the advantages of the ocean. The peninsula is blessed with the right soil, too; an easily drained, and therefore quickly warmed, sandy loam.

Fournier's efforts were doomed, alas, as were all early experiments with *Vitis vinifera* on the East Coast, by the vulnerability of European vines to phylloxera, mildew and the host of other native American pests, fungi, and viruses to which indigenous wild vines were immune or at least resistant. It was only in the nineteenth century, when these same pests, fungi and viruses had destroyed the vineyards of Europe (where they had been inadvertently carried on American vine specimens) that the necessary effort was made to identify and control them.

Regardless of Fournier's disappointment, other agriculture flourished on the North Fork in fields the Corchaug Indians had already cleared for their own crops of corn, beans, and squash. The new settlers, having divided the land among themselves, also planted corn, along with wheat and barley. They traded their excess grain with Connecticut, transport by boat being easier than carting over land to the west end of Long Island. Louisa Hargrave, writing in *The Long Island Historical Journal* in 1990, reports that Southold shipped apples and salt pork to the Caribbean at that time, in exchange for sugar and molasses. What little incentive there might have been for the settlers to persevere with European wine grapes, even in the face of nature's hostility, was no match either for that cheap molasses, easily converted into rum, or for a tax imposed on vineyards by the Duke of York's arbitrary government in New York.

Mixed agriculture remained the rule on the North Fork until the double impact of the Long Island Railroad and, in 1888, Daniel Hallock's invention of the potato weeder and digger brought fundamental change to the local economy. Hallock, whose family farm on the North Fork is preserved in its entirety as a private museum, introduced a simple technology that reduced labor costs and made Long Island potatoes competitive on the world market. The railway provided the means to carry them there. On the North Fork, potatoes became the principal—indeed, the dominant—crop, which attracted industrious and frugal Polish immigrants, who came to work in the fields at the end of the last century but soon owned the farms.

The Hargraves discovered the advantages of Cutchogue when Cornell faculty member John Tomkins told them about John Wickham, a descendant of one of Long Island's old farming families, who was successfully growing some particularly delicate varieties of European table grapes there. Wickham proved generous with his time and knowledge of the North Fork, Louisa Hargrave says, even as he tried to persuade them that starting a new type of agriculture in the area was a risk no young couple should take. But the Hargraves bought a sixty-six acre farm anyway, and began planting Cabernet Sauvignon, Pinot Noir and Sauvignon Blanc. The next year they added Chardonnay.

"We were romantics," Louisa Hargraves admitted to me when I was lunching with her and her husband. "We didn't know what we were doing, we didn't know what to expect, and no one could tell us. All the experts were wrong. We had to learn as we went along.

"It had never been our intention to own a vineyard and watch others work it for us; what we did, we did ourselves. And we were accepted here because our neighbors saw us at work every day in the vineyard. This was farm country, potato country—we were surrounded by hardworking families."

"Columella says 'enquire of your neighbors,' " added Alex, who claims to be guided as much by the texts of the ancient world as he is by anything else. "We had come into an active community which gave much thought to the problems of farming. Our neighbors' support and counsel were invaluable to us when we were getting started.

"We wanted the Jeffersonian ideal: to have a small farm, to connect with the land, and to use our minds. That has all come true. But there have been surprises along the way. We thought we'd have lots of time to pursue our other interests. We thought, for example, that winter would be three months' vacation. But that's when the vines have to be pruned. We had to have patience—for the vines to grow, for the wines to mature, for people to discover what we were doing.

"We might not be making a fortune, but we sell our crop and make a living. Anyone here can do the same if they put in the time. Our wine is no accident. It's what the North Fork can offer. We are thrilled when others here succeed. When people say we started a new wine region, we can only point out that the North Fork was here and waiting. Bordeaux was not created by one château. At most, we were a catalyst."

David Mudd, a retired airline pilot who had worked with the Hargraves and later put in a vineyard of his own, was another catalyst. He turned his experience to good account by setting up as a consultant, offering technical services to others who liked the idea of escaping from New York City on weekends to a little vineyard by the sea. More vines went in and more wineries were built. There are now roughly twelve hundred acres of vinifera grapes on the North Fork, supporting more than a dozen wine producers. There is a small acreage on the South Fork, too: most of it near Bridgehampton.

By 1988 the North Fork producers felt they had learned enough from their mistakes. With some degree of audacity, not to say presumption, they invited Paul Pontallier of Château Margaux and May de Lencquesaing of Château Pichon-Longueville, Comtesse de Lalande, together with Gérard Séguin of the University of Bordeaux II and Alain Carbonneau of the French National Institute of

Agronomic Research—at the time the two key figures in viticultural research in Bordeaux—to visit them on the North Fork and give a master class in their craft; to share, in effect, the secrets of making great wine.

The French came and in a series of formal presentations explained what they did in Bordeaux, and why. Wisely, they declined to be drawn into giving specific instructions to the Long Island growers. "There is nothing we can actually teach you," Pontallier said, modestly. "We can only explain what *we* do, how *we* work. In winemaking one must be neither too theoretical nor too dogmatic. A good wine is the result not of just a few broad decisions, but of close attention being paid to many small ones."

That said, the visitors did, nevertheless, spend several days touring vineyards and wineries and expressing privately their opinions on what they saw. To the surprise of the producers of the North Fork, the French took greater interest in their vines than in their fermenting tanks. It had been clear from the question and answer sessions after the presentations that North Fork growers and winemakers had assumed success to lie in knowing what to do with the grapes rather than with growing them.

I spent a few days on the North Fork at the start of the 1993 vintage, my first visit there since 1988. I was curious to see what impact, if any, the summer of the French had had.

"They made quite an impression," Richard Olsen-Habich, then of the Bridgehampton Winery, told me. "We really should have known everything we were being told—it was the kind of information that had always been available to us, after all. But, more than anything else, the visit helped us change our focus. Until the French came we had been so preoccupied with winemaking that we hadn't fully grasped the importance of what we were doing in the vineyard."

Kip Bedell, of Bedell Cellars, said much the same thing: "They got us thinking. I'm more conscious now of what I do and of the effect it has. I still experiment, but not, as I once did, for the sake of trying something new. If something works, I stay with it. I'm more consistent. Like everyone else, I'm paying much closer attention to the details. The result is that the quality of most North Fork wines has improved dramatically since 1988."

The French got the growers of the North Fork to recognize the importance of leaf spread to capture sunlight at a latitude more northerly than California, and encouraged them to strike a balance between leaf cover and fruit. They got them to understand that they must respond to the irregularity of their climate, reducing the crop in seasons when full ripening could present a problem. They affected thinking in the winery, too, if only by making winemakers conscious of the differences between their grapes and those of both Bordeaux and California.

Some of the Long Island winemakers at first adopted wholeheartedly the methods and practices used by the French (though the the latter had made it clear that what worked for them wouldn't necessarily work on the North Fork). That particular enthusiasm was short-lived.

"We eventually realized that, no matter what we do, we can't make Bordeaux wine out of North Fork grapes," Larry Perrine of Gristina Vineyards told me. "The varieties might be the same, but the character of the fruit is different. We had to find the appropriate way to handle it. Which meant we had to find and accept our own style of wine.

"For a start, our red wines are not as dense as Bordeaux classed growths; their texture is different. But then, even other Bordeaux wines are rarely as dense as the classed growths. I saw that if I racked my wines as often as they did theirs, drawing them off their lees and into fresh barrels every three months, the constant movement would tire them and make them flat, where Bordeaux's classed growths are made more accessible by that manipulation."

Taking a slightly different approach, Dan Kleck, winemaker at Palmer Vineyards, racks his young red wines as frequently as anyone in Bordeaux does. Letting air to them, he finds, opens them up and brings them forward. But he, too, sees the danger in exaggerating a Bordeaux–North Fork connection.

"We can't just follow what they do," Kleck says. "There's the Atlantic between us. We have to respect the character of our own North Fork grapes. We must work *with* that character, not against it.

"In Bordeaux they let the skins macerate with the new wine long after fermentation is over and they then age the wine for a couple of years in barrel. That won't work for us. I leave the skins with the wine no longer than absolutely necessary. I want to bring out the fruity, friendly, forward qualities of a Merlot, for example, so even when racking, I handle the wine gently, as if it were a relative of Pinot Noir rather than of Cabernet Sauvignon."

Larry Perrine shares this concern to preserve the wine's fruit. "On the North Fork, protecting the fruit is more important than worrying about tannin," he said. "Bordeaux wines need tannin because it's intrinsic to their very structured style. This is not Bordeaux."

Alex Hargrave, too, likes his wines to be approachably balanced from the beginning ("an unbalanced wine doesn't become balanced in the bottle" he says) and to go on displaying a vibrant fruit even as they mature. His 1992 Hargrave Vineyard Cabernet Franc has that soft, almost raspberry fruitiness of a fine Bourgueil—a Loire Valley wine also made entirely of Cabernet Franc. It's a style that gives a wine immediate appeal. The discreet fruit of the silky 1988 Hargrave Vineyard Cabernet Franc drunk with lunch on that September 1993 visit was still the core of the wine.

In most years, Bordeaux wines are more supple than the red wines of the North Fork because they are fleshier; an emphasis in North Fork wines on aroma and flavor helps compensate. This style is likely to take hold. At a dinner party I attended one evening in Cutchogue, Russell Hearns, the Australian wine-maker at the new Pellegrini Vineyards, produced, just for our interest, a 1992 barrel sample of an experimental blend of Cabernet Sauvignon and Merlot, a wine he had drawn off the grape skins well before fermentation in tank was complete and allowed to finish fermenting, separated from the skins, in small oak barrels. The technique is much used in Australia to make lively red wines with limited tannin but with good color, fruity aromas and exuberant flavor. Hearns's wine was delicious, and it had a better texture than I would have expected from such a short maceration.

As I visited various wineries during the week, I was often asked whether I had tasted that wine of Hearns, which clearly had made an impression. It's easy to see why it makes commercial sense: we all like the idea of wine being made for a long bottle development, but little of it ever has that chance. Research reveals repeatedly that most wine is consumed within hours of being purchased.

267

I anchored my week by tasting through a wide range of red, white and rosé wines from just about all the wineries and of every vintage from 1988 to 1992. The summer of 1988 had been a good one on the North Fork, followed by a particularly warm and sunny fall. On the other hand, 1989 had been dismally cool and wet and much of the fruit had failed to ripen properly; as a result some of that year's white wines were a touch austere, the reds on occasion slightly herbaceous. The year 1990 was as average as any on the North Fork can be, but 1991 was particularly warm until Hurricane Bob blew in at the end of August. The rain it brought was sorely needed, in fact, but it fell so fast and so furiously that it ran off almost at once. Cool and often cloudy, 1992 produced successful white wines with keen flavors; the reds were good, too, when producers had the patience (and the nerve) to wait to pick. Flavors in cool years are usually more intense, but waiting for the grapes to ripen, to accumulate the necessary sugar—on the North Fork one must sometimes wait until the end of October—can be nerve-wracking. A bad autumn storm can destroy a crop still on the vines.

Among the 1992 North Fork Chardonnays, I particularly liked those of Gristina Vineyards, The Lenz Winery, and SagPond Vineyards. (SagPond is an odd man out, really, because this winery has its vineyard on a well-drained South Fork knoll near Bridgehampton, but I include it for the sake of completeness). Chardonnays of 1991 that appealed to me were the Hargrave's Chardonette (a marketing name) and those from Pellegrini Vineyards, Bedell Cellars (its reserve in particular was easily the best 1991 Chardonnay tasted), The Lenz Winery's Gold Label, and Palmer Vineyards' Barrel Fermented.

A Chardonnay from the North Fork is usually more taut, slimmer and more citrusy than one from California; it's great with local fish for that very reason. Sometimes North Fork winemakers take fright at their wines' delicacy and use oak as a condiment rather than a means to expand the wine's base—but that's a common mistake everywhere in the world.

By and large, however, I found the Merlots, Cabernet Sauvignons and Cabernet Francs more interesting. I was impressed by the Cabernet Francs tasted at Hargrave Vineyard, and by Palmer Vineyards' Proprietor's Reserve Cabernet Franc 1990. There are many delightful Merlots: Pellegrini Vineyards' 1992 (Russell

Hearns' work again), Gristina Vineyards' 1991, and Bedell Cellars' 1991 and Reserve 1990. Other 1990 Merlots that caught my attention were those of Palmer Vineyards and of Jamesport Vineyards. Paumanok Vineyards' 1990 Merlot is lighter than some others, but was most attractively scented.

Cabernet Sauvignon on the North Fork seems to show less character than Merlot, but this might just be true of the style of the particular vintages I was tasting. At any rate, those I liked included the 1991s from Pellegrini Vineyards and Peconic Bay Vineyards; the 1990s from Gristina Vineyards, Palmer Vineyards, and Bidwell Vineyards; the truly elegant 1990 Cabernet Sauvignon of Bedell Cellars (Bedell is not one of the glamour wineries, but I found its wines to be among the most reliable); the 1989s of both Palmer Vineyards and Bidwell Vineyards (despite the stylistic constraints of that vintage); and the 1988s of Hargrave Vineyard and Pindar Vineyards. In 1989 Mattituck Hills made an attractive red table wine based on Cabernet Sauvignon and Merlot, though labelled without varietal identification. John Simisich, the proprietor of Mattituck Hills, continues to experiment (the 1991 was Cabernet Sauvignon and Pinot Noir) as he searches for a wine of broad appeal that will nonetheless be representative of the area.

Chardonnay, Merlot, Cabernet Sauvignon and Cabernet Franc are the North Fork's key varieties, but there are others planted—especially Riesling, Gewürztraminer and Pinot Noir. If they receive less attention—and acreage is dwindling—it is only because of lack of consumer support. (The words Chardonnay, Merlot and Cabernet create their own sales magic.) Yet some of the wines from these other varieties are charmingly impressive: Cygnet, for example, a proprietary blend of Riesling and Gewürztraminer from Bedell Cellars; Commonage, another proprietary white blend from Pellegrini Vineyards; Paumanok Vineyards' 1992 Chenin Blanc and the 1991 and 1992 Pinot Blancs from Palmer Vineyards; a delicious Blanc de Pinot Noir 1991, which actually is a rosé, from The Lenz Winery; and some late-harvest wines, including a 1991 Riesling from Paumanok and a 1992 Gewürztraminer called Finale from Pellegrini Vineyards.

Most North Fork wine is consumed in the restaurants of the summer communities on Long Island's South Fork and in New York City—a market that was difficult to breach at first but has now taken to its local wine region as happily as Paris takes to the Loire and San Francisco to Napa and Sonoma Counties.

And just as Parisians happily drive down to Touraine for a day in search of a riverside lunch, wine for the cellar, and *rillettes* for the kitchen, and as San Franciscans enjoy lunching on a terrace with a view of the vineyards, New Yorkers are beginning to discover the pleasures of a trip to the North Fork to shop for wine, eat a picnic on a patched-up jetty, and fill a basket with fruits and vegetables from a roadside stand to take back to the city.

Simple restaurants like the Jamesport Country Kitchen and Aldo's in Greenport are catering to palates a little more sophisticated than those of neighboring farmers (those who want local color can get an earful of small-town politics and gossip over breakfast at the Cutchogue Diner). Although the North Fork is hardly geared up for South Fork–style tourism—thankfully, some might say, there are no boutiques, outlet malls, trendy grocers or multimillion dollar "cottages"—motels and bed-and-breakfasts allow a weekend of winery visits and a tour of towns and villages that could well be a thousand rather than a hundred miles from New York City.

Luckily, too, the North Fork hasn't been spoiled by the excess of preservation and restoration that transforms the genuine into the quaint. Off the peninsula's two main arteries—one runs alongside Cutchogue's old village green, dotted with seventeenth-century houses, and the other leads to north-shore woods and Horton's Point lighthouse—there are eighteenth-century barns and stylish Victorian farmhouses, old churches and the occasional schoolhouse. The intrepid will find, hidden at the end of lanes that lead nowhere, once-white wooden frame houses, smothered by overgrown shrubbery and huddled around a creek, a boat shed and a welcoming if decayed shanty saloon with a deck hanging perilously over the water. It's the North Fork at its most serendipitous, and a glimpse of America at its most unaffected and unassuming.

REMEMBRANCE OF WINES PAST

W HAT WAS THE BEST WINE YOU EVER TASTED, THE ONE YOU WILL ALWAYS REMEMBER?"
It's a question I'm often asked when someone newly introduced first realizes how
I spend much of my waking time. How to answer? I think I'm expected to
château-drop, to say something glamorous about a Margaux '53, a Cheval-Blanc
'47 or a Mouton-Rothschild '45—a monumental wine, by the way, still flamboy-
antly vigorous when poured for me at a dinner at Mouton itself a couple of years
ago. (There's a real château-drop for you.)

But how does anyone compare that Mouton-Rothschild with a Cheval-
Blanc '47, last tasted in the 1970s, to decide which was "better"? And what would
be the point anyway? Such wines are almost always impressive, and usually
memorable. But that isn't the same thing as "always remembered," is it? In any
case, one's memory of a wine is rarely a mere abstraction of aroma and flavor.
Often it seems to reflect so well a particular context that later we are never quite
sure whether we remember the circumstances because of the wine or the wine
because of the circumstances. At times the two can even be ludicrously at odds.

Not long ago, while helping a friend clean up an apartment from which
the removal men had taken his furniture just hours before, I came across a bottle
of Barossa Valley Cabernet Sauvignon, a 1981 from the Hill-Smith estate, overlooked by the packers. We were tired and more than ready to stop. Fortunately,
one of us had a corkscrew and there were paper cups in a kitchen cupboard. We
sat on the floor, our backs to the wall. The wine was more than remarkable: it was
sleek and patrician and elegant beyond anything I'd expected. At that moment, it
was the most delicious wine in the world.

When mountains labor to bring forth a mouse, that can be memorable,
too. In the 1960s, when my company in London imported and distributed the

wines of Henri Maire—an important but highly promotion-driven wine producer in the Jura, in eastern France—I was asked, at short notice, to arrange a small dinner at a distinguished restaurant (my choice) for a few distinguished guests (my choice). The principle dish (Henri Maire's choice), prepared by none other than Raymond Oliver, at the time still reigning at Le Grand Véfour, was to be flown over from Paris hours before the event.

The object was to show—in London and Paris simultaneously, and with precisely the same dish—a wine that Henri Maire had shipped in barrel around the world. In the eighteenth century it had been a custom to send certain sherries to and from the tropics in the hold of sailing ships; the journey was thought to age fortified wines advantageously. Names of certain blends—Fine Old East India, for example—still allude to the practice. The wine Henri Maire had chosen to be despatched for two years before the mast, so to speak, was an Arbois rosé. He called it Vin Retour des Iles and proposed to offer it to his numerous guests at the Grand Véfour (and to my much smaller group in London) to demonstrate—I think—that Arbois rosé was serious wine and not to be confused with the pretty tipples in designer bottles then increasingly popular at restaurant lunch tables.

I chose to hold my dinner in a private dining room at Prunier's on St. James's Street. Simone Prunier, a consummate restaurateur, was a resourceful woman of limitless discretion, and I knew I could rely on her to pull together what seemed to me to be an adventure fraught with risk. We knew nothing of the dish to be sent from Paris except that it was to be *marcassin* (young wild boar) accompanied by a sauce. It would need only to be reheated.

We composed a menu around this dish: champagne and canapés to greet the arriving guests; a plain poached turbot with hollandaise (Prunier's, after all, was renowned for its fish but we didn't want to upstage Raymond Oliver); cheeses from the Jura area—the Franche-Comté—to follow the *marcassin;* and a sumptuous pineapple ice, to be brought to the table packed inside the original fruit, enveloped in a veil of finely spun sugar. I selected Henri Maire wines for the fish and the cheese that would allow the special bottling of rosé every chance to be the star.

The dish, transported expeditiously by Air France from restaurant door to restaurant door, was something of an anticlimax: I can describe it only as minced wild-boar patties in a brown sauce. Unfortunately, the wine offered neither compensation nor distraction. Henri Maire had decided, at the last minute, that there was barely enough Vin Retour des Iles for the swelling number of his guests at the Grand Véfour and therefore none—not a single bottle—was sent to London. I was asked to serve the standard Arbois rosé instead. I have to say, it was a perfectly satisfactory wine. But it was not, as Dr. Johnson once said of a perfectly satisfactory dinner, what you would ask a man to. Least of all at Prunier's.

Who knows what vinous perspectives the actual Vin Retour des Iles might have opened up for us? In a brief but charming new book, *La Légende du Vin*, subtitled (in French, of course) *A Short Essay of Sentimental Enophilia*, Jean-Baptiste Baronian, French novelist, essayist, critic and editor, says that those who appreciate wine find in every glass a trace of a history, of a civilization, and of a gesture that bind together a time and a place.

A few years ago I tasted, on an exceptional occasion in California, the 1771 and 1791 vintages of Château Margaux. Both wines were a vibrant strawberry color and astonishingly fresh; their bouquet was extravagantly scented. In the eighteenth century, wine, like fruit, was bottled for preservation, not aging, and it was common practice to perk the aroma of red Bordeaux with powdered orrisroot, the rhizome of iris. It was used then, as it still is (but in perfume, not in wine) to contribute a scent of violets. In any case, both wines were made before Cabernet Sauvignon, with its distinctive pungency and dense garnet color, had replaced Malbec as the principal grape of the Médoc.

With Fragonard, Couperin and Beaumarchais as touchstones, anyone speculating on how an eighteenth-century French wine tasted back then would imagine something with very much the delicacy, the luminosity, and the perfumed intensity of those wines. I confess, though, that foremost in my own mind as they slipped down my throat was the thought that I was drinking—in Los Angeles, the quintessential twentieth-century city—wines made by men alive in Bordeaux at the time of the American and French Revolutions. Just to look at Chardin's painting of a bowl of raspberries can be an eighteenth-century experience. But in

273

GERALD ASHER

absorbing alcohol converted from fruit sugar two centuries earlier, I was actually sharing calories transmitted in solar energy that had also warmed the faces of Thomas Jefferson and Marie-Antoinette.

But *most* memorable of my life? Were it not that people casually met might assume I was making fun of them, I would in fact explain that it was, and still remains, unidentified. I drank it at a mountain inn near the Simplon pass in the early summer of either 1962 or 1963. From 1955 until 1970 I spent weeks on end visiting suppliers all over Europe to taste and select the wines my firm brought to London. For much of that time there were neither *autoroutes* nor *autostrade*, and I drove a Triumph TR4 (which I'd had refinished in deep Burgundy red instead of its original British racing green) to get myself quickly from place to place. Well, that was the rational explanation at any rate.

I'd spent the night at Sion, in the Swiss Valais, after an evening of *raclette*—molten slivers of the local cheese draped over hot potatoes—and the cooperative's Fendant, a flowery white wine with which we were having a modest success in England. I was on my way to Verona, and had set off early to be sure of reaching Milan by evening.

There was little traffic on the road—the Simplon is more often used as a rail route—and by noon I was high in the Alps with the Swiss-Italian border behind me. It was early June, and for most of the way wildflowers were scattered along the roadside. At the higher altitudes, drifts of snow still lay dazzlingly white in the midday sun. The exhilaration of the climb—the TR4 would respond with its distinctive soft roar as I changed through the gears on those endless, steep turns— the crisp air, the brilliant light, and the grandeur of the mountains, made me feel I was on top of the world. And I almost was, literally. But I was also hungry and had many curving miles ahead of me to Domodossola, where I planned to stop for a late lunch.

Then an inn appeared. It was small, but comfortably appealing. The deliciously simple set lunch of sautéed veal scallops and buttered noodles with a salad of green beans was typical of what one finds in the mountains. My glass was filled with a light red wine poured from a pitcher, left on the table. I was relaxed, carefree, and happy. Oh, how ruby bright that wine was; it gleamed in the sun-

274

light. I remember clearly its enticing aroma—youthful, but with a refinement that surprised me. The wine was sweetly exotic: lively on my tongue, perfectly balanced, and with a long, glossy finish. It was the sort of wine that Omar Khayyam might have had in mind for his desert tryst. The young woman who had poured it for me was amused when I asked what it was. It was, she said, *vino rosso.*

I sat there trying, without success, to put my finger on the grape. It was probably one of those sub-Alpine varieties already then disappearing into odd pockets of vineyard in remote valleys—Bonarda, perhaps, or Ruchè. Or perhaps it was, more conventionally, a Brachetto, a Freisa or a Grignolino, any one of which was likely to show more than its usual appeal if grown near that altitude. Whatever it was, the wine had been made with uncommon care. It was exquisitely graceful.

I shall always remember that wine, though I have never learned what it might have been. Italian friends have suggested Vercelli, from the Novara hills, just a way farther south; and others, Valtellina, farther east. No wine I've tasted since from either has come close.

But the pleasure in any wine is subjective: we each bring something to what is there in the glass and interpret the result differently. Perhaps, on that June day more than thirty years ago, I had contributed an extra-large dose of well-being. Who can say?

275

WINE OF THE GODS

I'D PICKED OUT A SMALL ISLAND WITH DIRECT FLIGHTS FROM ATHENS FOR A QUIET WEEK IN THE AEGEAN, IMAGINING, I SUPPOSE, THAT IT WOULD BE INACCESSIBLE TO EVERYONE IN THE WORLD EXCEPT ME. Needless to say, the beaches were crowded by day and by night the narrow whitewashed alleys of the island's one small town throbbed with disco.

I rose late each morning, lunched under a canvas awning behind the minuscule cathedral, and spent my afternoons with the *Herald Tribune* under a tree in a public square the size of a suburban patio. With the evening star the first of the Day-Glo tank tops would appear, the little square would fill with suntanned limbs, and the plinka-plonk of bouzouki would begin drifting from the bars and cafés. Later, the music would get louder, the dancing more frantic. As the crowd got tipsier, girls would occasionally shriek with excitement and the young men would get boisterous.

276

An Athenian friend of a friend, a woman who kept a house on the island, told me over dinner on my third or fourth evening of a few remote beaches in coves difficult to reach by land. Local fishing boats called in on them, but none had a jetty or quay to receive the harbor craft I saw listing out of port every morning, crammed with tourists and tape players. She gave me directions to one I could reach on foot in at most three quarters of an hour. "There's even a bar of sorts," she said.

Next morning, with book and beach mat, I climbed a high ridge a mile or so behind the town, passed a herd of goats making what they could of the scrubby pasture on the far side, and then followed a barely visible track as it twisted down through coarse grass and rushes towards the sea. The ridge, curving behind me, extended down into the water, isolating a beach of fine sand. It was deserted except for a fisherman beating his catch of octopus on a rock, slapping them down, rubbing them against the rough surface, and dashing a crock of seawater over them from time to time. I had no urge to take a closer look, and settled at a distance to read and to sun myself.

A collection of flotsam was arranged against the side of the hill to give shade. Rickety posts sunk into the sand supported a canopy of reeds over a few wooden chairs and tables, bleached and partly rotted by sun and sea spray. It was the bar, and after a while I went over and sat down at one of the tables. By then the octopus beater had left and I could hear nothing but the ripple of tranquil water. A small sail grazed the horizon, far away where sea and sky melded together in a blue haze.

A boy brought me some wine, pale golden and mildly resinated. Without my asking he also brought a few olives and a hunk of dense, slightly sour bread. A ray of sunlight, piercing the reeds overhead, was shattered by the wine glass. It was hot, I was drowsy. The distant sail was now at hand, and, once close enough, a man jumped down to swim and wade ashore. It could have been Dionysus himself, stepping from his raft, or Noah, released from his ark and relishing again the feel of sand between his toes. Noah and his vineyard seem remote from us now, and Dionysus, smiling languidly in the shade of a vine-sprouting mast—as he once had arrived in the Aegean, guided by dolphins—is a total stranger; yet both still influence our lives in ways we scarcely recognize and rarely understand.

I sipped my wine and broke the bread, thinking how essential they had been to life around that sea. Most of us have a special feeling for bread—even when it's stale we shrink from throwing it out; and though we make a show of not taking wine too seriously and joke about its little rituals, we pour it and drink it with particular attention. Without thinking, we receive guests with an offering of bread and wine—though these days one might be disguised as cheese crackers and the other as a glass of Lillet—regardless of whether we or they are either hungry or thirsty. And we do it because the role of bread and wine in our lives is older than history. The Eucharist itself is rooted in a far more ancient belief that to eat bread and drink wine was to partake of the body of the corn god and the blood of the vine god. "The drinking of wine in the rites of a vine-god like Dionysus," wrote Sir James Frazer in *The Golden Bough*, "is not an act of revelry, it is a solemn sacrament."

Sacrament or not, breaking bread and drinking wine, one with another, is the most basic act of community. Is it Athenaeus, the third-century Greek writer, who suggests that civilization began when men came together to eat food rather than fight over who would possess it? Certainly it is he who describes, though quoting an earlier author, the custom of first consecrating the dish to be eaten, following which "each man was permitted to drink a little [wine] from a bowl, and the one offering it [to another] would say 'Good dinner to you!' " We rarely pass a loving cup now, but is our ritual of saying grace, of raising a glass to each other, or wishing the company *bon appétit* so very different?

When describing how an early king and his companions had received a group of traveling strangers, Athenaeus says, "... wine seems to possess a power which draws to friendship by lightly warming and fusing the soul. Hence they did not even ask their guests too soon who they were, but postponed that until later, as though they honored the mere act of hospitality, and not the individual and the personal in us."

As Greeks, they would have respected strangers who could well have been gods. Gods. We are entertained, even amused, by the ancients and their mythological gods; but the Greeks used their myths to come to terms with truth and paradox too profound and too disturbing to be considered, let alone revealed, in any other way. They were able to grasp the meaning of their world better than we do ours.

Wine, in any case, was at the center of their mythology and of their universe as a metaphor for Dionysus and for the duality of being. It was a symbol of renewal, of the cycle of death and rebirth. The god's myth, expressed in his cult through music and sometimes frenzied dance, combined calm and uproar, horror and ecstasy, as well as both the light and dark sides of human nature. At times it allowed and even encouraged sexual license and wild abandon.

But if wine could bring violence, it also brought ineffable joy. Dionysus, born of a god and a mortal mother, drew heaven and earth together. Wine was man's portion of the divine, promising him life at its most intense. In the words of Walter Otto, author of the classic study *Dionysus: Myth and Cult*, celebrants of the Dionysiac rites were "thrust out of everything secure, everything settled, out of every haven of thought and feeling, and . . . flung into the primeval cosmic turmoil in which life, surrounded and intoxicated with death, undergoes eternal change and renewal." Wine, in short, was seen by the ancients as nothing less than the paradox, the mystery and the miracle of life itself.

It meant life to them in a literal sense, too. The vine finds sustenance where there appears to be none, as do the ivy and the pine tree, both plants also sacred to Dionysus. (The ivy was worn as a garland, while pine resin often scented the Greeks' wine and still does.) In the Dionysus myth and its enactment in the cult, celebrants strike barren rock with the *thrysus*, a rod of ivy-wood tipped with a pine cone, and cause streams of water and springs of wine to gush forth. Dionysus, after all, is god of water, of moisture in general, not just of wine: his annual festivals began with his epiphany in the mountains where rains were heaviest. According to Plutarch, he would appear in midwinter on Parnassus as a newborn child in a cradle, and it was there that the women went to find him. In spring, with new growth visible everywhere, his festivals reached a climax when he reemerged from the sea as a young man, pulled ashore, at Athens and Smyrna, in a boat mounted on wheels.

In this century, before forklifts and containerized cargo ships, French dockworkers each drank two and three liters of red wine a day. They didn't drink it to forget their troubles, and still less for the bouquet and flavor. They drank it because a liter of wine, with roughly seven hundred calories, replaced not only lost moisture but also the energy they burned in hard physical labor. In our automated, fossil-fueled, calorie-conscious age we forget that most people once struggled to obtain the calories needed to fire their bodies. Wine, as much as bread, was an important, a vital, food to the ancient Greek.

Furthermore, it protected and healed him as effectively as it nourished him. The ancient Greek might have been ignorant of the bacterium and the bacillus, but he knew from experience how effective wine could be as an antiseptic. Hippocrates—our physicians still make an oath to him when they qualify to practice—had little but wine to rely on for most of his remedies. Recently, we have again been reminded of benefits—obvious to the ancients—inherent in the moderate, daily consumption of wine.

So potently did wine bind sustenance and healing to religion that the highly charged act of offering it was only further heightened by its association with economic power. In the sixth century B.C., when trade had overtaken marauding and mutual raiding as the chief source of revenues of the Greek city-states, wine was the principal commodity. It brought to ancient Greece the accumulation of wealth that made possible the surge in the arts and the sciences known to us as the classical age.

It's no wonder, then, that wine, or rather its more easily depicted symbols—the vine and the cup—should have figured so prominently in the arts and artifacts of that age; nor should we be surprised that it continued and continues to do so. A fine wine cup, substituting for what it would normally contain, became an object of such esteem that its possession lent enormous prestige. It is not by chance that to those we wish to honor we present a silver cup: for millenia it has been the traditional reward of victors. A bold two-handled version in the British Museum, wrought in Anatolia nearly four thousand years ago, could be the prototype for every such prize given since.

But as one might expect, given the duality of Dionysus, there was a dark side to wine's sixth-century success. As commercial vineyards expanded and flourished, subsistence farmers and their families were dispossessed to make room for them. Migrating to the towns—as in all times since—they yearned angrily for what they had lost. In desperation they sought comfort from their nature god and lent Dionysus's cult a new and violently rebellious aspect. The ascendant landed aristocracy, fearful, instigated or at least willingly acquiesced in the tyrannies that sprang up in the Greek world at that time in response to this social ferment.

Dionysus the healer and nourisher, provider of relief and comfort, revealed himself as a god of personal liberty, too. Or that, at least, is the way the oppressed perceived him. It was an attribute so potent that Nietzsche, two and a half thousand years later, borrowed their mythic vocabulary in making Dionysus his symbol of the inner force that encourages each of us to respond to the world, freely, in his or her own way. Nietzsche contrasted Dionysus to Apollo, the god who imposed conformity, regulation and order. Apollo, all cold perfection, moves, as a respected historical geographer wrote recently, "only among the best people"; but Dionysus, ever exhilarating, ever outrageous, ever for the individual, ever for life, offered liberty to all without distinction. Isn't it clear why authority everywhere demeaned Dionysus, presented him as a god of foolish, drunken revelry and either subverted his cult in order to tame it or ruthlessly repressed it as obscene?

A particularly egregious episode in second-century B.C. Rome—another period of farm dispossession—began a decline that marked the end of the Republic and the imposition of imperial rule on free citizens. A harlot was rewarded handsomely for giving unsupported evidence of rites allegedly so vile that the government was able to justify not only a ban on the cult but the execution of many thousands of its political opponents. The consuls made speeches filled with innuendo about hidden "conspirators," talked of treachery and offered rewards to those who would name names. To our ears, more than two thousand years later, their words form the depressingly familiar litany of a repressive regime. Especially chilling are those warning the citizenry against sheltering or assisting intended victims in any way, or even sympathizing with them.

"I have thought it right to give you this warning," a consul told the assembled Romans, "so that no superstitious fear may agitate your minds when you see us suppressing the Bacchanalia and breaking up these criminal gatherings."

The Jews meanwhile used wine for the sacrament of blessing God's name, but did not see it as a metaphor for Him—their monotheistic religion had need of neither metaphors for God nor of gods as metaphors. Yet they too set bread and wine apart from other foods. While the obligatory blessing over bread extends to all other food to be eaten with it at the same meal (because bread is humanity's mainstay), the blessing over wine is more than a form of grace because the family table, to a strictly observant Jew, is an altar at which wine is fundamental to the fulfillment of his religious obligations. It is at his table, silver wine cup in hand, that he welcomes the Sabbath into his house, greets every festival, and sanctifies the celebration of all family occasions.

Such a controlled and formal role for wine seems at first far removed from the Greeks' perception of it. But a closer look at the major festival of Passover, celebrated, like Easter (and like the Great Dionysia), at the first full moon after the spring equinox, reveals what once can only have been an allusion to birth and to life's origins in the sea—the *Seder*, the Passover meal, begins, for most Jews, with a hard cooked egg served in a pool of salt water. There are also references to nature itself in the bitter green herbs that must be present—they are the kind of salad herbs once usually picked wild.

In a study of food in the Bible published by the *Annales* school of historians in Paris, Jean Soler points out that this festival, commemorating the exodus from Egypt and the birth of the Jewish nation, probably began as a feast of renewal in which participants ate foods that recalled their most distant origins. "The bitter herbs," he says, "must be understood . . . as the opposite of vegetables produced by agriculture." Roast rather than boiled meat is eaten, he explains, because boiling implies an ability to make pots to cook in, a skill acquired late.

Passover, interestingly enough, is the only Jewish festival at which those present are *obliged* to drink wine copiously—at least four cups each. And like the Dionysiac rites, one might add, it is a festival that celebrates liberty: "We were Pharaoh's slaves in Egypt," runs one verse of the Haggadah, the story of the exodus read at every *Seder*, "but now we are free."

It was at just such a *Seder,* celebrating birth, freedom and life's renewal, that Jesus pointed to the wine and said, "This is my blood." His disciples would have understood, surely, the Judaic significance of those words—Jews believe blood is life, is sacred, and belongs to God alone. But how would those words have reverberated, as they later did, in the ears of a Greco-Roman world with its own perception of wine and life and divinity, a world in which our division of the religious from the secular would have seemed artificial?

It was a world in which the early church, taking account of customs and rituals that were the very fabric of the communities it sought to convert, had to find ways to adapt and adopt, sometimes to avoid generating popular discontent—the singing of stirring Christian hymns springs from the joyous music and chanting that had accompanied pre-Christian rites: the church drew the line, however, at dancing—and sometimes to comfort those anxious not to offend their old gods in accepting the new. If, for example, the devotees of Venus (protector of marriage and therefore, by extension, of the married home) wanted to continue to offer and eat fish in her honor—Venus, like Dionysus, arose from the sea—why then, the church would make it Christian to do so on Friday, a day still dedicated to Venus in Latin-rooted languages. At a more modest level, every village adopted a saint to merge with the local god or goddess who formerly had given his or her protection to the community, its flocks and its fields. From Cyprus to Northumberland those patron saints endure in place-names to this day.

In the ancient religious rites, wine—humanity's portion of the divine— had brought the celebrants into the presence of the god. Even when Christian, much of the Greco-Roman world continued to think of wine that way. Ramsay MacMullen describes in his book *Christianizing the Roman Empire*, A.D. *100–400* the many adherents to the new Christian creed who took wine to the tombs of the martyrs on saints' days and, to the great concern of Ambrose and Augustine, drank there till evening, believing that without wine their supplications would not, could not, be heard. But for them, spiritual descendants, at least, of the men who had drunk from Athenaeus's common bowl and of those who had accepted wine from the hands of kings, wine was already a metaphor for god—for life itself—so the doctrine of Holy Communion through wine become sacred as the blood of God needed no impossible new leap of faith.

I woke from a light sleep to find the man from the boat standing almost beside me under the canopy of reeds. He had dried himself on a coarse cotton cloth dangling from a string in the sun and was stepping into a pair of old pants he must have left at the bar. He was obviously at ease there but looked around as if choosing a place to sit. I invited him, with a gesture of my open hand, to join me and share my bottle. Another glass appeared for him, and when I had filled it he raised it to me.

"*Yassou,*" he said, smiling.

"*L'chayim,*" I replied. To life.

INDEX

A

Aging, 38, 58, 99–100, 109,
  112–13, 123–24, 144–46, 237
Australia, 136, 182, 267

B

Barbaresco, 52–61
Barolo, 52–54, 56
Barrels, 58, 111–12, 115, 206
Beaujolais, 37, 121
Books, 62–71
Bordeaux, 66, 68, 94, 95, 155–57,
  172–80, 182
Botrytis, 30, 200, 201
Bottle shapes, 95
Bouquet, 112–13
Burgundy, 35, 119–31, 242–43

C

Cabernet Franc, 159, 268
Cabernet Sauvignon
  California, 82–92, 94, 159
  North Fork, 279
  Oregon, 247–48
  Washington, 190–99
California
  Cabernet Sauvignon, 159
  Chardonnay, 160–71
  Edna Valley, 23–31
  Napa Valley, 27, 30, 82–92,
    213
  Santa Cruz, 148–54

  Sauvignon Blanc, 230–38
  Sonoma County, 151
  Zinfandel, 211–20
Catawba, 43, 44, 45, 48, 49, 50
Chablis, 29, 34
Chambourcin, 50
Champagne, 29, 36, 43, 66, 68,
  97–107
Chardonnay
  California, 26–31, 160–71,
    231
  North Fork, 268
  Oregon, 246–47
  Washington, 191
Châteauneuf-du-Pape, 37, 78
Chianti, 37
Clarete, 113–14
Clones, 160–71
Corbières, 72–81
Côte-Rôtie, 181
Crete, 15–22
Crozes-Hermitage, 187–89
Crus
  Burgundy, 119–20, 122–23
  Champagne, 101–2
Cynthiana, 46, 51

D

Decanting, 93–96

E

Edna Valley, 23–31

F

Fermentation, natural, 91
Food, pairing wine with, 32–39, 122, 203–4, 230–31
France
    Bordeaux, 172–80
    Burgundy, 119–31
    Champagne, 97–107
    Corbières, 72–81
    Côte-Rôtie, 181
    Crozes-Hermitage, 187–89
    Haut-Brion, 172–80
    Hermitage, 181–87
    Sauternes, 200–210
Fumé Blanc, 233–34

G

Gewürztraminer, 36, 247, 269
Graves, 232, 233

H

Haut-Brion, 172–80
Hermitage, 181–87

I

Ice wine, 152
Intensity, 37
Italy
    Barbaresco, 52–61
    Barolo, 52–54, 56
    Orvieto, 249–60

L

Labrusca, 192–93
Long Island, 261–70

M

Mâcon Rouge, 34

Madeira, 19, 32, 176
Malaga, 35
Malmsey, 15–22
Merlot, 159, 190–99, 247–48, 268–69
Missouri, 40–51
Moselle, 35
Muscadet, 32

N

Napa Valley, 27, 30, 82–92, 213
New Zealand, 234
North Fork, 261–70
Norton, 40–41, 45–46, 51

O

Oak, 111–13, 181
Oregon, 239–48
Orvieto, 249–60

P

Petite Sirah, 153
Phylloxera, 25, 64, 76
Pinot Gris, 246
Pinot Noir, 26, 86, 232, 239–48, 269
Port, 13, 34–36, 66, 68, 94–95, 137–47, 201
Portugal
    Port, 137–47
    vinhos verdes (green wines), 221–29
Pouilly-Fumé, 232, 234
Pressurage à froid, 207–8

R

Religion, wine and, 276–83
Ribera del Duero, 108–18
Riesling, 37, 191, 247, 269

S

Sancerre, 232, 236
Santa Cruz, 148–54
Sauternes, 200–210, 232, 233
Sauvignon Blanc, 86, 230–38
Sauvignon Musqué, 236–37
Scale, 37
Seyval, 50
Sherry, 35, 68
Shiraz, 136, 182
Sitia, 15–16
Sonoma County, 151
Spain, 108–18
Syrah, 80, 132–36, 182, 184

T

Tannins, 123–24
Texture, 36–37

U

United States.
      See California; Long Island;
      Missouri; Oregon; Washington

V

Vidal, 50
Vignoles, 50
Vinhos verdes (green wines),
      221–29

W

Washington, 190–99
Wine tasting, 63, 132–36, 155–59,
      271–75

Z

Zinfandel, 37, 211–20